Clinical Interpretation of
Objective Psychological Tests

Clinical Interpretation of
Objective Psychological Tests

CHARLES J. GOLDEN, Ph.D.

Assistant Professor of Medical Psychology
University of Nebraska Medical Center
Omaha, Nebraska

GRUNE & STRATTON
A Subsidiary of Harcourt Brace Jovanovich, Publishers
New York   San Francisco   London

Library of Congress Cataloging in Publication Data

Golden, Charles J   1949–
   Clinical interpretation of objective psychological tests.

   Bibliography: p.
   Includes index.
   1. Psychological tests. I. Title.
[DNLM: 1. Psychological tests. BF431 G616c]
BF176.G64   150'.28   78-25778
ISBN 0-8089-1163-5
© 1979 by Grune & Stratton, Inc.

Grune & Stratton, Inc.
111 Fifth Avenue
New York, New York 10003

Distributed in the United Kingdom by
Academic Press, Inc. (London) Ltd.
24/28 Oval Road, London NW1

Library of Congress Catalog Number 78-25778
International Standard Book Number 0-8089-1163-5
Printed in the United States of America

Contents

Acknowledgments   vii

Preface   ix

1. Wechsler Adult Intelligence Scale   1
2. Alternate Tests of Intellectual Performance   36
3. Tests of Achievement   45
4. Minnesota Multiphasic Personality Inventory   57
5. The Sixteen Personality Factors Questionnaire (16PF)   107
6. Benton Visual Retention Test   121
7. Bender-Gestalt   129
8. Neuropsychological Tests   143
9. Halstead-Reitan Neuropsychological Battery   159
10. Standardized Version of the Luria Neuropsychological Tests   202

Index   227

Acknowledgments

In an undertaking of this size it is difficult to fully acknowledge all those who helped prepare the manuscript. Specific thanks are due to Dr. Fred Strider, Mary Ann Strider, and David Osmon for wading through the early drafts and making appropriate comments. I owe an immense debt to numerous secretaries at the University of Nebraska Medical Center for providing typed copies of many drafts. A final acknowledgment is due to the psychologists who put together and provided the basic research on the instruments described in this book. In each case, their efforts represented many hours of detailed analytic work as well as many hours of drudgery. Their contribution to the field of psychological testing and to clinical psychology as a whole is not reflected in their listing in the references. Without their work and their inspiration, there could have been no book.

Preface

Despite extensive changes in the attitudes of psychologists towards testing, the use of psychological testing in the evaluation of psychiatric, medical, and normal individuals remains a major skill expected of the thoroughly trained applied psychologist in clinical, school, or industrial work. Psychological testing, in addition, remains the primary function of many psychologists trained at the Master's level. Changes in attitudes towards testing, however, have brought about substantial modifications in the clinical interpretation of psychological tests. This has resulted from a more complete understanding of the role of psychological tests, their limitations, and their advantages. Such changes also reflect the increasingly sophisticated research that has appeared in the area.

Although many psychologists are aware that such changes have taken place, there does not exist any single source that presents the status of the clinical interpretation of the major psychological tests. One can turn to books concerned with single tests, but these are generally disappointing in the area of clinical interpretation and often inappropriate to the teaching of the clinical interpretation. One can turn to the literature itself, but there one is faced with countless thousands of articles of varying validity and usefulness. These, too, suffer from an emphasis on the psychometric and experimental properties of tests rather than their clinical usefulness with the single patient.

The present volume is an attempt to remediate this problem in the area of adult objective psychological testing. The emphasis throughout the volume is to present the basic clinical knowledge and strategies necessary for the competent use of the most widespread and important tests in adult clinical psychology today. The tests have been selected from the four major areas of psychological testing: intellectual evaluation, achievement, personality, and organic brain dysfunction. The tests chosen are those most frequently used in each area as well as those which promise to be useful in a significant clinical area likely to be faced by the average psychologist. The references chosen have been limited to those that would be the most useful to the reader looking for a more in-depth evaluation of a given test beyond that presented in this volume.

The book has been written so it can be understood by the individual without any specific background with a test or with psychological testing in general. As a result, the book can be used profitably with a number of different populations: as an introduction to the clinical interpretation of psychological tests for the undergraduate major or psychology graduate student; as an update for the professional psychologist at the masters or doctoral level; and as a survey and introduction for the professional outside psychology who is interested in psychological testing. In the latter capacity, the book should be of particular interest to psychiatrists, social workers, physicians, and rehabilitation professionals.

It is hoped that the book will give the reader a respect for the complexity of clinical interpretation, an understanding of the possibilities of each of these tests in a clinical situation, and a basic introduction to the way in which the clinical interpretation is accomplished. In this way, the volume can contribute to the training of better clinicians as well as providing the nonpsychologist with a better understanding of the clinical foundations and methods associated with objective psychological testing.

Clinical Interpretation of
Objective Psychological Tests

1

The Wechsler Adult Intelligence Scale

The original version of the test that was to later become the Wechsler Adult Intelligence Scale (WAIS) was devised in 1939 by David Wechsler at the Department of Psychiatry in Bellevue Hospital (New York). The test was intended to serve as an alternative to the Stanford-Binet which was primarily designed as a test of children's intellectual functioning. The original Wechsler-Bellevue scale did away with the concept of mental age which was so prominent in the assessment of children's intelligence, and introduced the concept of a deviation IQ which measured an individual's standing relative to his or her peer group.

In 1956, the original Wechsler-Bellevue was replaced by an extensively altered test called the Wechsler Adult Intelligence Scale. The WAIS corrected deficiencies in the original test, such as a restriction of item difficulty that made it difficult to assess certain intellectual characteristics, as well as replaced poor items difficult to score or interpret. In addition, the new WAIS had a much more extensive standardization sample which included a wider geographical representation and a wider representation of nonwhite individuals. Within five years the WAIS was one of the most used instruments in the U.S. At present, it is the most frequently administered adult intellectual test and is used in nearly all mental health and educational settings.

PURPOSE OF THE TEST

The major purpose of any intellectual examination is to assess the individual's level of intelligence. The initial purpose was to identify individuals who were mentally retarded or who possessed very high intelligence in order to offer them appropriate educational or work placement or type of therapeutic approach. The WAIS, however, offers the examiner the possibility of analyzing scores on different subtests and allows for the identification of particular areas of strength and weakness in the individual. These resulting patterns can be used to provide vocational training, or to make diagnostic decisions in a more refined and specific manner than can a general IQ score.

Diagnostic decisions aided by the WAIS include the diagnosis of brain damage (McFie, 1975), the diagnosis of psychiatric disorders (Rappaport, Gill, and Shafer, 1970), and the assessment of such conditions as chronic alcoholism (Gudeman, Craine, Golden, and McLaughlin, 1978). In each of these cases there is more reliance on the pattern of subtest scores rather than the overall IQ's generated by the test.

ADMINISTRATION AND SCORING

The WAIS consists of eleven subtests, six of which are classified as verbal and five of which are classified as performance. Each is administered according to detailed instructions offered in the WAIS manual (Wechsler, 1955). Wechsler emphasizes the importance of sticking to the instructions as they are presented in the manual. Thus, proper administration requires extensive familiarity with the test manual, test materials, and testing situation.

Several general considerations are appropriate to all the WAIS subtests (as well as most of the test described in this book). Testing should be done in a well lighted, well ventilated room. Furniture appropriate to the size of the individual to be tested should be available, and the individual should be able to remain comfortable for the full testing time. Optimal seating arrangements place the examiner on one side of the table and the examinee on an adjacent side so that they sit at a 45° angle (Delprato and Jackson, 1975).

The examiner and examinee should be comfortable with one another; general introductions, or discussions about the subject's occupation and reason for testing, an explanation of the testing and its purpose, and a relaxed, unhurried atmosphere can often serve to do this. The testing situation should be one of general unconditional positive regard. No performance attempted by the subject is "wrong," and all performance, whether right or wrong, should be followed by encouragement and praise to motivate the subject to do his or her best. Specific feedback which gives answers, however, such as saying "good" only after correct items, should be avoided as it tends to increase most test scores (Isenberg and Bass, 1974; Kratochwill and Brody, 1976; Sattler, 1969; Willis and Ehrlick, 1975). With this limitation, the examiner should do all he or she can to make the testing situation a positive and rewarding experience.

Wechsler suggests that test material should not be available for the examinee to touch or see until the proper time in the test. This can be generalized to include all distractions, whatever their source. Testing should be done in a quiet room, one which does not have sudden loud noises nearby. The room itself should be tastefully decorated but free of any serious visual distractions such as moving sculptures. Telephones and any bell systems should be disconnected if present. A sign on the door should instruct others to avoid intrusions.

In general, all tests should be administered in the order given in the manual (and discussed here). The order may be changed, however, for specific reasons. An individual with a poor educational background, for example, who is very sensitive about his or her lack of knowledge might be very agitated if the tests began with the Information subtest. Beginning with a performance subtest might be more effective in establishing the subject's cooperation.

The WAIS is generally begun by telling the subject: "This is a test of your abilities and skills. It is used to determine your IQ, but I am more interested in what information about your skills we can derive that will be of use in (whatever the purpose of the examination). There will be both difficult and easy questions on the test. Don't be upset if you feel you've missed any questions because no one is expected to get them all right." These instructions, of course, can be amended or revised to fit individual preferences and to make the testing situation as acceptable as possible to the examinee.

Information

This is the first subtest of the WAIS. Test questions should be read directly from the manual, starting from item five. If the subject gets either item five or six correct, credit is given for items one through four. If both five and six are missed, items one to four must be given. If items two through four are missed, the test should be discontinued. Zimmerman and Woo-Sam (1973) suggest that one should also consider discontinuing the entire test, as subjects with performance at such a low level are not offered an adequate evaluation by the WAIS.

All the items concern specific questions of fact. As a result, the test is fairly easy to score. The reader should note that several questions (on US population, height of women, number of senators) have answers that change from year to year. In general, population estimates should be within 30 million of the correct answer (about 220 million at this time); the average height of women should be within about two inches of the current value; and the number of senators should be exact (currently 100).

Questions may be repeated if necessary. If subjects ask about guessing or state they are unsure, they should be encouraged to guess or give their best answer. Spontaneous corrections to answers are acceptable, unless the answer is accidentally given by the examiner or the subject returns with the answer after a break. All answers to this and the other verbal tests should be recorded verbatim, as the subject's verbalizations, whether right or wrong, may add some additional qualitative information to our understanding of the person.

The test should be discontinued after five incorrect answers. The examiner may "test the limits" by administering the test beyond this point in order to ascertain if the subject has additional knowledge. Additional correct answers, however, cannot be included when determining the patient's IQ. This technique should not be used with subjects likely to be embarrassed or upset by a continuing inability to answer.

If a subject gives more than one answer, one that is correct and another wrong, the subject must be made to choose between them. If several answers are given, but all are generally correct and not contradictory, the examiner may choose to score the best answer.

Comprehension

This subtest is an attempt to establish the degree to which the subject understands basic social customs and situations. In the more advanced items, ability to interpret proverbs is also included.

The test administration begins with item three. If any one of the items three through five are missed, however, items one and two are administered as well. All questions should be read directly from the manual. They may be repeated but only as they are written; the examiner is not allowed to paraphrase or change the question. Since many of the items require judgment, answers may be ambiguous. In these conditions, subjects should be encouraged to give more information by being told, "go ahead," or "tell me more about this" (Wechsler, 1955). The test is discontinued after the subject misses four questions in a row.

The Comprehension subtest (along with Similarities and Vocabulary) can be very difficult to score. Even experienced test users, for example, may disagree over borderline responses in this subtest (Klinger and Saunders, 1975). For this reason, it is very important for the examiner to be very familiar with the scoring criteria and to insure that a scorable answer is elicited. Examiners must also be careful to use the scoring criteria objectively. Donahue and Sattler (1971) have found that examiners tend to give higher scores on these items if they like the subject.

Testing the limits may be done by continuing the test after four wrong answers, or by more specific questions into the nature of answers on ambiguous questions. Since such questions may be leading, the answers cannot be used in determining how many points the subject earned but can be useful in forming an impression of the subject. Testing the limits may also involve paraphrasing questions to see if different answers are elicited. Answers to this test should be recorded verbatim as they are often as revealing as some projective test items.

Arithmetic

Wechsler (1955) specifically warns examiners not to introduce this test as a test of arithmetic. The words arithmetic or mathematics often cause patients to expect severe failure. Wechsler suggests simply saying: "Now, let us try these" (Wechsler, 1955, p. 37). The test is begun on question three. Items one and two are administered only if both items three and four are missed. Subjects can get credit for a question only by giving the correct answer within the time limit shown. Hence, all items must be timed. Timing is begun when the examiner finishes reading the question. A question may be repeated exactly as written, if necessary, but the timing is not stopped. Answers not given within the time period are counted as wrong. Paper and pencil are not allowed.

Spontaneous corrections are allowed if they are given within the time period. Testing is discontinued after four consecutive failures. Testing the limits may also be used with this subtest. This can include allowing longer time for items on which the subject is actively working. This has the secondary effect of allowing the subject to feel that a correct answer has been reached, although it is not credited on the test. Additional items may also be given beyond four consecutive failures. Again, these cannot be included in the scoring.

Similarities

This subtest involves finding similarities between two objects. The test is begun with the first item. The format for each question is, "in what ways are a (object one) and a (object two) alike." If the first question is missed, the answer is given to the patient in order to illustrate what is wanted. Thereafter, no additional help is offered the subject, although they can be encouraged to expand on an ambiguous or borderline item as in the Comprehension test. Questions may also be repeated. The test is discontinued after four consecutive failures. In this test, the inexperienced examiner may have difficulty telling immediately whether a borderline response is scorable; in these cases, the answer should be counted as scorable and not as a failure. This may result in giving too many questions, but is preferable to giving too few questions. When the test is scored, no credit is given for answers given after four consecutive failures. This general procedure is applicable to Comprehension and Vocabulary also.

Testing the limits consists of additional questions or encouraging the subject to give more answers, even if he or she is not sure how good they are. The subject may often know better answers but does not recognize that they are better. As with the other subtests, however, such answers may not be used to increase a subject's score.

Digit Span

This test consists of two sections: Digits Forward and Digits Backwards. For Digits Forward, the subject is told that some numbers will be said which the subject should repeat afterwards exactly as they are given. The first item involves three digits. The most difficult item involves nine digits. If the subject gets a series correct, the examiner goes on to the next longer series. If an item is missed, a second item of the same length is given. If this is done correctly, the examiner moves on to the next longer series. If the second item of a given length is missed, the test is discontinued.

Digits Backward is given in much the same way. In this subtest, the subject must repeat the numbers given in the reverse order rather than exactly as stated. Item difficulty varies from two to eight numbers, and the administration is otherwise identical to Digit Forward. The test is ended when the subject misses two items of the same length.

On both Digits Forward and Digits Backward, additional items may be given in a testing the limits analysis. If a subject has missed all items, one may also attempt a two digit or one digit item to determine the severity of disorganization in the patient and to see if the instructions were understood.

Vocabulary

This is the last of the verbal tests. It consists of 40 items that are presented verbally as well as on a written card presented to the examinee. The subject is told that the test requires the subject to give the meaning of some words. In general, each word is presented with the statement "What does (word) mean?" The test starts with the fourth word. If any of the items four though eight are missed (0 score), the first three items are also given. If an answer is ambiguous or incomplete, the examiner should encourage the subject to tell him or her more. The test is discontinued after five consecutive failures. Much of the discussion regarding scoring and questioning discussed under the Comprehension and Similarities subtests are applicable to Vocabulary as well. As with the other tests, additional items or questioning may be used in a Testing the Limits procedure to further evaluate the subjects' competency in this area.

Digit Symbol

Digit Symbol requires the subject to match empty spaces under the symbols one to nine with symbols assigned to those numbers in a table at the top of the work page. An example of a Digit Symbol-like task is shown in Figure 1-1. The subject is first shown the task, the examiner states that each number is associated with a symbol, then instructs the subject to place the appropriate symbol in the empty box below each number. The examiner then goes over the first three items verbally and shows the subject what to do. The subject is then allowed to do seven additional sample items. These ten items serve as the practice portion of the test. At this point, the subject is told to fill in as many squares as he or she can without skipping any items (Wechsler,1955). After the examiner says begin, the subject starts and is allowed to continue for 90 seconds. If the subject skips any, the examiner instructs him or her to do them in order without skipping any. At the end of the 90 seconds, the subject is told to stop. No additional items that may have been done by the subject are counted in the score.

Wechsler provides special instructions for left-handed clients whose writing hand covers the table that gives the association between the numbers and symbols. In this case, a second key (from another record form of the WAIS) is placed before the subject so that the key can easily be seen. The examiner should stress for all subjects that perfect reproduction of figures is not necessary, especially if an inordinate amount of time is spent on such activities. If the subject stops at the end of the first line and does not immediately go to the second line, the examiner should instruct the subject to "Go to the next line and continue until I tell you to stop."

1	2	3	4	5	6	7	8	9
□	○	+	/	△	▽	\	X	L

2	9	3	7	8	6	4	1	5

Figure 1-1. Example of a Digit Symbol task. The upper table is used to fill in the lower items.

Subjects should not be allowed to erase; if they find an error, they can simply write over it.

Testing the limits may involve a readministration of the test if the examiner suspects that an initial low score was due to not understanding the task. They may also ask the subject to read or write the numbers (to insure they know them) or to write the symbols in order (to be sure that the symbols are visually perceived). These techniques can help clarify the source of the subject's problems when there is a poor performance.

Picture Completion

This task involves a set of pictures included in the WAIS kit, each of which has an important detail missing. The subject must identify the missing detail in each picture. All items on the test should be administered regardless of failures. For the first and second items, failure is followed by an explanation of what is wrong. For one additional item, if the subject finds some essential part missing, the examiner should say, "Yes, but what is the most important thing missing"(Wechsler, 1955). This, however, can be done for only one item. Answers should be given within 20 seconds, a more than ample time period if the subject is aware of what is missing.

Subjects need not identify the missing detail in verbal terms. The subject may describe the use of the piece, or point to where the detail is missing. The examiner may question the subject to determine if an answer is correct. The major scoring criteria is that the subject recognizes where something is missing and what it is. If a nut were missing from a screw, for example, the subject could say "the thing that holds the screw on," or point to the end of the screw, or say "nut," or "the square thing that goes there," or any other similar answer and still get credit.

Testing the limits is less appropriate with Picture Completion. One can see if the subject has missed items because he or she doesn't understand what the picture is. The subject may be asked to list all missing elements if there is a tendency to concentrate on unimportant details. None of this information, however, can be used in scoring.

Block Design

This task employs nine blocks, all of which are painted identically with all red sides, all white sides, and sides half red and half white, divided along the diagonal. The task requires the subject to duplicate ten designs in the Block Design booklet using the blocks. The task is similar to that used in many children's block toys. If the subject brings this up and is upset about it, it is useful to point out the strong relationship of Block

Design performance to engineering skills (Zimmerman and Woo-Sam, 1973).

The initial designs use four of the nine blocks which are provided. (Blocks not in use should be left in their box.) The first design is done in blocks by the examiner without showing the card with the design on it. The subject is given four additional blocks and allowed to copy what the examiner has done. If the subject fails, the examiner makes the design again out of the subject's blocks, mixes them up, and asks the subject to try the design again. The examiner then goes to the second item whether the subject succeeds or not. The examiner shows the subject the design on card 2, then tells the subject that he or she will make the blocks match the picture. After this is completed, the blocks are mixed up and the subject is instructed to do the design from the picture. If the subject fails, the demonstration is repeated and the subject given a second chance to do it.

After the first two trials, no additional help is given the subject. Design three is presented and the subject is told to make a design like this and to tell the examiner when he or she is finished. This procedure is followed for each design, except for design seven. Here the subject is told that the design requires nine blocks, all of which are placed before the subject. The test is discontinued after three consecutive failures. Failures on items one and two requires failing both chances to do the item.

There are definite time limits for all items (60 seconds through design six, 120 seconds for designs seven to ten) that must be adhered to by the examiner. If a subject is nearly finished, however, the examiner may allow the subject to continue although a correct answer is not scored. Spontaneous corrections within the time limit are allowed. In some cases, subjects may forget to tell the examiner when they are ready. If this occurs in the early cards, which do not give a time bonus, the subject should be reminded at the end of 60 seconds that the examiner is to be told when the item is finished.

Testing the limits can involve telling subjects after they finish that there is an error and asking them to correct it. Allowing extra time can often give valuable information as well.

Picture Arrangement

This subtest involves the arrangement of pictures so that they tell a logical, coherent story. Most people find the task interesting and challenging. The test materials consist of eight sets of cartoon pictures varying in length from three to six pictures. On the back of each card is a number denoting the sequence in which the pictures are to be laid out and a letter that is used to describe the sequence in which the pictures are arranged by the subject.

When the first item is presented to the subject, they are told that the pictures tell a story about a bird building a nest and that they are to place the cards in the correct order. If the item is missed, the examiner shows and explains to the subject what the correct sequence is. Then the pictures are placed in the mixed up order and the subject given a second chance to do item one. Item two is then presented with the instructions to put those cards in the right order. If this item is missed, the examiner again demonstrates and tells the correct story (about building a house). The subject is then given another chance on item two. If both items one and two are never correctly done, then the test is discontinued. The subject is otherwise given all the Picture Arrangement items. Each item is simply presented to the subject and they are told to put the cards in the right order.

There are definite time limits for each item. The examiner may allow the subject to exceed the time limits as a testing the limits procedure; however, such performances get no credit in the scoring. It is important to keep an accurate time since several items (seven and eight) offer time bonuses and no credit is given for overtime performances.

Testing the limits may also involve getting the subject to tell the story he is laying out; this can serve as a projective test and a measure of the subject's social competence. If there is a basic error in the subject's analysis of what the pictures represent, correcting this and then allowing another attempt can also be a way of evaluating the subject's social and intellectual skills.

Object Assembly

Object Assembly serves as the last Wechsler subtest. It consists of four jigsaw puzzle items which the subject must complete within specified time limits (two minutes for the first two items and three minutes for the last two items). Timing is extremely important on this test as time bonuses are available for each item. A screen is set up between the examiner and examinee for each item. The items are laid out behind the screen as detailed on the examiner side of the screen. This can be time consuming if the examiner is unsure of the order and the pieces; hence, previous practice is recommended so this can be done efficiently without undue waste of time.

For the first item, the subject is told that if the pieces are put together correctly, they will make something. Then the subject is told to go ahead and put the pieces together as quickly as he or she can. For later items, the instructions are simply to put the pieces together as quickly as possible. For all items, the subject is given credit only for performance under the time limit. If they have failed to finish by that time, it is necessary to score from the final configuration. Since scoring can be somewhat difficult initially, this may entail stopping the subject at the end of the time period so that partial credit may be given.

Scoring for partially finished figures involves the number of correct juxtapositions as defined by the WAIS manual. This involves placing together any two pieces in the correct way. The pieces need not be in the correct place overall, however. Thus, the scoring can take some time, especially with an inexperienced scorer. Testing the limits by giving extra time is an allowable procedure, but only when scoring has been finished.

SCORING THE WAIS

Each subtest is scored according to specific rules given in the manual. For Information, Picture Completion, and Digit Symbol the raw score is the number of items correctly answered. (It is important to remember that five of the verbal tests do not begin with item one and that credit is given for the skipped items.) For Arithmetic, it is the number of correct answers plus two possible points for fast performance on the last two items.

Three subtests, Comprehension, Similarities, and Vocabulary, employ a scoring system that rates the quality of each answer. A high quality answer scores a two, a low quality answer a one, and an incorrect or unacceptable answer no score. The criteria for judging quality on each answer is given in the manual; it is extremely important that the examiner be familiar with these criteria and stick to them as closely as possible. It is also necessary that the examiner be aware when an answer is borderline or incomplete so that the subject may be encouraged to expand or explain the answer. Proper questioning during testing makes scoring of these items much easier. For all three of these subtests, the final raw score is the sum of the scores on each item.

Digit Span is scored by simply summing up the number of digits forward and the number of digits backwards the individual can remember. On Object Assembly, Picture Arrangement, and Block Design, scoring is a combination of the number of correct answers and time bonuses. On Picture Arrangement and Block Design, each correct answer is worth four points. If a person gets a correct answer after first missing the item on items one and two, the correct answer is worth two points. For designs seven through ten of Block Design and seven and eight of Picture Arrangement, additional points are given for fast performances according to Wechsler's tables in the manual. In addition, Picture Arrangement gives partial credit (two points) for nearly correct answers listed in the manual for items six, seven, and eight. Partial credit answers, however, are not eligible for time bonuses.

Object Assembly offers partial credit and time bonuses for each item. Time bonuses are only available for fully correct answers. Partial credit is given for any pieces correctly placed together at the end of the time period as defined in the manual. This test is easily the most difficult performance test to score. For all three tests, Block Design, Picture Arrangement, and Object Assembly, the total raw score is the sum of the scores on the individual items.

DETERMINING SCALE SCORES

After raw scores have been calculated, scaled scores are determined. All scale scores are based on the performance of 500 subjects between the ages of 20 and 34. The mean score of this group has been arbitrarily defined as ten, the standard deviation as three. All scaled scores are based on this group no matter what the age of the subject. Raw scores are changed into scale scores by using the conversion table available on all WAIS record sheets.

Because of the scale transformation used, the scale scores give direct information on a patient's level of performance compared to the reference group. Fifty percent of all subjects will get scores from 8 to 12. Sixteen percent of all subjects will get scores below 7, and 16 percent will score above 13. Two and one-half percent will score above 16.

DETERMINING IQ's

Scaled Scores on the six verbal tests (Information through Vocabulary) are summed up to give a *Verbal Weighted Score*. Similarly, the five performance tests (Digit Symbol through Object Assembly) are summed up to get a *Performance Weighted Score*. These two scores are summed up to give a *Full Scale Weighted Score*. These three scores are then found in the appropriate IQ conversion table for the patient's current age. In these tables, the IQ equivalent of each weighted score is given.

There are situations in which the whole Wechsler is not given. In these situations, weighted scores must be estimated. The estimation formulas are as follows:

$$\text{Verbal Weighted} = \frac{\text{Sum of Scaled Scores of Tests Given}}{\text{Number of Tests Given}} \times 6$$

$$\text{Performance Weighted} = \frac{\text{Sum of Scaled Scores of Tests Given}}{\text{Number of Tests Given}} \times 5$$

BRIEF FORMS OF THE WAIS

Short forms of the Wechsler are usually given in situations where only an IQ estimate is needed or the abilities reflected in certain subtests are only of interest. They are often used in psychiatric settings where a quick screen is desired so that subjects who need more extensive testing can be identified and given the entire WAIS. The accuracy of these versions differs with the number of tests used. For example, Maxwell (1957) and Silverstein (1970) found that any combination of five tests could be used to estimate overall IQ with a .95 or better correlation. They also found similar accuracies for many different combinations of four tests, the best being a combination of Information, Vocabulary, Block Design, and Picture Arrangement. A combination of only Vocabulary and Information or Vocabulary and Block Design can correlate greater than .9 with full scale IQ. As a result, many different forms of an abbreviated WAIS can be used with confidence, especially if four or five scales are involved; the tests employed can be chosen on the basis of a clinician's needs in a given situation. For smaller batteries, however, it is recommended that the Maxwell and Silverstein articles be consulted.

One disadvantage of brief forms is the restriction of information available. As we shall see, there is only little interpretive value in the size of most IQ's, much more information comes from subtest patterning and from observing the subject's performance on different tasks. Such tests are at best screening devices from which no definite conclusions can be reached. As long as these objections are kept in mind and the abbreviated form is used for a logical, psychologically reasonable purpose that aids in the evaluation of patients, there is no reason to avoid such forms. Care must be taken in such situations to insure that others who see the test results (e.g., teachers, psychiatrists) are aware of the limitations of a short battery.

CLINICAL INTERPRETATION: THE INDIVIDUAL SUBTESTS

Each subtest of the Wechsler is hypothesized to measure certain major intellectual skills. As a result, analysis of how a patient performs on each subtest can yield valuable information for understanding a patient and for answering applicable referral questions. One important caution must be recognized, however: no subtest is a pure measure of any simple intellectual skill. All subtests represent combinations of skills, with some skills more heavily weighted on some tests than on others. It is important to recognize when interpreting test results that low scores may be due to a variety of reasons ranging from the very obvious to more subtle dysfunctions. For this reason, many users of the WAIS place a great emphasis on observing the patient while they do a subtest. Testing the limits is frequently used as a way of separating alternate theories about why a patient did badly.

As a result, an analysis of individual subtests does not give us final answers but rather enables us to generate hypothesis about the subject's performance. These hypotheses can then be tested by looking at the manner in which the subject performed the other subtests, the qualitative indices gained from observing the patient, and from testing the limits. If we hypothesize that block design is performed poorly because of poor spatial skills, for example, we would expect that the designs generated would be rather bizarre, including significant rotations. If, in fact, an individual was just slow but accurate, this hypothesis might have to be modified or dropped. Similarly, a poor spatial ability would show up in the performance on Object Assembly, and if this score is above normal, again we would have to reexamine the hypothesis.

In this way, hypotheses generated by each subtest can be confirmed or altered. This enables the clinician to form a picture of the individual's strengths and weaknesses. Combined with other analysis techniques, we are then able to accumulate extensive information on a patient's performance.

Information

Information serves primarily as a test of an individual's fund of general knowledge. It represents information to which we would expect the average individual with an average educational background to have access. The test measures long-term, remote memory, and the ability to assess and use that memory. In general, it is also related to an individual's reading background. Poor performance may be associated with a poor educational or cultural background as well as with low intelligence. Significantly low Information scores in an individual who was once normal or near normal suggests severe deterioration in intellectual function which may be related to severe psychosis or degenerative brain disorders. The score will also be low in individuals suffering early brain damage of the left hemisphere or involving both hemispheres. In such individuals, the score may reflect the individual's attainment at the time of the injury. In adults with deterioration late in life, the Information subtest may be the highest score. In these cases, it suggests the person's earlier IQ level. This can serve to help measure the amount of deterioration a person has suffered in cases involving insurance compensation for injury.

Schizophrenics will typically do less well on items involving reasoning rather than simple recall (Norman and Wilensky, 1961). Individuals from alternate cultural backgrounds are also likely to do poorly, as are individuals from poor educational backgrounds (Finlayson, Johnson, and Reitan, 1977; Walker, 1970).

Comprehension

Comprehension evaluates an individual's ability to understand common social customs and situations, and to provide for appropriate activity as well as the reasons behind such activities. It assesses one's awareness of social norms and practices, and one's ability to abstract the reasons behind them. The test also evaluates long-term memory and experience, and the ability to verbalize these factors. The test also involves the individual's judgment: to select from alternative answers and to provide those that are most acceptable and logical (Rapaport, Gill, and Schafer, 1970).

Poor performance on Comprehension can be associated with long-term dysfunction such as early brain injury or childhood psychosis. A poor or alternate cultural background can also cause low scores. (In such cases, one must assess whether the answers given are reasonable for the individual's cultural and educational background.) Comprehension is in general less affected by educational background than is Information.

There is some evidence that socialization is a strong factor in comprehension. As noted above, one must be able to view the logical choices and select those most reasonable, a process which implies knowledge of one's culture. In addition, Hunt, Quay, and Walker (1966) have reported correlations between Comprehension and socialization. Wechsler (1958) found adolescent sociopaths performed at the mean or lower on Comprehension, suggesting general agreement with this hypothesis.

Comprehension will generally be relatively high in brain injured adults, reacting in the same manner as does Information. It can also be used to estimate premorbid level of functioning and, except in severe deterioration, is among the highest scores. Psychotics will generally score lower on Comprehension than Information and Vocabulary because of the judgmental decisions more inherent in Comprehension. Comprehension as the highest score is not unusual in intelligent adults, especially if educational levels do not match their intellectual levels.

One advantage of the Comprehension subtest over the other subtests is its ability to elicit a number of important qualitative remarks from individuals. Otherwise hidden pathological conditions may show up in a bizarre response or responses on Comprehension. For example, an individual may say we register marriages so that the government can keep track of children who are to be sent to secret camps. A particularly antisocial youth suggested that when one sees a fire, one should watch carefully so one can see the people die. Such responses may almost be diagnostic in and of themselves. Preoccupation with bizarre ideas may result in lowered scores, or may only show up in one or two items so that the individual has a normal or even superior score overall.

Good scores on the test suggest someone in touch with social reality and with the day-to-day world. These scores are particularly important in individuals with otherwise poor profiles. For example, the mentally retarded individual with a higher Comprehension score can probably operate on a higher social level than suggested by the person's overall IQ and may be an excellent job candidate because of this ability. Poor scores, however, may not mean the opposite. Testing the limits is useful in attempting to isolate the causes for a given Comprehension score.

Arithmetic

The understanding of number concepts is an important part of intellectual development, especially in a highly numerical, science oriented civilization. Arithmetic provides a basic measure of an individual's ability to work with Arithmetic problems in logical and daily problems. In addition to obvious arithmetic kills, the test also requires verbal understanding (translating the verbal problems into arithmetic operations and back again), memory (especially in older and brain injured patients), and concentration. Educational background and experience with arithmetic appear to be an important aspect of the test's performance.

Before going ahead with a discussion of this test, it is necessary to consider the problem of an individual's reactions to the test. Many individuals react quite dramatically to the problems, often stating that they are stupid and cannot do such things, and even refusing to try what are otherwise simple problems. Such a strong emotional reaction in what are otherwise normal individuals, lowers scores, often to the lowest score on the test. In many cases, these scores must be discounted in determining the individual's intellectual capabilities. The score is important, however, in making vocational choices for the person; such an individual would not do well in College Math or as an engineer without a good course in how to relax when doing arithmetic. The reactions may also be a clue in how the individual handles strong frustration.

Arithmetic may be a low score in mentally retarded individuals as well as brain injured persons. Individuals with concentration problems may also do poorly. Transient high anxiety states may cause low scores on this test and on Digit Span (Knox and Grippaldi, 1970; Keiser, 1978; Firetto and Davey, 1971). Digit Span, however, appears to be more sensitive to this general anxiety than is Arithmetic (Rapaport, Gill, and Schafer, 1970).

It should be emphasized that Arithmetic is not a particularly good measure of arithmetic skills (the ability to add and subtract and so on). Individuals will often do better on a pure test of mathematical skills, such as the Wide Range Achievement Test, discussed later, than they do on Arithmetic where they lack paper and pencil and there is greater emphasis on memory, concentration, attention, and verbal skills. If one is interested in actual grade level skills, such tests as the Wide Range Achievement Test are much more appropriate.

Arithmetic will often be poor in organic disorders of many kinds, with particularly low scores achieved in left hemisphere injuries. The test involves such a wide range of skills, however, that low scores may be found in almost any kind of injury.

Similarities

Similarities relates to an individual's ability to form verbal concepts—specifically generalizations—when given two members of a given verbal class (e.g., tools or clothing or living beings). The test requires memory, concentration, and the ability to relate the two objects to a common class. These relations may be done at two levels: concrete (you wear them) or abstract (clothing). The more abstract a person's associations the higher the score on the test. The individual must be able to concentrate on the essential details of the objects compared, and must have the verbal skills to form the relevant verbal concepts.

Similarities provide a measure of higher cognitive skills. The individual who does well is often able to work well with verbal abstract ideas and to handle simple reasoning. The impaired patient is often one who has low verbal skills or who is able to respond only in a concrete fashion. In the poorest cases, the individual is not able to see any relationship at all, even in the simple items. This implies an individual operating at a very low, reactive level with few generalizations to link things together. Low scores may also suggest low emotional control (Rapaport, Gill, and Schafer, 1970).

Generally, Similarities varies little from a subject's mean score in most diagnostic groups (Zimmerman and Woo-Sam, 1973), although there is considerable individual variation. One exception to this is a brain injury in the left temporal lobe or left parietal lobe which may interfere with an individual's ability to form categories. The test also has characteristics similar to Vocabulary, Comprehension, and Information, however, which tends to keep the scores up because of prior experience and learning (long-term memory). This skill is generally not affected except by long-term deterioration or extremely severe brain dysfunction. On the other hand, the test requires new learning and abstracting, especially in the more difficult items. These complex skills are quite sensitive to deterioration in brain damage and in emotional disorders. Thus Similarities represents a "swing" test which may stay up or go down depending on the severity of the injury and the nature of the disorder. As a result, comparison of Similarities to the more stable, long-term memory tests (Vocabulary, Information, and Comprehension) and to the more abstract, deterioration sensitive tests (Digit Span, Block Design, Digit Symbol) can provide a good barometer of actual deterioration as opposed to simple anxiety affects. For example, McKeever, May, and Tuma (1965) found that high Similarities scores were good prognostic signs in predicting early release in schizophrenic patients.

It is rare that answers to Similarities questions will indicate a specific pathology. As a result, such answers should be attended to closely. Zimmerman and Woo-Sam (1973) in a review of the Similarities literature, suggest that schizophrenics tend to deny the presence of similarities between objects more so than brain damaged individuals who simply have no answer. This result has not been generally confirmed, however. Such denials appear to be more common in paranoid schizophrenics with current acute exacerbations rather than in all schizophrenics. Similarly, the performance of the brain damaged differs considerably with type and extent of lesion (see section on Organicity).

Digit Span

Digit Span is a measure of immediate auditory memory. The test requires the ability to attend and concentrate as well as remember. In Digits Backward, there is the additional skill of reverse sequencing, which appears to be largely spatial rather than verbal in nature. Digit Span is not a general measure of memory skills. Other memory skills—delayed auditory memory, visual memory of all kinds, logical memory, and the like— are not measured by the test, nor is there necessarily a correlation between Digit Span performance and other measures of memory.

Digit Span is very sensitive to both anxiety and brain deterioration (McFie, 1975; Golden, 1978; Keiser, 1975; Firetto and Davey, 1971; Walker, Sannito, and Firetto, 1970; Walker and Spence, 1964). Scores are quite depressed in anxiety states, but are relatively normal in schizophrenics without cognitive deterioration (Wechsler, 1958). Digits Forward and Digits Backward are affected by left hemisphere brain damage, especially in the temporal lobe, while localized right hemisphere injuries, especially in the right frontal lobe, might affect Digits Backwards alone.

Rapaport, Gill, and Schafer (1970) have suggested that extremely low Digit Span scores relative to all other scores may indicate a depressive psychosis or deteriorated schizophrenia, whereas a good Digit Span score relative to all other scores in a schizophrenic suggests an absence of anxiety.

Vocabulary

Vocabulary is generally recognized as the best single estimate of intelligence. It is assumed that the individual has had an equal chance in terms of education, cultural background, and verbal interactions with others in making this statement. To the extent that the assumptions are true, it has been found that Vocabulary alone can correlate up to .9 with full scale intelligence. Vocabulary measures one's ability to learn words and express their meanings. It is one of the primary "hold" tests among the Wechsler subtests that resist change with mental deterioration and aging.

Low Vocabulary scores are often the result of poor general intelligence, poor educational background, different cultural background (especially where standard English is not an individual's first language), or early brain injury. Like the Comprehension and Information subtests, brain injury (especially in the left hemisphere), will not affect the individual's level of Vocabulary at the time of the injury, but will affect future learning. Thus, Vocabulary can often be used to evaluate premorbid intelligence in the individual injured in adulthood and to estimate the age of injury in an individual injured as a child. The one exception to this rule is general deteriorating disorders such as Alzheimer's Disease (Golden, 1978).

High vocabulary scores may reflect high verbal intelligence and good education: an inquisitive, curious individual who likes to read, and has a sensitivity to new verbal experiences. Since Vocabulary is not affected by many pathological conditions, however, a high Vocabulary score does not necessarily imply a currently intact individual A low score, in contrast, generally implies mental retardation or a serious pathological condition in individuals with an adequate cultural and educational background.

Digit Symbol

Digit Symbol measures a wide variety of skills. It is the most sensitive subtest of the WAIS to motor problems in the dominant hand. It also measures basic learning skills; the ability to associate a symbol with a number. This involves visual memory as well as the ability to maintain a course of action in a speeded, sometimes tense race against the clock. As a result, the test is also sensitive to high levels of anxiety. Because of its sensitivity to memory and motor deficits, the test is also useful in detecting brain dysfunction.

Consequently, low scores may suggest a number of conditions ranging from anxiety to brain damage. The test is generally sensitive to age effects as well. Unlike most of the verbal tests, this test does possess the ability to be administered to culturally and educationally deprived individuals. (This is also true for Block Design.) Testing the limits, as described earlier, and close observation can be useful in identifying such factors, although in some cases the problems may be so intertwined that only a general dysfunction can be recognized. Extremely good scores on Digit Symbol are rare in most pathological conditions.

The correlation with anxiety is best seen with current, situational anxiety rather than a general trait of anxiety. Thus, attempts by the examiner to keep the testing situation and the examinee relaxed can be useful in producing better scores.

Picture Completion

Picture Completion is a measure of an individual's ability to perceive and visually organize a sketch and then recognize that an essential element of some kind is missing. In addition, one must be able to avoid distractions and inessential details. Since familiarity with the objects pictured is necessary, there is a strong cultural component in the test. For example, while the author lived in Hawaii, he found many subjects who did poorly, simply because the items were so foreign to their experience.

Of all the performance tests, Picture Completion is the least sensitive to focal brain disorders. Thus, in serious left hemisphere injuries which affect the traditional scores that measure premorbid intelligence (Comprehension, Vocabulary, Information), the Picture Completion score becomes the best estimate of that premorbid intelligence.

Paranoid patients may express the belief that nothing is missing from pictures relatively frequently. Weiner (1966) has suggested that schizophrenia can be recognized in Picture Completion by the type of errors that are made. For example, on an animal with a missing tail a schizophrenic might answer udders, tongue, or sex organs. On a violin without a string peg, the schizophrenic might say the violinist was missing, while a normal might suggest the bow or strings. Rapaport, Gill, and Schafer (1970) suggest that extremely poor performance is suggestive of deteriorated schizophrenics and depressed psychotics. Moderate impairment suggests schizophrenia in general, while normal performance is suggestive of neurosis in a psychiatric population.

Block Design

Block Design is the purest measure of spatial (nonverbal) reasoning in the WAIS. As a result it is an excellent measure of nonverbal intelligence and general spatial skills necessary for such tasks as engineering. The subject must begin with the picture presented, break it down in some manner so that the placement of blocks can be determined, and then place the blocks in the correct manner. In this task, the test requires strong visual analysis skills and visual-motor coordination. In the more difficult items, speed as well as concentration and attention are also demanded to get a maximum score. The test also allows the examiner to observe how the subject goes about problem solving; impulsively, with great planning, hit and miss, or a combination of these techniques.

Organic impairment often affects Block Design performance extensively. This is especially obvious in diffuse injuries and injuries involving either parietal lobe. In most brain injuries, Block Design will be below the subject's mean score and often be the lowest of all the performance tests. In schizophrenics, however, Block Design tends to stay at or above the subject's mean score (Wechsler, 1958). As a result, Block Design is an excellent measure for discriminating schizophrenic from brain damaged performance as was recently demonstrated by Golden (1977).

One disadvantage of Block Design is its difficulty for low intelligence subjects as the test does not have any really easy items. On the other hand, several very difficult designs help the test to discriminate well among individuals with high nonverbal intellectual skills. A second major advantage lies in the qualitative impressions about the subject that can be gained by attentively watching the subject's performance, something sometimes missed by many examiners.

Picture Arrangement

Picture Arrangement provides the evaluation of several major skills: visual perception of individual pictures, organization of a series of pictures, awareness of social sequences, planning skills, ability to form and test hypotheses (possible stories), flexibility, and general ability to sequence material in a logical order. One drawback of the test is its dependence on social sequences which may differ from culture to culture; consequently, a cultural bias is possible on the test and must be considered in any evaluation.

Picture Arrangement is considered by many as a measure of what Wechsler (1958) called "social intelligence" (Edinger, 1976). Wechsler found that adolescent sociopaths did very well on this test, while schizophrenics varied considerably. Brain injured patients do not show as great a loss on Picture Arrangement as they do on the other performance tests (except Picture Completion). It can be affected by injuries to the right frontal areas, however, and may be down more than the other performance tests in certain left hemisphere injuries which disrupt social or verbal skills.

Some insight into a subject's manner of thinking may be gained from having the subject explain incorrect stories as this may indicate some defects in social competence or the understanding of cause and effect relationships. This information can be valuable in a qualitative evaluation of a subject.

Object Assembly

Object Assembly requires visual analysis and visual-motor skills from a subject. The subject must recognize what the object is from the pieces presented or at least their interrelationship. Then, it is necessary to put the pieces together in a manner that creates the object involved. As in Block Design, one is able to watch how an individual faces a relatively difficult problem solving task.

Both organic and schizophrenic patients may do poorly on Object Assembly. The Object Assembly score is often one of the higher scores in mentally retarded subjects however. Wechsler reported that neurotics show impairment on Object Assembly, but Ladd (1964) failed to find any deficit. Rapaport, Gill, and Schafer suggest that depressed individuals tend to do poorly on the test, which may be related to the heavy emphasis of time bonuses used in scoring Object Assembly.

INTERPRETING PATTERNS OF SUBTEST SCORES

Interpreting differences between subtest scores is often important in the analysis of a WAIS profile. For example, one may be interested in whether a person's ability to interpret visual information and to find inconsistencies (Picture Completion) is significantly different from the person's ability to analyze a visual configuration and to reproduce it in blocks (Block Design). Such a comparison might allow us to infer that the individual can visually analyze what is put before him or her, but is unable to perform the motor skills necessary to reproduce the pattern (construction dyspraxia, a major symptom of many organic brain disorders). Similarly, one might ask if a score on a test not sensitive to anxiety (Vocabulary) is stronger than a score on a test sensitive to anxiety (such as Digit Span). This allows us to infer the presence of a significant amount of anxiety or other similar disorder.

Such comparisons lie at the heart of interpreting the pattern of scale scores. The comparisons allow us to infer the source of the problem in a lower scale score on one of the tests. The process basically involves comparing the two or more tests involved, and attempting to identify which skills are measured by one test and not the other. These are the skills which are then likely to be impaired, or conversely, the skills which are strong. When such comparisons are made over all of the scales which significantly differ from one another, a pattern will usually emerge giving the clinician a strong idea of the individual's relative strengths and weaknesses. This pattern of skills can then be used to predict and to diagnose approximately for the referral question.

These comparisons have some difficulties associated with them. The major problem is that the subscale scores are not all reliable; that is, one cannot be sure that the score the patient received is his or her real score. Thus, when two subtests differ by only one point, it may be that there is really no difference at all, and that the apparent difference was created only by chance events and the unreliability of the subtests.

As a result of this problem, scores on each pair of tests must differ by a certain number of scale scores before the difference can be considered significant. Specifically, scores must differ anywhere from three to five scale points before the difference is significant at the .05 level. The size of the difference depends on which two subtests one is comparing. This, however, is a rather burdensome arrangement, as the user would have to consult a table everytime he or she wanted to know whether the difference between a given pair of scores was significant. In actual practice, most clinicians simply work from the assumption that all differences of a given size are likely to be significant, a practice that appears to work well. More conservative clinicians will generally assume that a four-point difference is necessary for significance, while many others simply assume that a three-point difference is sufficient enough to establish a clinical difference.

INTERPRETATION OF IQ's: THEORETICAL ISSUES

The interpretation of the meaning of an intelligence quotient has become one of the more controversial issues in clinical psychology. This controversy has centered around biases in the test against individuals with certain cultural and educational backgrounds. As noted earlier, several of the subtests are performed more poorly by individuals with low education or from different cultures in the absence of any reasonable expectation of an intellectual difference between two groups. The mere fact that education and culture affect a test result does not make it a bad test, however. The problem arises when the test is misinterpreted. If an individual with a poor educational background gets a low score on Information, for instance, we may just conclude that the individual has had little educational opportunity (which in this case is true). If we were to conclude that the person was brain damaged, however, we would be in error because our *interpretation* of the test score was wrong.

Thus, in interpreting any IQ score, several factors must be considered. These can be best expressed as an equation: IQ score = Actual Intelligence + Environment + Motivation. This simply means that any IQ score we calculate is a combination of an individual's actual intelligence plus or minus a factor for the person's environment (culture, education, language, experience) and a factor for the individual's motivation. Note that this equation makes no assumption about the nature of actual intelligence. The equation applies whether one believes that intelligence is an interaction of environment and biological skills, biological skills alone, or determined by background alone.

Environment includes all the exogenous factors that influence intellectual development. Psychometric theories assume, in general, that the individual taking the test has had average chances to gain an education, to interact with other people, to learn standard English, and to generally experience life as a child and adult in the dominant American culture. To the extent that this assumption is not true, then the obtained IQ on the WAIS (or any other test) will deviate from the actual IQ of the individual. If the total experience of the individual has been greater than that offered others, the obtained IQ will be too high; if the total experience has been too little, then the obtained IQ will be too low. In both of these circumstances, the obtained IQ will have to be adjusted if we contend that we are measuring "actual IQ" instead of how well one performed on the test.

Motivation is also an important factor. Again, we make the assumption that an individual has an average level of motivation to do the test. This, of course, is not true. Some cultural groups or other subgroups do not place an importance on IQ tests or test performance in general. Some individuals with psychiatric disorders may not be motivated to do anything, let alone an intelligence test. On the other hand, the child from a home which places a strong emphasis on education may be highly motivated to do well and perform higher as a result. Minor deviations from average motivation do not affect test scores greatly. Individuals whose motivations are seriously deficient, however, or who may be motivated to deliberately do badly, will get much lower scores than they are capable of achieving. In these cases, the test results must often be rejected as generally uninterpretable (except for the observation that the patient is unmotivated). Patients with high motivation may do somewhat better than expected, and the results must be regarded as an example of the person achieving at his or her best. One exception to this must be noted: if the person is too highly motivated and concerned about his or her performance, the anxiety generated by the individual's concern may actually lower performance. This can often be seen most dramatically in the Digit Symbol and Digit Span scores.

Thus, we interpret any IQ (or any scale score) by looking at the actual score on the test, estimating the person's environmental background (through interview as a rule), estimating the individual's motivation (by observation during the testing), and estimating the patient's "actual IQ" from these factors. Which of these factors is of importance in interpretation of a given case differs considerably depending on the situation. If we are asked "Which person of these two will do better in a school situation today without any additional training?," the person with the actual higher verbal IQ would probably be the best bet. If we were asked "Which person who is doing badly now would benefit by additional training?," we would ideally pick the person with a high "actual IQ" (discounting cultural effects) and a high motivation, since they would more likely be interested in such education. If we are asked, "Can this person take care of herself?," we might look at actual performance, since that is where the individual is now. Each situation must be approached on the basis of the parameters of that situation.

INTERPRETING IQ's: PRACTICAL FACTORS

All Wechsler IQ's have a mean of 100 and a standard deviation of fifteen. Thus 50 percent of all people will have an IQ in the range from 90 to 110, the range of average or normal intelligence. Sixteen percent of the population has an IQ below 85, and about 2½ percent have IQ's above 130. IQ's at or above normal do not generally have the behavioral implications of low IQ's. At these levels, a person's desire, personality factors, creativity, and emotional factors make more of a behavioral influence than does IQ. Thus, the individual with 105 IQ may become a success while the person with 130 IQ is a failure. For reference, however, the average high school graduate will have an IQ of about 100; the average BA an IQ of 110; the average MA an IQ of 120; and the average Ph.D. an IQ of 130. Thus, it is highly unlikely that the individual with IQ 95 would get a Ph.D., but well within possibility that such an individual would get a BA. Such predictions, however, must be tempered with the recognition that some individuals with IQ 95 probably do have doctoral degrees.

Performance and Verbal IQ's can be interpreted in much the same way as Full scale IQ's. High verbal IQ's predispose individuals towards careers with high verbal content (psychology, most other social sciences, law, etc.) while higher performance IQ's imply such careers as engineering, mathematics, architecture, or surgery. Since most individuals have Performance and Verbal IQ's that are relatively close together, however, such differences usually are not major in determining a career; such factors as interest, vocational aptitude, parents' occupation, and so on are much more significant determinants.

Low IQ

The lower an IQ is below normal, the more important it becomes in limiting an individual's choices. At extremely low levels, the person has no choice and little ability; he or she must be cared for continuously. At the higher levels, IQ plus a number of social factors determine the extent and independence of a person's adjustment.

IQ's in the range of 70 to 84 are generally considered borderline or marginally intelligent (Maloney and Ward, 1976). Such individuals are able to achieve reasonable social and vocational competence if they are given proper education and training and have sufficient job opportunities. Many are never recognized by others as being lower in intelligence because of the ability to interact with others at a normal level (social competence). In general, their intellectual attainments limit their socioeconomic status. Sometimes they will drop out of school because of frustration, but they are capable of finishing most American high school programs. The lower level of intelligence along with lower socioeconomic status may dispose these individuals to a higher degree of stress and lower level of medical care, which may lead to more frequent hospitalizations and serious physical and mental problems.

IQ's in the 55 to 69 range are typically defined as mild mental retardation. Since 1973, however, the American Association of Mental Deficiency has defined mental retardation as an IQ below 70 along with a significant deficit in adaptive behavior, both of which developed before the age of 18 (Grossman, 1973). Thus, in addition to the IQ deficit, the person must show an inability to adapt to his or her environment. In the adult, this is usually defined as the ability to achieve social and economic self-sufficiency (Maloney and Ward, 1976). Using this double definition, the rate of mental retardation is significantly reduced.

It is important to recognize that social adaptability depends a great deal on both the individual and the society to which he or she must adjust. A highly stressful, technological society would thus create a larger number of mentally retarded individuals than would a more agrarian, less stressful environment. The incidence of mental retardation will vary from locale to locale and country to country as a result. The urban psychologist must recognize that the individual living in a rural setting may be perfectly adapted there even if a problem arises when the person comes into the city.

Individuals with IQ's in this range, as well as lower IQ's, are more likely to develop psychiatric disorders than others. This is theoretically due to their inability to handle as much stress or complexity as a person of normal abilities because of a lack of adequate cognitive skills to handle the problems. In such cases, disorders may range from neuroses to acute psychotic-like problems. It is necessary for the psychologist and other professionals working with the person to take into account the role of IQ and transient situational stress in the development of these disorders, rather than assuming a long-term underlying psychotic disorder.

In working with the person with an IQ in this range, it is also necessary to assess such factors as motivation, attitudes, past experience, and the like in addition to intelligence when making recommendations for training or other types of disposition. The consideration of any secondary deficits such as motor dysfunction, perceptual problems, and health disorders are also important, as these additional strengths or weaknesses can make a big difference in prognosis. Individuals with higher scores in such tests as Comprehension and Picture Arrangement should be considered better risks because of a higher understanding of social and practical situations. In suggesting training or job opportunities, a careful analysis of skills, by carefully examining subtest patterns, is imperative.

IQ's in the range below 55 are variously described as moderately retarded (40 to 54), severely retarded (25 to 39), or profoundly retarded (24 or below). IQ's below 40, however, must be estimated on the WAIS as Wechsler does not provide Tables for such IQ's. In addition, the number of easy items on the Wechsler for lower IQ is practically nonexistent; as a result the accuracy of IQ's below 55 is questionable. If one needs to know how far an IQ is below 55, the test of choice is the Stanford-Binet (see Chapter 2 in this volume).

Individuals with moderate mental retardation may be able to hold jobs, but many have difficulty in learning self-help skills. Individuals with severe or profound retardation are generally severely brain damaged and unable to care for themselves. Special help from trained individuals is necessary for the care and teaching of these groups.

THE PIQ-VIQ DIFFERENCE

Much has been written about the significance of differences between the PIQ and VIQ. In general, however, little has been learned. One of the problems of looking at this difference is the assumption that the performance and verbal IQ's measure different things. Even a casual analysis of the test, however, reveals this to be false. For example, nearly all the performance tests involve verbal components. Instructions are primarily verbal, although some demonstrations are given. Social competency as measured by Picture Arrangement usually has a strong verbal component. Digit Symbol involves numbers and symbols similar to letters and offers a clear advantage to the literate individual. Picture Completion must be understood purely through verbal instructions. On the other hand, Arithmetic skills are strongly spatial in nature, as educators have tried to show with the "New Math". Reversing digits in Digits Backward is a spatial skill. An overlap arises when one tests brain injured patients; the left hemisphere controls verbal skills which causes low verbal scores, but it also controls right hand motor skills necessary to do Digit Symbol, Block Design, Picture Arrangement, and Object Assembly. Finally, all the tests are influenced to some degree by the assumed general underlying intelligence factor many biological and neurological theories of intelligence define. The overall relationship between the scales is shown by their high intercorrelation (.77) and the high correlation of both scales with full scale IQ (.96, .93) (Wechsler, 1955).

Despite these factors which act to keep the performance and verbal IQ's alike, there are generally differences between them in almost all individuals. In general, these differences are small (less than ten points), and probably due largely to chance variations in scores and rounding errors in translating from raw to scale scores. In some individuals, however, these differences are considerably larger. In some cases, this may be due to one very poor score, such as Arithmetic, which lowers an otherwise high IQ. In these cases, the difference is due to a specific problem in one area. In other cases, large differences (greater than ten points) may reflect differential aptitudes that may arise because of environment or culture (individuals from alternate cultures may average as much as 15 points lower in verbal as opposed to performance skills), teaching (an educational curriculum that emphasized one skill over the other, usually verbal skills in bright individuals), or simply an inability to do better in one sphere of endeavor as compared to the other.

One extensive area of research has attempted to relate PIQ-VIQ differences to brain damage. As can be recognized by the reader, the presence of significant differences in normals for the reasons cited above make it difficult to ascribe large differences only to brain damage. Many have attempted to prove, however, that there are greater differences in brain damaged groups. Although some positive studies have been reported supporting this contention, in general no definitive pattern or highly reliable diagnostic sign has been found (e.g., see Golden, 1978; Todd, Coolidge, and Satz, 1977). While it can be said that strong verbal-performance differences may be associated with brain damage in some cases, such differences are often not present. Golden (1978) indicates that the differences are more likely in acute, focal brain disorders and less likely in both chronic and diffuse brain disorders. Since most brain damage seen by psychologists falls into the latter group, the sign is of limited value.

Given that the difference is not a good indication of brain damage versus normality, others have looked at the ability of the difference to predict right versus left brain damage. These studies have hypothesized that since the left hemisphere controls verbal functions, individuals with left hemisphere injuries should have low verbal scores as compared to performance scores. Similarly, since the right hemisphere controls non-verbal functions, individuals with right hemisphere injuries should have lower performance (nonverbal scores). An impressive number of studies have supported this contention (Balthazar, 1963; Balthazar and Morrison, 1961; Black, 1974; Dennerll, 1964; Doehring, Reitan, and Klove, 1961; Fields and Whitmyre, 1969; Goldstein and Shelley, 1973; Russell, 1972). Despite this support, an equally imposing list of studies has failed to support the use of the PIQ-VIQ difference in lateralization (Heilbrun, 1959; Meyer and Jones, 1957; Pennington, Galliani, and Voegele, 1965; Reed, Reitan, and Klove, 1965; Smith, 1966).

An examination of the studies supporting and contradicting the PIQ-VIQ hypothesis reveals some basic problems in the difference score. It appears to work only in localized lesions rather than extremely massive lesions (as these will tend to disturb the function of the brain as a whole), and works better with acute as opposed to chronic injuries. Lesions in the parietal-temporal area of both hemispheres tend to produce better results. Frontal lesions may indeed even fail to affect average IQ at all (Smith, 1966).

Reasons for the failure of the test in many situations suggest that the PIQ-VIQ difference can only be used as a general indicator suggesting a hypothesis to the clinician. Such hypotheses must be confirmed by closer examination of the test results and the nature of the errors made by the patient. If performance scores are lower than verbal scores, for example, because the right (dominant) hand is paralyzed, one is much more likely to have a left hemisphere injury, as the left hemisphere controls the right hand. Similarly, left frontal lesions which are massive may disturb an individual's ability to follow directions and will cause both scores to be equally low. A subtle right frontal injury may affect Digits Backward alone, causing the performance IQ to be higher than the verbal IQ.

WAIS PATTERNS AND THE DIAGNOSIS OF BRAIN DAMAGE

Many advocates of the WAIS recognized quite early that simple differences in performance and verbal IQ's were not sufficient for the diagnosis of brain damage, recognizing many of the same problems cited above. These researchers attempted to find alternate ways to diagnose brain dysfunction. The most famous of these concerns the "hold" and "don't hold" tests. The theory behind this approach suggested that some tests on the WAIS were very sensitive to brain damage; they would be affected every time a brain injury was present. Other tests, the theory said, were hold tests. These scores would not go down in brain damaged subjects. Thus, if one would compare the hold to don't hold tests, one could tell if there was a relative decrease in the don't hold tests. If there was a decrease, then there was brain damage. Numerous combinations of hold and don't hold tests were suggested for these formulas. All ended up with one basic result: they didn't work (Golden, 1978).

The reasons for this failure were numerous. First, tests sensitive to brain damage (such as Digit Span or Digit Symbol) are the same tests sensitive to anxiety, psychiatric disorders, distraction, lack of motivation, and nearly every other disorder which interferes with the assessment of intelligence. As a result, there is no way to tell the brain injured from the anxious from the psychotic patient using these formulas. The formulas did work relatively well with normals, however. The problem is that the psychologist never has to say whether a "normal control" is brain damaged. One is almost always working with a choice of diagnoses such as brain damaged or schizophrenic.

A second major reason for the failure is that each of the don't hold tests are unaffected by a great number of brain disorders. Originally, the don't hold tests were developed from populations consisting primarily of diffuse organic brain syndromes. In these individuals, scores on all the don't hold tests were down. In focal injuries seen in general hospitals or neurological settings, however, only one or none of the don't hold tests (e.g., Digit Symbol), may be impaired. In essence, the problem boiled down to the observation that the hold and don't hold tests differed considerably depending on the type and focus of the brain damage.

From the recognition that the WAIS is differentially affected by different lesions has come research looking for patterns of WAIS scores which signify different lesions. With this method one determines the pattern of impaired test scores. This pattern can then be matched against patterns expected in different kinds of brain injury. If the pattern matches what would be expected in a given brain injury, then the person is likely to be brain injured in that part of the brain.

The most ambitious use of the WAIS in this manner was reported by McFie (1975). McFie outlines the basic patterns expected in different types of localized brain injuries. Left frontal lesions are characterized by a loss on Digit Span with a mild or no loss in the verbal IQ. Such injuries will also be accompanied by a deficit in verbal associative learning. Right frontal lesions are characterized by deficits in Picture Arrangement, on memory tasks involving designs, and sometimes in Digits Backward (Golden, 1978). Left temporal lesions produce losses in Similarities and the Digit Span test; right temporal lesions cause a drop in Picture Arrangement and design memory. Meier and French (1966) have also suggested that a loss in Object Assembly may be seen. Left parietal injuries will cause losses on Arithmetic, Digit Span, Block Design, and sometimes Similarities (Mahan, 1976). Right parietal lesions will affect memory for design, Block Design, and Picture Arrangement. (Tests for design memory are discussed later.)

Diffuse injuries will generally cause a loss on most of the tests sensitive to brain injury: Digit Span, Arithmetic, Picture Arrangement, Object Assembly, Block Design, and Digit Symbol. (Digit Symbol will tend to be down in all brain injuries, as well as in many intact individuals.) Injuries to subcortical areas will generally affect tests with strong motor components: Digit Symbol, Block Design, Object Assembly, Picture Arrangement, in this order. Injuries which involve more than one of the areas discussed above will produce various combinations of the test deficits depending on the precise location of the deficit.

Deficits which are caused by brain injury early in childhood, especially before age two, will show a considerably different pattern of scores than the adult. As a rule, the individual will have an IQ below 80 and often in the range of mental retardation. The tests traditionally referred to as hold tests (Information, Comprehension, and Vocabulary) will generally be the lowest tests in the record. This is due to the inability of the early brain injured child to fully take advantage of educational opportunities and from day-to-day learning. Often the highest scores in these subjects will be on Digit Span, Picture Completion, Arithmetic, and Block Design. Recognition of this pattern allows the psychologist to differentiate between relatively early brain damage and brain damage occurring later in life.

As a test of organicity, the WAIS is not accurate enough to be used alone. Combined with a test of visual memory, such as the Benton Visual Retention Test, the WAIS can be useful as a screening instrument for deficits in individuals known to be brain damaged. It is not diagnostically effective enough, however, to be used to make the diagnosis of brain damage versus no brain damage with confidence. It has been shown, however, to be a highly useful instrument to add to a more extensive neuropsychological test battery such as the Halstead-Reitan (see later chapter on this test).

PSYCHIATRIC DISORDERS: DIAGNOSTIC APPROACHES

It is questionable whether the WAIS, or any other intelligence test, should ever serve as a primary diagnostic instrument for psychiatric disorders. Diagnostic inferences made from other tests such as the MMPI which is discussed later, however, can be confirmed or supplemented with information gained from the WAIS. If one has diagnosed a psychosis, for example, an analysis of WAIS performance is useful in determining the degree to which the psychosis interferes with the person's cognitive skills. Knowledge of cognitive skills (or their lack) can also aid in the understanding of a potential psychiatric disorder and its possible relationship to intellectual rather than emotional problems. Finally, unsuspected psychiatric disorders can occasionally be recognized during an intellectual examination.

In evaluating psychiatric disorders, it is particularly important to focus on signs of emotional disorders that are spontaneously offered by the patient in terms of bizarre answers to questions on tests like Comprehension and in terms of ineffective learning strategies on Block Design or Object Assembly. Observation of high anxiety states may also be made, especially on Digit Symbol and Digit Span. In addition, especially poor performance on Vocabulary, Similarities, Information, and Comprehension in the absence of a history of mental retardation, may also imply a serious psychiatric disorder. In determining the possible meaning of symptoms observed on the tests, testing the limits, as described earlier for the subtests, can be a useful additional feature.

ADVANTAGES AND DISADVANTAGES

There are a number of significant advantages in choosing the Wechsler Adult Intelligence Test as a measure of intellectual ability. First, it offers an IQ which is the standard against which all other IQ tests are currently measured. Consequently, the use of nearly any other test is validated on the observation that it correlates with WAIS IQ. Under these conditions, use of the WAIS itself seems to be more logical whenever this is possible. Secondly, unlike most other adult intelligence tests, the WAIS yields more than a full scale IQ. It also provides subtest scores which yield significant information about adult functioning that can be used to help answer numerous referral questions. Thirdly, the test remains the most comprehensively normed adult intelligence test available today. Finally, the WAIS is one of the most heavily researched instruments available to the psychologist. Normative data and validity studies are available for numerous psychological service settings, patient populations, and administration conditions. While only a small part of this literature is relevant to any one setting or population, the information is available for the psychologist who needs it.

The WAIS does have distinct disadvantages, however. First, the test is unsuitable for large group testings. Its individual administration format makes it difficult to screen large numbers of patients in psychiatric and other settings that process numerous patients. In these situations, a briefer screening test of some kind, usually designed to correlate with the WAIS, is employed (see Chapter 2).

A second drawback is the problem of administering the WAIS to black, chicano, and other cultural groups in the US. The test remains heavily influenced by cultural and language concepts which reflect the life of the average American but not that of most minority groups. As a result, many minority educators and psychologists have suggested that the WAIS is biased against minorities and they advocate the use of so-called "culture fair" tests or tests designed specifically for a minority culture (see Chapter 2). For example, Williams (1975) has suggested the use of the BITCH (Black Intelligence Test Corrected for Honkies), a test specifically designed for the black culture.

A third drawback of the WAIS is its susceptibility to the improvement of scores with retesting. As no alternate form of the test exists, this makes it difficult to use the WAIS in situations in which frequent reevaluation is indicated. It should be noted, however, that this is a drawback in many of the intelligence tests that currently exist.

The final, and possibly most serious deficit in the WAIS, is the tendency of the WAIS to overestimate low IQ's when compared to the

Wechsler Intelligence Scale for Children (WISC) and its 1976 revision, the Wechsler Intelligence Scale for Children–Revised (WISC-R). The problem lies in the fact that there are far too few easy items on the WAIS. An individual given a score of zero, the lowest possible, may actually be operating at a level much lower than that. Such lower levels are not tested on the WAIS, however. This difference may cause significant problems. For example, a 15-year-old child may test at an IQ of 65 on the WISC, making the child eligible for special classes. The same child, at 16, may take the WAIS and earn an IQ of 75. Although the child has not changed at all, he or she is no longer eligible for special classes.

Consequently, users of the WAIS must be cautious in interpreting scores of adults who test below an IQ of 80 on the WAIS, especially if the person has scores of zero on any subtest, as this suggests an individual operating at a lower level than IQ 70. In these cases, the user may estimate the correct IQ at about ten points lower than that actually achieved. If further documentation is needed for legal or other purposes, it is suggested that the Stanford-Binet be used (1972 norms) as this will provide the most accurate estimte of a low IQ in an adult.

CASE EXAMPLES

Case 1. This case was referred to the author because of a "psychotic episode" in which the patient apparently threatened his family and employer. Because mental retardation was indicated in the patient's history, the patient was evaluated on the WAIS (Table 1-1). As the reader can see, the patient earned a verbal IQ of 50 and performance IQ of 48. There were no signs of psychosis on the test. The patient was highly cooperative but only able to respond slowly and on a very concrete level. Discussion of the case with the staff social worker indicated that the patient's problem began when he was expected to master a new job, one that was clearly above the patient's learning potential. It was hypothesized and later confirmed that the patient was probably reacting to extreme frustration due to the expectations of his parents and employer, both of whom assumed he was smarter than he actually was. (One reason for this may have been the patient's Comprehension score which is significantly above all his other scores.) The patient was transferred to a job more in keeping with his skills and was able to adapt without problems.

Case 2. This patient was referred by neurosurgeon to investigate possible changes in the patient's cognitive skills related to a suspicion of generalized cerebral atrophy due to presenile dementia (Alzheimer's Disease). As can be seen in Table 1-1, the patient's scores are quite variable. Vocabulary, Comprehension, Arithmetic, Similarities, and Information were uniformly high, while Digit Span was extremely low. There were significant drops in the performance tests on Digit

Table 1-1
Scores for WAIS Cases

	Case 1	Case 2	Case 3	Case 4
Information	1	14	6	12
Comprehension	4	14	6	13
Arithmetic	1	12	4	6
Similarities	0	13	3	6
Digit Span	0	6	5	5
Vocabulary	1	15	5	14
Picture Completion	1	14	7	10
Digit Symbol	0	6	6	4
Block Design	0	10	7	8
Picture Arrangement	0	7	4	8
Object Assembly	0	12	5	9
Verbal IQ	50	116	72	100
Performance IQ	48	110	73	102
Full-scale IQ	<48	114	71	101

Symbol, Picture Arrangement, and to a lesser extent, Block Design. The performance IQ was significantly below the verbal IQ. The patient was cooperative but tended to be somewhat apathetic; however, she did everything that was asked of her.

This analysis of the test results reveals a pattern inconsistent with generalized cerebral dysfunction. On the verbal tests, only the very poor score on Digit Span stands out, as do the Picture Arrangement and Digit Symbol scores on the Performance Test. The pattern as a whole was more consistent with bilateral impairment of the frontal lobes, which was suggested to the physician who referred the patient to a neurologist. A CAT-scan and subsequent surgery later confirmed a bilateral, slow growing tumor involving both frontal lobes.

Case 3. The patient was referred for determining eligibility in a program designed for adult, mentally retarded individuals. As the reader can see (in Table 1-1), the patient earned an IQ of 71, somewhat above the 69 cutoff. Since the WAIS is known to somewhat overestimate these scores, however, it was suggested to the agency that the patient was still eligible. Retesting on the Stanford-Binet yielded a score of 66, which was low enough to qualify the individual for the program.

Case 4. This case represents a fairly typical profile of an individual six months after a tumor was removed from the left parietal area. There remained significant but small deficits in Arithmetic, Block Design, and Similarities, with a slightly lower score on Digit Span. The person's overall IQ is about 100 at present. If we estimate his IQ from the Comprehension, Vocabulary, and Information subtests, however, we find that the patient's prior IQ was about 115, suggesting a drop of 15 points or one standard deviation. Thus, although the individual's IQ is "normal," his current level of functioning reflects a large and serious decline.

2
Alternate Tests of Intellectual Performance

Although the WAIS is unquestionably the major test of intellectual performance in use today, a number of other tests are available which can be useful in specific circumstances. These tests will be discussed briefly in this chapter along with indications for their use. It should be noted that each of these tests offer approximations to the WAIS IQ, not exact equivalents.

STANFORD-BINET

The Stanford-Binet preceeded the WAIS as the major measure of child and adult intelligence. The Binet was originally designed as a test of children's intelligence, but was later extended to allow the assessment of adult intelligence. The original Binet used the concept of mental age to assess intelligence. Briefly, this approach attempted to establish the age at which the skills possessed by the individual would be considered normal (defined as 50 percent of an age group having a given skill). When the mental age of the individual was divided by the chronological (true) age, the resulting quotient would be an IQ. An IQ over 100 would indicate a brighter than average individual while an IQ below 100 would indicate a duller than normal individual. Recent editions of the test, however, have adopted the deviation IQ approach pioneered by Wechsler. Binet's IQ's have a mean of 100 and a standard deviation of 16.

Administering the Stanford-Binet

The Binet tests are arranged in year levels ranging from two years to superior adult. The first problem facing the examiner is to establish where to begin the test in order to determine a basal level, a year grouping in which the examinee can pass all tests. Beginning too low will both lengthen the test and often insult the patient. Beginning too high may convince the patient that the test is very difficult and cause undue anxiety. One useful way to establish the starting point is to administer the Vocabulary test; this generally provides a good basal level. This method is best used with adults who are suspected of a possible mental retardation. Adults with normal or better intelligence may be started at the average adult level as a rule.

If the individual does not pass all the tests at the level chosen, it is necessary to administer the levels previous to the one chosen. If the individual only missed one test at the level chosen, it is generally necessary to go back only one level. If the examinee misses all or most of the tests at a given level, however, it may be necessary for the examiner to go back more than one level depending on the examiner's assessment of the examinee's abilities. After a basal level has been established, testing is continued until all the tests at a given level are failed. Administration instructions for each subtest can be found in the Stanford-Binet manual. Readers may also find Pedrini and Pedrini (1970) of use.

A general rule in administering the Binet is to make sure that all tests are administered and scored as directed. As the test can be long with some patients, there is a tendency to skip tests or administer them incorrectly which invalidates the Binet IQ. Some minor alterations in test procedures may be used with physically handicapped individuals, although IQ's generated from such procedures must be viewed with caution. The reader interested in such modifications is referred to Sattler (1974).

After completing the test, the examiner must allot credit for each test. The individual is given full credit for all years up to and including the basal level year. Thereafter, credit is given for each test passed at each level according to the values for tests at each level which differ from one month value for tests at the initial two year old level to six months value for tests at the highest (Superior Adult III) level. The months credit earned at each year level are summed to get a total score. This is then located in the appropriate table in the Binet manual to yield an overall IQ.

Interpreting the IQ

The Binet IQ can be interpreted much as the WAIS IQ, except for the use of a standard deviation of 16 rather than 15. Thus, at IQ levels of 70, the Binet IQ is two points lower than the WAIS IQ; at 52 the difference is three points; at 36, four points, and at 20, five points.

Comparability of the WAIS and Binet IQ's

The median correlation between the WAIS and Binet is about .78, suggesting a high degree of relationship. The tests tend to deviate at the high and low ends of the scale: Binet IQ's tend to be significantly lower in individuals with IQ less than 70 and significantly higher with individuals who have an IQ higher than 130. The Binet as a rule correlates higher with the verbal tests because of a greater emphasis on verbal functions than is seen in the WAIS.

Pattern Analysis

Although the Binet was not specifically designed for a pattern or scatter analysis as was the WAIS, the success of the procedure with the WAIS has encouraged many authors to develop systems for doing scattergrams or pattern analysis of the Binet. Several major systems of this type are described for the reader in Sattler (1974). These systems are applicable to the mentally retarded population not best served by the WAIS.

Advantages and Disadvantages

The primary advantage of the Binet is in establishing an IQ for adults suspected of mental retardation. As noted in the last chapter, the WAIS tends to overestimate low IQ's, a serious problem in a borderline individual of about IQ 66 who may have a WAIS IQ greater than 70. In these cases, and in cases of all lower IQ's where an exact IQ is desired, the Stanford-Binet is the test of choice.

On the negative side, despite the attempts to develop scattergrams and the like for the Binet, pattern analysis in adults is considerably more difficult and tentative than with the WAIS. As a result, the Binet is rarely the test of choice for normal adults. The Binet is also somewhat more difficult to administer and score than the WAIS, a factor which is also responsible for the popularity of the latter.

AMMONS FULL RANGE PICTURE VOCABULARY TEST

The Ammons Full Range Picture Vocabulary Test consists of pictures representing complex scenes or situations. The patient is given a word and must pick the picture that best represents the word. The test covers a wide age range with norms from age two to adult. The patient is given a stimulus word orally or can read it in written form. The test is able to evaluate the full range of intelligence. Two forms are available, each with a separate set of four pictures. The same pictures are used for all items, making the test easy to give and score. Of the studies currently available, the correlations range from .49 to .92 with WAIS IQ (e.g., Sydiaha, 1967; Granick, 1971) with the majority of studies yielding correlations in the range between .7 and .9.

A related test is the Quick Test. The Quick Test consists of three sets of picture plates, each with four pictures representing complex scenes or situations. Each plate has a series of 50 words associated with it. The words are presented to the examinee orally or in a written form. All words are given to all subjects, with total administration time for all three sets averaging around 50 minutes. The three sets are highly intercorrelated, however, and one may choose to administer only one 50 item word list in a time of 10 to 15 minutes. Tables provide transformations to IQ's, but the test is only appropriate for individuals with average or below average IQ's rather than the full range of IQ. Tables provide equivalent IQ's for ages six through adult levels.

Interpretation

IQ's on the Quick Test correlate with full scale WAIS IQ's from .34 to .88 with the lower correlations occurring in brighter populations for which the Quick Test is inappropriate. Among psychiatric patients, the correlations average about .80 (e.g., see Ogilvie, 1965; Davis and Dizonne, 1970; Quattlebaum and White, 1969; Borgatta and Corsini, 1960).

While IQ's based on Vocabulary give the best estimate of any test in determining full scale IQ, these scores are not as sensitive to pathology as are WAIS scores. Thus, they will tend to estimate premorbid intelligence rather than the impaired intellectual performance seen in organic brain injured patients and other severely pathological groups. IQ's will tend to be higher, as a consequence, than the WAIS equivalent, and considerably higher in some cases than the person's level of adaptive functioning. Thus, the IQ's provide a weak measure of current adaptive skills. When used as a screening test, any IQ below 80 should be an indication for a full WAIS as should any historical or neurological signs of organic brain dysfunction.

SHIPLEY-HARTFORD SCALE

The Shipley-Hartford Scale consists of two subtests. It was originally developed to screen for mental retardation in psychiatric patients, and has also been used for the diagnosis of organicity. A major advantage of the test lies in the fact that it can be group administered rather than administered as an individual test. The test can be easily administered by technicians and other nonprofessionals as well.

The two parts of the test consist of a multiple choice vocabulary test in which a meaning must be selected from one of four alternatives. The second part of the test consists of items with series such as "EFGH——." The patient must fill in the last part of the series. Intelligence scores may be determined by taking the patient's raw score and using tables to determine an equivalent IQ. An organic deterioration index is derived by comparing the IQ derived from the verbal score to an IQ derived from the series items which theoretically measure abstract skills in the patients. These latter skills are hypothesized to be sensitive to brain damage while the Vocabulary test is theoretically insensitive to brain damage. Thus, the ratio between the two scores is a measure of the probability of organicity. When the ratio goes below 70, the patient is said to be brain damaged.

Interpretation

Correlations between the WAIS and Shipley-Hartford IQ's range from .73 to .86 in numerous studies, averaging around .80 (see Monroe, 1966; Pringle and Haanstad, 1971; Mack, 1970; Bartz, 1968). One of the most serious problems with the Shipley, however, is its low correlation with the WAIS at IQ's below 93. Watson and Klett (1968) reported that at this level, the two IQ's were correlated at a level of only .23, far too low for any kind of clinical interpretation. Since most screenings are aimed at recognizing low intelligence, the Shipley would not be applicable in most clinical uses. If used, one would have to give full WAIS evaluations to all the patients with IQ's under 93. If the Shipley is used, the reader is referred to the conversion tables of Paulsen and Lin (1970) who present conversion tables with age corrections not available in the standard table.

There are also questions about the Shipley-Hartford as a test of organicity. A number of studies have reported that the Shipley fails to discriminate between organic, psychiatric, and normal patients (Aita, et al., 1947; Parker, 1957; Savage, 1970). In general, the percentage of patients identified as organic increases greatly with increasing severity of a psychiatric disorder (Yates, 1954). Overall, the test does not appear to be useful in most circumstances even as a gross screening test or organicity (Golden, 1978).

RAVEN'S PROGRESSIVE MATRICES

The Raven's Progressive Matrices was intended as a "culture fair" test of intelligence based on purely nonverbal and noncultural items. The test consists of a design with a piece missing. The examinee must select

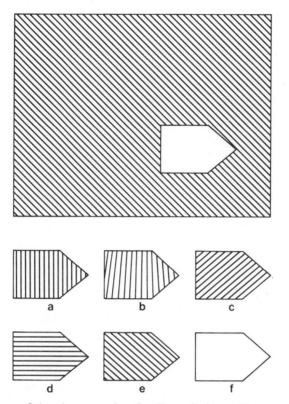

Figure 2-1. An example of a Raven's item. The proper piece to fill in the upper drawing is chosen from the six alternative pieces at the bottom.

from six choices the correct design to be the missing piece. An example of a Raven's type item is seen in Figure 2-1. The test requires such abilities as spatial skills, recognition of design, abstract skills, ability to recognize numerical and spatial relationships, and concentration and attention skills. The overall performance on the test has been found to relate to educational level (Colonna and Faglioni, 1966).

The Raven's Matrices may be administered by anyone, even non-professional technicians. The instructions are easily explained. For each of the 60 items, the patient simply points to the piece that fills in the missing hole. Two sample items are included, and few subjects except very deteriorated individuals have difficulty in grasping what is necessary. The test has no time limit, but rarely takes over an hour. The patient may mark his or her answer on an answer sheet or this may be done by the examiner. An alternate version is available for children and is also of use with severely retarded adults.

Norms for the test are available for ages 8 through 65. The norms are scanty, however: equivalent scores are presented for seven percentile levels rather than direct conversion to IQ equivalents. Peck (1970) presents more extensive percentile norms for age groups from 25 to 65. These percentiles may be changed into IQ's by converting the percentiles into standard z scores (using tables available in many statistics books), multiplying the z by 15 and adding the result to 100.

Interpretation

Raven's IQ's have been reported to correlate from .43 to .93 in populations including organic and psychiatric patients. In general, the Raven's is more sensitive than the verbal IQ to pathology and less sensitive than the performance tests. Thus, the degree of deterioration in a population greatly influences the reported correlations. In addition, the Raven's has a low ceiling so equivalent IQ's are difficult to estimate for bright individuals. Correlations tend to be higher in populations with lower mean IQ's.

Poor performance on the Raven's is associated with brain dysfunction which causes difficulty on such tests as Block Design. Thus, scores will tend to be lower than overall WAIS IQ's in individuals with specific losses in these skills who retain verbal and verbal conceptual skills. This underestimation may cause the examiner to expect less of the patient. The difficulty in estimating IQ's because of the lack of extensive normative data, especially in American populations, is also a major problem in using this test.

PEABODY PICTURE VOCABULARY TEST (PPVT)

One of the more common brief tests of intelligence is the Peabody Picture Vocabulary Test (PPVT). The PPVT is easily administered and requires only a pointing response from the patient. The examinee is told a word and shown four pictures representing simple objects or concepts. The examinee must point to the picture representing the word to be defined. The test consists of 150 words and 150 sets of four pictures. A second word list (form B) exists which can be used with the same 150 pictures. The test has the potential use of estimating IQ's of individuals with severe speech or physical handicaps, although this has not been extensively researched. Test administration can be fast as the examiner need only administer items above the subjects basal level. If the basal level (highest level with six consecutive items correct) is determined accurately (by estimating the individuals IQ), the test can be completed in under 15 minutes. Even when this is not done, the test rarely takes more than 30 minutes to reach a ceiling (missing six of eight consecutive items).

cant3o**I**eat

Interpretation

The PPVT IQ averages a correlation of about .75 to .80 with WAIS IQ's (Bonner, 1969; Shaw, 1961; Pool and Brown, 1970). PPVT IQ's tend to overestimate WAIS IQ's, especially in lower IQ ranges. Thus, if used as a screen, subjects with IQ's lower than 80 should receive full WAIS evaluations. As noted earlier, Vocabulary tends to be a stable test in adult brain damage. As a result, the IQ's of organic patients may be seriously overestimated by the PPVT. It does offer a useful measure of "premorbid IQ," however, when this is necessary to determine degree of disability or for diagnostic purposes.

CONCLUSIONS

The alternate tests of intellectual function are often employed in situations where the time and personnel required to take a WAIS are not available or would be economically unreasonable because of the small amount of return for the effort involved. The brief tests enable the clinician to identify those subjects who can most benefit from further evaluations with such tests as the WAIS. In addition, the tests offer an alternative to the WAIS in situations where the WAIS is inaccurate, such as patients with retarded IQ's for whom a more exact IQ score is needed. The tests can also serve as substitutes in testing physically or speech handicapped individuals for whom it is impossible to take the WAIS.

When substituting an alternate test for the WAIS in a desire to save time, a number of considerations must be involved. First, the limitations of the brief tests must be considered carefully. For example, the Shipley-Hartford, probably the easiest and fastest alternative test, is inaccurate with low IQ patients. Thus, the Shipley might serve only as an initial screen to differentiate normal individuals (greater than IQ 93) from individuals with lower IQ's. At this point, another individually administered screening test such as the Quick Test or PPVT might be necessary to further identify individuals who need more extensive examination. Use of these alternatives for all clients could eliminate the Shipley entirely but they are difficult to give to large numbers of individuals since they are individually administered. In some settings, the initial screening is done simply by contact with the person rather than a test like the Shipley-Hartford. With an experienced psychologist, psychiatrist, or other skilled professional performing the initial screen, this can be as effective as a group screening test.

As the reader can see, a number of alternatives are possible in any given situation. Before adopting any of these tests, the clinician should carefully consider the advantages and disadvantages of each approach, analyzing such factors as staff availability, present screening procedures, purpose of the exam, type of population (organic, psychiatric, normal), and the needs of the population. The use of a procedure or set of procedures that is inadequate for the person being tested is rarely justified, nor is overly extensive testing (which the patient must pay for) likely to be of benefit to the patient. A balance of these factors can provide professional and practical uses of these alternative examinations.

3
Tests of Achievement

Tests of school achievement have long been used by the clinical psychologist to evaluate the role of education in symptoms demonstrated by the patient. There are, however, few achievement tests which fit into the testing requirements of the psychologist. Ideally, such a test would be comprehensive, yet short enough to fit into a larger test battery; easily administered without an extensive background in education, scorable in an objective and consistent manner, and applicable to a wide range of individual adults with backgrounds ranging from little or no educational skills to holders of advanced postgraduate degrees. At present, there are two primary tests which meet these requirements: the Wide Range Achievement Test and the Peabody Individual Achievement Test.

WIDE RANGE ACHIEVEMENT TEST

The Wide Range Achievement Test (WRAT) was first presented in 1936 as a standardized assessment of educational skills. The authors of the test stated that it was designed to be an adjunct to tests of intelligence and other psychological characteristics. The test was immediately accepted by numerous clinicians in education and psychology. Two subsequent revisions (1946, 1965) served to keep the test up to date. All three versions of the test examined three major areas of educational achievement: reading, spelling, and arithmetic. The 1965 version was set to evaluate individuals from the prekindergarten level to the college graduate. Two forms of the test (one for above 12 years, one for below 12 years) were devised to provide maximum speed in the testing situation. Altogether, the test takes about 30 minutes to administer.

Administration

Each version of the test (level I, level II) consists of tests for spelling, arithmetic, and reading. For each form the spelling test is administered first. Initially, the individual is shown a series of figures (lines, circles, triangles, etc.) which they are told to copy. The subject is allowed 60 seconds to copy 18 marks. Then the individual is asked to write his or her name on a line on the answer sheet. The first part of the test is given to anyone who fails to get at least five words correct on level I spelling. As a result, these sections are skipped when testing the adult until the third part of the spelling test is given.

For both levels of the test, the third spelling section consists of words which are said by the examiner and written by the client. For each word, the examiner says the word and then uses it in a sentence. The subject is allowed 15 seconds to write the word unless he or she has a motor handicap which impairs writing speed. The examiner may allow sufficient time to compensate for the handicap in these cases. The test is discontinued after ten consecutive errors. In general, subjects should be encouraged to guess if they hesitate in writing a word.

The words for level I and level II differ in that level I has many more easy words and level II many more hard words. All adult subjects are given level II, unless a poor performance is elicited where it was not expected; then it is often useful to follow up with level I to gain more information.

The Reading Test consists of three prereading tasks that are not generally administered to adults: identifying two letters in the subjects own name (written in the spelling section), identifying ten letters, and naming 13 letters of the alphabet. These tests are only administered when the individual fails one of the first 11 words in level I (most difficult word: *how*), reading pronounciation, or one of the first ten words in level II (most difficult word: *form*).

In the reading pronounciation section on both levels, the subject reads from a list of words presented on a test booklet. For convenience, we have usually given the subject a clear form to read from while marking his or her answers on the subjects form. The subject is given ten seconds for each word. The subject may be asked to repeat a word when the examiner is unsure what the subject said or if it is a borderline response listed in the test manual (Jastak and Jastak, 1965). The subject should also be encouraged to guess when he or she is unsure. The test is discontinued after ten consecutive errors. As with the other tests, level II is administered unless an unusually low score is expected. The manual provides the allowable pronounciations.

The arithmetic test consists of a basic oral part and the written mathematics section. The oral part consists of counting 15 dots, reading five digits, showing three and eight fingers, comparing two numbers, and three oral addition and subtraction problems. If a score of less than five points is achieved on the written part, the oral questions are given. Credit for these items is otherwise automatic.

The written section contains problems ranging from simple addition to advanced algebra. The subject is told to do the problems as quickly as possible. The subject is also informed not to spend too much time on one problem as skipping is permitted. The subject is given ten minutes. As a rule, most subjects reach their upper limit by the end of ten minutes. In cases where there is a suspicion that overly slow and meticulous performance has prevented the subject from reaching the limits of his or her skills, extra time can be allowed but should not be included in the standardized score. Any additional items solved correctly, as well as the subject' manner of performance, can be used in making recommendations in the case. As with other tests, level II is normally given the adult subject.

Scoring

Scoring is relatively simple for the WRAT. For level II tests, the subject gets five points for copying the shapes and spelling his or her name, although this is usually not given. Thus, for most subjects, the total score will be the number of correctly spelled words plus five. For reading, 15 points are given for the initial prereading items plus one point for each word pronounced as given in the manual. For Arithmetic, ten points are given for the oral items plus one point for each correct written item within ten minutes.

Scoring for level I is generally the same, except 20 points are given for the copying and writing of name in Spelling, 25 points are given for the prereading items, and 20 points are given for the oral arithmetic items.

After the raw scores have been determined, these may be translated directly into grade level equivalents by using tables printed on the test form. Separate tables are printed for level I and level II. The grade level scores may be translated into a standard score equivalent to the WAIS IQ by using tables in the test manual. Thus, the standard scores have a mean of 100 and a standard deviation of 15. Tables are available through all adult age levels, although "45 and over" is included as a single group. The tables in the manual may also be used to determine age appropriate percentiles.

Scoring Issues

Grade level scores can be rather misleading in the adult. Low scores, representing primary and junior high school levels, tend to indicate levels of performance in school that are somewhat standard across the nation. Any given school may, however, teach the material included as a given grade level in the WRAT as much as two years before or after the grade suggested by the WRAT. Scores in the high school or college level are much more questionable. For example, if an individual takes no math after the ninth grade, as is allowed at many schools, a math score at eighth or ninth grade level might be regarded as normal. In a recent sample collected by the author a group of midwestern high school graduates showed only a tenth grade average rather than a twelfth grade level concurrent with their years of school. In many adult education programs the levels required for graduation are at the ninth grade level in some subjects, depending on state requirements. Thus, a score of tenth grade on one section might be perfectly adequate for the individual.

Given the problems in interpreting grade level scores, standard scores would appear more meaningful. They do not entirely take care of the problem of educational opportunity, but they do give a standard reference group against which the subject can be measured. Moreover, the scores are comparable to IQ's. Thus, we can compare whether achievement levels for the individual are comparable to the individual's intellectual level. Jastak and Jastak (1965) have shown that there is a high level of correspondence between WAIS IQ's and WRAT standard scores. In general, differences of ten points or more appear to be clinically meaningful. If the IQ is higher, the person is performing at a level significantly below expectations. In these cases, one must consider the possibility of learning disabilities in the adult (see below). If the educational level is higher, the scores suggest either a late brain injury (discussed below) or a person able to take maximum advantage of their skills. These individuals are often highly motivated, but may also be under a great deal of stress to perform at levels above their capabilities. In either case where there are large discrepancies, one must seriously consider the possible role they may play in any presenting psychiatric disorder.

In evaluating differences between IQ's and WRAT standard scores, differences on Spelling and Reading should be given more weight than differences on Arithmetic. As noted in the chapter on the WAIS, many individuals are adversely affected when asked to do mathematical problems. This can create wide swings in scores due to anxiety rather than intellectual factors. This is reflected in the somewhat higher correlations between Reading, Spelling, and the WAIS (about .85) compared to the correlation between the Arithmetic and WAIS (.75). As might be expected, verbal IQ's offer much better correlations with the WRAT scales than do performance IQ's.

Educational Interpretations

As noted above, the WRAT can give the psychologist a rough idea of the individual's standing in terms of school grade level and compared to other individuals his or her age. While grade level scores are only approximate, they may be combined with the standard score and IQ's to make educational recommendations. Individuals with low grade level scores but greater ability as implied by the IQ are often good candidates for adult education courses leading to a high school degree if the patient does not possess such a degree. Areas where the individual is outstandingly low (compared to ability and in absolute terms) might indicate where remediation is needed. The patient with normal intelligence, for example, who has trouble reading might be helped in vocational placement if such training was offered. These are also individuals for whom a learning disability evaluation is indicated (see below).

In other cases, individuals with low scores, grade level and standard scores, might not be encouraged to attend college. For example, one patient we saw with an acute anxiety disorder in her first year of college was found to be reading at a substantially low level (7th grade) despite good grades in a rural school. It was clear that the stress of going to college when she did not have the educational skills had led to her problem. Returning her to school would only have resulted in the return of the problems. The psychological report suggested either remedial training prior to school or getting the patient to form goals more consistent with her abilities in order to avoid future problems.

Learning Disabilities

The diagnosis of learning disabilities is and has been a controversial and unclear area. A learning disability has been defined as being at least two grade levels behind age expected grade level in a specific area. The individual must have normal intelligence and the disability cannot be due to poor motivation, poor cultural background, blindness, or loss of hearing.

In adults, the definition requires several facts to be established: (1) The person must have an IQ in the normal range (85 or greater); (2) The person must show a specific deficit in some educational skill below that expected by the person's intelligence. For the skills measured by the WRAT, this means a standard score at least 15 points below the individuals IQ. In addition, the grade level achievement of the individual should be at least two grade levels below the person's final grade level in school; (3) The deficit cannot be due to cultural problems, emotional disorders, blindness, loss of hearing, or unwillingness to study in school.

The first point is most easily established by the WAIS. In individuals whose problem is verbal, however, only the performance tests or a test like the Raven's Matrices may be employed to estimate IQ. The second point requires a significantly low score on one or more of the subtests of the WRAT or other standard measure of specific learning areas. The requirement that the standard score be at least 15 points below the IQ insures that the deficit is not due to intellectual loss alone. For example, an individual of 40 with an IQ of 85 would be expected to earn a grade level of 5.9. Although this is obviously low, it is consistent with the IQ and not a surprising deficit. Such an individual would have to have a grade level of 3.1 before fitting the definition. This avoids classifying many performances normal for the individual as learning disabilities. Similarly, an individual with IQ 126 would possibly have a learning disability at a grade level of 10.7, which is usually a "normal" performance.

The grade level requirement is made so that inadequate schooling is not diagnosed as a learning disability. No matter what an individual's IQ, we cannot expect them to show educational performance above the actual training they received. The third requirement is inherent in the basic definition of learning disabilities. This needs to be established through an examination for emotional problems (as discussed in later chapters), a thorough history, and appropriate evaluations for sight or hearing if they are suspect. Any emotional disorder must be evaluated carefully to determine if it caused the learning problem or was the result of the learning problem and the subseqeunt stress and frustration engendered by such problems. A good history and interview are the best tools in establishing those relationships. Ancillary tests such as the MMPI are also useful in establishing such disorders.

It is necessary to evaluate carefully the nature of the disorder for those individuals in which a learning disability is diagnosed. This can be done by more extensive testing. Neuropsychological testing aimed at identifying specific deficits are often helpful in this regard (see Golden, 1978). Referral to an educational specialist is usually appropriate for educational programming or vocational training, when appropriate, unless the clinician is experienced in designing such programs.

It should be emphasized that learning disabilities may play a major role in the development of psychiatric disorders. Such conditions can lead to extreme frustration and stress which in turn can lead to failure, acting out behavior, depression, anxiety, and other psychiatric symptoms. Thus, when they are found in individuals with such problems their possible etiological role must be closely evaluated. As noted above, a careful history from the individual and collateral sources can be useful in making such a connection. In individuals where this is found to be the case, psychotherapy is strongly recommended to allow the patient to gain insight into the nature of his or her problem.

Brain Damage

Achievement tests are used by a variety of clinicians interested in the diagnosis of brain damage. The most common role of the achievement tests are as indicators of the patient's past status. In the individual with a normal premorbid status, their achievement level should be consistent with the individual's IQ, especially if normal or above normal educational background is present. When an individual receives a brain injury as an adult, the IQ will go down, the degree depending on the severity and the location of the lesion (see the WAIS chapter). Achievement scores remain remarkably stable, however, except in very severe and obvious disorders. Thus, in most brain injuries there will be a gap between IQ and standard scores on the WRAT which can be used to estimate the degree of impairment. Deficits on such tests as the Halstead-Reitan can be used similarly.

Achievement tests may also be used to diagnose specific types of brain injury. For example, some parietal-occipital injuries are characterized by losses in spelling skills, even of relatively simple words (Golden, 1978; Luria, 1966). Losses in the ability to carry in multiplication and subtraction may be associated with right hemisphere injuries when all other mathematical skills are intact. Disorders of reading may be associated with temporal-occipital injuries in the left hemisphere. Using these signs, the WRAT can be a useful adjunct to other tests in the assessment of brain dysfunction.

Advantages and Disadvantages

The WRAT has a number of advantages as a test of achievement. It can be given quickly, without difficulty. It has been standardized on a large normative population and has been shown to be useful in clinical practice over a number of years. It is generally accepted as a standard measure of achievement by others, both in psychology and education.

The test also has some significant disadvantages, however; the only measure of reading skills requires intact motor skills and an "American" accent. Individuals with physical disorders which interfere with speech as well as individuals with foreign accents are not able to take the Reading subtest. The Mathematics subtest measures basic skills, but not whether the person can use them in day to day situations. (In this regard, it is often useful to compare the score on the WRAT with Arithmetic on the WAIS.) When these questions are significant, an alternate test of achievement one can consider is the Peabody Individual Achievement Test (PIAT).

PEABODY INDIVIDUAL ACHIEVEMENT TEST (PIAT)

The PIAT was published in 1970 by Dunn and Markwardt as a wide range screening instrument in the areas of reading, spelling, mathematics, and general information. Unlike the WRAT, only two out of five subtests require the subject to select from one of four multiple choice responses printed on frames enclosed in two hard cover, loose leaf notebooks. The test shares several advantages with the WRAT: it can be administered quickly by nonprofessionals, it offers an easy to use, attractive format, and it is appropriate for a wide range of ages and levels of functioning. Unlike the WRAT, however, norms are available through age 18.

Administration

The five subtests of the PIAT are given in a nearly identical manner and scored in an identical manner. For each subtest, the examiner starts at an item representing the highest difficulty which the subject should be able to complete without trouble. In the first subtest (Mathematics), this is determined by what the examiner knows of the individual, his age, grade level completed, IQ, and performance on other tests. In later subtests, this can be estimated by assuming equal performance as on the previous subtest.

After the first item is determined, the examiner tests in a forward direction until the subject misses an item. If five items have been correctly answered in a row at this point, then the examiner continues forward. If five items have not been answered consecutively in a correct manner, the examiner works backwards from the initial item until five consecutive items have been correctly answered. At this point, the examiner returns to the most advanced item completed so far and continues forward until five of seven consecutive items are missed. At this point, the subtest is completed and the examiner should move on to the next subtest.

The subtests are given in the following order: Mathematics, Reading Recognition, Reading Comprehension, Spelling, and General Information. For three of the subtests, Mathematics, Reading Comprehension, Spelling, the subject must choose from one of four possible answers presented. For mathematics, an oral problem is given, as well as presented graphically or written verbally depending on the question. For Reading Comprehension, a statement is read by the subject who must then match it to a collection of four drawings, one of which represents the statement the subject has read. For spelling, the subject is given a word (included in a sentence as well) and then must select the correct spelling from among four choices.

The Reading Recognition Test requires subjects to read words and pronounce them correctly as in the WRAT reading test. The general information test presents questions similar to those in the Information subtest of the WAIS. The subject must answer the questions verbally. The examiner may ask for clarification of answers in this test when the scoring is unclear or one is directed to do so by the scoring criteria that accompany each item.

The questions may be repeated for all items if the subject asks. Spontaneous corrections by the subject are allowed. The last answer given is the one scored. The examiner, however, should never indicate whether an answer is correct either verbally or nonverbally. All questions, directions, and other material read to the examinee must be read verbatim from the materials provided in the PIAT kit rather than recited from memory. At no time may the examiner embellish or abbreviate the instructions in any manner, even when repeating an item.

Scoring

To score each subtest, one must first determine the basal and ceiling items. The basal sequence is the five highest numbered consecutive items which the subject got correct in the entire protocol. Thus, if the five highest consecutive correct items were items 55 to 59, these would be the basal items. If the subject got items 55 to 59 correct and 65 to 69 correct, then 65 to 69 would be the basal items even if the subject missed one or more of the items between 60 and 64. The ceiling sequence is determined by the lowest set of seven consecutive items in which the subject missed five items. Again, if the subject missed five items in the sequence 43 to 49 and in the sequence 53 to 59, the lower sequence, 43 to 49, is considered the ceiling sequence even if items 50 to 52 are all correct.

The *basal item* is the lowest of the basal item sequence, and the *ceiling item* is the highest item missed in the ceiling item sequence. The *critical range* are all of the items from and including the basal item up to and including the ceiling item. To obtain the raw score for any subtest, the number of errors made in the critical range are subtracted from the number of the ceiling.

Once the raw scores are determined, they may be changed into grade level scores, percentiles, and standard scores as with the WRAT on the basis of the individuals age. For adults, the highest age level presented, 18 years, is used. In addition, percentile ranks are presented for grade level. These are useful with individuals who did not complete school. The tables help adjust for the lack of schooling to some degree, although not for differences in age between an adult subject and a youngster at a given grade level.

In addition to the individual scores, the examiner may calculate a total score (sum of the raw scores on all five tests) and its percentile, grade, and standard score equivalents.

Interpretation

For the adult subject, a difference of more than 15 raw score points between any two subtests is likely to indicate a significant advantage or disadvantage for a given subject. This is useful in categorizing the subject's strengths and weaknesses. Of particular interest are findings which indicate a significant difference between the Reading Recognition and Reading Comprehension subtests. A difference in favor or Recognition suggests an individual whose reading is primarily by rote, and who has difficulty understanding things he or she might be expected to understand. A difference in favor of Comprehension suggests someone either with a motor speech impairment, a foreign background, or someone who has learned primarily by reading rather than speaking and interacting with others. The latter explanation is useful to explore with high IQ psychiatric or other patients who may tend to isolate themselves and use books as an escape.

Differences in favor of Information over the other tests may suggest an individual whose learning has primarily been outside a formal school setting. As with the WAIS Information, this subtest can give a good estimate of intellectual skills.

Other interpretations made with the PIAT alone are generally equivalent to those outlined for the WRAT. For the Reading Recognition and WRAT Reading, correlations on the order of .9 or better have been reported, as have similar correlations for PIAT and WRAT Spelling. PIAT Reading Comprehension correlates highly with WRAT Reading (.9), as well as PIAT Reading Recognition (on the order of .7). The relationships between PIAT and WRAT Arithmetic is questionable, however. A review by Kieffer and Golden (1978) found that the two tests correlate about .5, a substantially low correlation for two tests purporting to measure the same things. There is no equivalent in the WRAT for Information.

The difference between the WRAT and PIAT mathematics is important to examine. Kieffer and Golden (1978) suggest that this difference may be due to the emphasis in the Peabody on daily problem solving skills rather than the emphasis on pure math seen in the WRAT. In this case, it would appear that the Peabody is more useful as a measure of an individual's ability to use math in a day to day situation than in planning possible placement in a school situation. The WRAT, on the other hand, would probably predict school placement well but not the ability of the child to use the knowledge. Thus, a difference in scores between these two subscales could have significant meaning depending on the referral questions and goals for the patient.

The user of the PIAT should pay particular attention to the Spelling test as well. As the PIAT requires spelling recognition rather than spelling ability, there will be children in which the score on the PIAT would be substantially higher than the WRAT score, although in general these two skills correlate highly. In cases where some of the WRAT/PIAT difference are suspected, it is sometimes useful to administer both tests to the same child.

Advantages and Disadvantages

The primary advantage of the PIAT lies in its applicability to a handicapped population. The Reading Comprehension subtest, in particular, offers an excellent measure of reading skills in the speech impaired individual. This ability is particularly important because of the significance of reading skills in many jobs and educational placements. This advantage also extends to the Mathematics and Spelling subtests, but is less important since additional time may be given on those tests to correct for motor impairment. The advantage is quite important, however, in individuals with significant paralysis or any other disabling motor or sensory condition affecting the dominant hand. In addition, norms are provided for grade level as well as age.

There are several disadvantages with the PIAT as well. First, the test only provides norms through age 18 and the twelfth grade. This is a handicap with adults, especially those with a college education. In these individuals, the WRAT is usually the test of choice. A second disadvantage is the interpretation problems with the Mathematics subtest in situations where one wishes to make an educational placement rather than evaluate the individuals ability to function in common situations. Finally, the Information test is redundant with WAIS information. As a result, many clinicians do not administer it.

CASE EXAMPLES

Case 1.   LC, a 36-year-old man, was evaluated after a significant industrial accident which resulted in a gross motor disability. He had worked as a lugger in a meat packing plant, a job which required considerably physical strength but little education as he had dropped out of school in the eighth grade. Testing indicated an IQ of 115 and achievement scores of 100, 103, and 95 on the Reading, Arithmetic, and Spelling subtests of the WRAT, unusually high scores given the individual's poor schooling. It was felt that the individual had considerably greater talent at school type work than was indicated by his past schooling. Since the patient could no longer work at his former job, it was suggested he get his General Education Degree (which was no problem given his WRAT scores) and go into some area of interest to him at college or a technical job training school. The patient eventually secured a degree in electronics and was employed in a situation where his disability made little difference.

Case 2.   LD, a 16-year-old female, came from a family tnat placed a great emphasis on education. As an adopted only child she was constantly pushed to do well in school by her mother, a college teacher and father, a lawyer. She was referred for evaluation because of a suspected learning disability and an increasingly difficult behavior problem at school. Initial testing revealed a 100 IQ and achievement test scores which were all normal (98 to 106). From the achievement and IQ testing, no evidence of a learning disability was found. Indeed, her performance was quite normal for her age. A further evaluation revealed that the parents considered normal progress a failure. The parents continuing harassment (not letting her date, go to movies, or do other things she liked because of her poor school record) and pressure were leading to the behavioral problems. Family therapy was recommended to correct this problem before it got more serious.

Case 3. HJ, a 20-year-old male, was referred because of an acute psychotic breakdown which occurred in his third year of college. The patient earned an IQ of 135 and standard scores above 130 on all the subtests of the WRAT. After resolutions of the acute symptoms, the patient was unsure whether he could do the academic work at college. It was suggested that his problem was not academic, but rather an inability to relate to other people (based on MMPI results). We suggested a return to school along with continued medical and psychotherapeutic intervention on an outpatient basis. The patient was able to finish school without difficulty under this regimen.

Case 4. AS, a 21-year-old male, was a sophomore in college who was flunking all of his classes after having a basically good record. While he had an IQ of 120, his reading recognition score on the PIAT was equivalent to a standard score of 115, while the Reading Comprehension score was 85. This suggested a severe problem in Reading Comprehension. Further testing and investigation indicated a significant problem in understanding written material. The patient was studying by reading books four or five times, rarely leaving his room except for meals as this was the only was to keep up. The testing revealed, however, fully normal skills when the material was presented auditorily. The current problem was apparently caused by an increase in required reading material and the patient's inability to continue to withstand the stress he was under. We arranged to have written material presented orally to the patient, as well as for oral administration of tests. The patient's grades increased from a near F average to Bs and As within the course of two months.

4
Minnesota Multiphasic Personality Inventory

Beginning in the 1930s, McKinley and Hathaway began to assemble a large pool of objective personality items for the purpose of creating a diagnostic instrument that would aid in the classification of psychiatric patients. From a final pool of about 1000 items, a set of 504 items were selected that were considered reasonably independent of one another. These items were given to normals and to patients with various psychiatric diagnosis. The purpose at that time was to create a scale which would represent each diagnostic group tested: Hypochondriasis, depressives, psychopathic deviates, hysterics, paranoids, obsessive-compulsives, schizophrenics, and manics. It was hoped that individuals with a specific diagnosis would get a high score on the appropriate scale, thus yielding a quick diagnosis.

Unfortunately, the scales did not work as expected. Individuals with a given diagnosis showed high scores on several different scales, making the task of diagnosis much more difficult. Furthermore, it became recognized that the group labeled schizophrenic was not a homogenous group but was rather highly heterogenous. Thus, the labels attached to the scales did not mean what they appeared to mean: a high score on psychopathic deviate, for example, does not mean that one is a psychopathic deviate.

Despite this failure, the MMPI has become the most used objective test of personality and, in recent years, probably the most used personality test, surpassing even the traditional leader, the Rorschach Inkblot Method. It has proven itself to be highly adaptable to different environments, psychiatric systems of nomenclature, and theories of personality. It has become the premiere screening instrument used in psychiatric, medical, and community mental health facilities.

PURPOSE

The original purpose of the MMPI, as noted above, was to help establish psychiatric diagnosis at a time when there was a belief that the psychiatric nomenclature was as useful as the medical diagnostic nomenclature which has proven so useful in the treatment of physical disease. This was done by devising scales empirically found to be related to a given disorder, whether or not the item possessed face validity. It has been found that scores on the individual scales are associated with a number of traits and behaviors. The analysis of these traits has become a major thrust of MMPI research. Rather than pointing at a definitive diagnosis, the MMPI allows the psychologist to form a picture of an individual's behaviors, traits, underlying dynamics, level of adjustment, contact with reality, attitude towards the world, and characteristic beliefs. From this picture of the individual, such material as diagnosis, prognosis, likely future behavior, and other information may be determined on the basis of personality theory, clinical experience and research, and research relating to diagnostic categories. The MMPI can be used to suggest modes of treatment appropriate to an individual, whether that treatment is medical (primarily drug therapy), psychological, or social. Finally, the MMPI provides an objective measure of individuals or groups of individuals which may be used to measure behavioral change in therapy or because of environmental conditions. The MMPI is useful both in clinical work and research.

ADMINISTRATION AND SCORING

Unlike many of the personality instruments of its time and subsequently, the items in the MMPI were not determined on the basis of any single theory but were intended to comprehensively review all symptoms and attitudes that might be of interest in psychiatric disorders. Consequently, the MMPI includes questions involving a wide range of items, many of which do not have any clear relationship to specific psychological disorders.

The scales in the MMPI were derived empirically as well. Rather than assign items to a particular scale because it belonged there, the authors administered the test to selected psychiatric groups. The items on each scale consisted of those items which differentiated the clinical group from normal control groups. Thus, while some of the items may make sense, a good number of the items do not, except in the sense that they did manage to differentiate the clinical group. As a result of this, each scale consists of items which are highly face valid (obvious items) while also consisting of items which are not face valid (subtle items).

In addition to the original eight clinical scales, four validity scales were also developed which allowed for the clinician to investigate individuals who might be lying, faking bad, faking good, or who do not have the reading ability necessary to take the test. To these original 12 scales, two additional scales were later added, Masculinity-femininity and social introversion, both of which became part of the regular MMPI. Beyond these scales, hundreds of additional scales can be scored and used for a wide variety of purposes.

Administration

The MMPI can be administered either as a group or individual instrument by any normally intelligent person with a minimum of training. Unlike most of the other instruments discussed in this book, the test need not be given by a psychologist. In actual practice, the test is given by clerks, psychological technicians, nurses, and others so as to minimize the time spent on the test by the Ph.D. In addition, scoring may also be done by a minimally trained assistant or clerk.

There are four basic forms of the MMPI. Two are intended for individuals with serious disorders unable to take the test normally, while two others represent the forms most often used. Other forms of the test exist, but all are put together on the same basis of one of these versions.

The boxed version of the MMPI consists of 550 MMPI items on individual cards. These items are then placed by the subject behind dividers labeled True, False, and Cannot Say. Most administrators emphasize that the Cannot Say category should not be used in general, that the patient should answer simply whether True or False is most accurate. This emphasis is important as too many Cannot Say items make the test unscorable. It is often useful in this version to have the individual reconsider Cannot Say items after the test is completed. This form of the test should only be used for individuals who simply cannot fill out a normal answer sheet under any conditions, but still are lucid enough to answer the questions. The test is scored by transferring the patient's answers to an answer sheet and then using appropriate scoring overlays. As might be expected, this form is highly time consuming for the scorer.

The second special form of the MMPI is a tape recorded version of the test. The subject listens to the questions and then puts his or her answer on an answer sheet in between the questions. Alternatively, the examiner may have the subject tell him or her the answer and the examiner may mark it down. This form is for subjects who are generally alert and able to respond in a reasonable time but who are illiterate or semiliterate. (Generally, a sixth grade reading comprehension level is considered necessary to take the MMPI.) For subjects who are not alert and do not respond in a reasonable amount of time, it is often necessary to stop the tape. For such subjects, it is sometimes more efficient for the examiner to read the test to the subject in order to allow for variable response times. We have found this technique useful with highly labile patients who are unable to concentrate for more than a few items at a time. Answers to items are recorded on the appropriate test form and scored as described below.

The most common form of the MMPI is the group booklet form. Two alternate forms exist: one printed in a soft paper booklet and a second printed within a hard bound cover. The paper form consists of 566 items, 16 of which are repeated for scoring purposes. The most common answer sheet for this form is two sided (with questions 1 to 300 on side one) and designed to be scored by an IBM-805 scoring machine. The test may also be scored by hand scoring templates. Several scales have two templates, however, one for the front side and one for the back side, making scoring difficult. In addition, this form of the test requires that the individual have a normal sized desk to work on.

The alternate form (form R) has hard covers enclosing the pages and is spirally bound. The covers may be opened and used as a desk; this enables one to test subjects who have no desk, such as patients in a hospital bed. The answer sheet to form R fits over pegs on the cover that hold the sheet in place so that items and the proper answer column are lined up. Thus, the subject need not match items to item numbers (which are not included on the answer sheet.) Another advantage of this form is its easy transformation into a short form; to score all the standard scales one need only administer the first 399 items. In the paper booklet form, a short form of the test includes the first 360 items plus items 371, 374, 377, 383, 391, 397, 398, 400, 406, 411, 415, 427, 436, 440, 446, 449, 450, 451, 455, 461, 462, 469, 473, 479, 481, 482, 487, 502, 515, 521, 547, 459, and 564. Administering such a hodge podge of questions is awkward at best.

The advantage of a short form capability lies in the time reduction necessary to do the test. In a psychiatric population, the test as a whole will take anywhere from 1¼ hours to 3½ hours, while the short form may be completed in 45 minutes to 2½ hours. The short form can be administered, as a rule, within one or two sessions, while the longer form may take three or even four sessions. Thus the short form can generate data considerably faster, an important consideration if results are desired quickly and there are limitations on the subject's time (as in an acute care medical or psychiatric facility). The disadvantage of the short form is caused by an inability to score some of the experimental or additional scales if they are desired.

Form R is scored by templates placed over the answer sheet when the scoring is done by hand. The form may also be scored by the National Computer Systems in Minneapolis, Minnesota.

Scoring the MMPI

Raw scores for the scales are determined by templates placed over the appropriate answer sheet or by computer. (Computer programs will also, as a rule, do all the additional steps to be described below.) Raw scores for several of the scales are corrected according to the size of the K score, one of the validity scales to be described below. This is done for scales measuring Hypochrondriasis, Psychopathic Deviate, Psychasthenia, Schizophrenia, and Mania. The amount of K correction added to each scale was determined empirically for each group by investigating what K, if any, could be added to maximize the discrimination of clinical and control groups. The K correction formula and Tables are listed on each MMPI profile form.

After the proper K corrections have been determined, the raw scores for each scale are plotted on the MMPI profile sheet. The scales are plotted in the order listed in Table 4-2. Table 4-2 also lists the name of each scale, the abbreviation for each scale, and the appropriate scale number used in MMPI profile coding.

Table 4-2
MMPI Scale Names, Numbers, and Abbreviations

Scale	Number	Abbreviation
Lie		L
Validity		F
Correction (Bias)		K
Hypochondriasis	1	Hs
Depression	2	D
Hysteria	3	Hy
Psychopathic Deviate	4	Pd
Masculinity-Femininity	5	Mf
Paranoia	6	Pa
Psychasthenia	7	Pt
Schizophrenia	8	Sc
Mania	9	Ma
Social Introversion	0	Si

Table 4-3
Scores for Sample Case

Scale	T Score
L	40
F	55
K	59
1	29
2	39
3	40
4	60
5	69
6	87
7	83
8	103
9	59
0	54

Profile Coding

After the profile has been plotted on the MMPI sheet, the profile may be coded. The coding offers a shorthand which can be used to describe the profile to others in an efficient manner. These profile codes are useful to know since most MMPI books and much research use these codes to describe individual as well as group research. The major system at present will be described (Welsh, 1948).

First, the scales are listed in order by the size of the T score on the profile sheet. Only the clinical scales (those with numbers in Table 4-2) are listed in this manner. The scales are listed by their numbers. So, for example, we might have a subject with the T scores suggested in Table 4-3. In order, we would list these scales:

8 6 7 5 4 9 0 3 2 1

Then, the symbols listed in Table 4-4 are placed after the last scale score which is equal to or greater than the number associated with each symbol in Table 4-4. For example, the symbol ' follows the last scale score which is equal to or greater than 70 (in this case, Scale 7). No symbol is placed after a scale with a T score less than 29, or to the left of the highest score, or the right of the lowest score. If there is no scale between scores *80 and 70,* for example, the symbol for 80 (") is simply followed by the symbol for 70 ('). Thus for our patient:

8*67" '54–90/3:2 #1

Underlining is used to connect all scales within one T score point of each

Table 4-4
Symbols for MMPI Profile Codes

Symbol	Scores equal to or greater than
*	90
"	80
'	70
—	60
/	50
:	40
#	30

other. After the list for the clinical scales, the validity scales are listed by their symbols (F, L, K, ?) in the order from the highest T score to the lowest. For our subject:

$$K \; F/L:?$$

These are put together to yield:

$$8*67'''54-90/3:2\#1 \; K \; F/L:?$$

The reader will find that practice with these symbols will soon lead to quick coding skills.

CLINICAL INTERPRETATION

In examining each of the MMPI scales, the clinician generates hypotheses about his or her subject. These hypotheses are suggested on the basis of the research and clinical experience with the MMPI. After completing the analysis of all the scales and scale configurations, some of the hypotheses stand out because of their repetition in several places. In general, these form the major inferences about the patient which the MMPI can generate. Secondary hypotheses, consistent with these inferences, can then be drawn from the remaining hypotheses, while hypotheses inconsistent with the picture are either discarded or used to modify the overall impression of the patient. In turn, the picture generated can be integrated with knowledge about the patient's life, demographic characteristic, referral problems, and so on. In addition to this, the clinician may add inferences on the basis of personality theory and current knowledge about the development of specific psychological disorders. An extensive picture of the individual may be generated in this way and used to answer referral questions and make suggestions for treatment or prognosis.

In general, this process begins with the validity scales. These enable the clinician to determine whether a profile is valid or questionable, as well as determine the test taking attitude and approach of the patient. The validity scales may also suggest some of the major psychodynamics of the patient, such as the presence of strong repressive or denying tendencies. The information from the validity scales gives one a general outlook of how to view the patient's profile. For example, if the validity scales suggest that the individual avoids saying negative things about him or herself, then clinical scales suggesting severe psychopathology must be taken quite seriously as such an individual may not be able to recognize that their responses are bizarre. Similarly, if one has the impression that the individual tends to exaggerate, a higher profile might be considered in a less severe light.

After the validity scales have been examined, the clinical scales are considered. Each of these is interpreted in order to generate additional hypotheses about the individual. Then, the patient's high point pattern (those scales higher than all other scales) is investigated. This pattern is generally given a heavy emphasis because these are the individual's predominant characteristics. The inferences from the other scales are used to modify this high point impression, or to enable the clinician to select among the possible high point interpretations. In some cases, several high point patterns may be present which must be integrated together. In this way, a picture of the MMPI possibilities is drawn which can be integrated with the demographic, personal and interview data.

One major aspect of this process must be kept in mind by the novice interpreter. The most common error in MMPI interpretations is for the clinician to hold to one single interpretation for a given scale or configuration. In actual practice, this is never the case. All profile scores and configurations have more than one interpretation. Thus, one must be alert to the evidence generated by all the scales, not just a single high score or high point pair. For example, while one high point pair may suggest paranoid schizophrenia, if this is combined with scores indicating good contact with reality, the enjoyment and seeking out of other persons, and a generally positive affective state, one must look for alternate explanations rather than holding to the standard interpretation. This flexibility is essential if the clinician is to gain a maximum amount of information from the MMPI.

As the reader can see, the interpretation of the MMPI is not simply an automated process of looking up "the" interpretation of a profile. It is an important clinical task which requires insight, a good knowledge of psychopathology, a grounding in personality theory, and the intelligence to integrate these factors with the possible interpretations of the MMPI scales and configurations, and to then integrate these observations with knowledge about the patient gained from history, behavior, interviews, and the like. As a result, this is not a process that can be done by a computer. The computer is limited to standard interpretations and is not capable of the integration necessary nor is it capable of combining the results with the person's individual characteristics, behavior, or history. The computer cannot recognize unique situations, nor can it adjust for differences across populations, a major factor that any clinician who has worked in such diverse settings as VA hospitals, general medical hospitals, mental health centers, and psychiatric hospitals can recognize. Consequently, despite the proliferation of computer programs and their use, the computer is no substitute for clinical judgment and interpretation of the profile.

THE VALIDITY SCALES

The MMPI has four scales used to measure the validity of the profile: ? (Cannot Say), L (Lie Scale), F (Unusual item endorsement), and K (Test Taking Attitude and Correction Factor). In addition to their role as validity scales, these scales also offer information about the patient's personality.

Cannot Say (?) Scale

This scale involves a counting of all unanswered questions or questions answered both true and false. Many clinicians emphasize to their patients that all questions should be answered either true or false, depending on which is most accurate. In this way, most cannot say responses can be eliminated. It is also useful to scan a subject's answer sheet after the test is completed and to have the subject go over the questions again to eliminate these responses. All but a few can usually be removed. A profile is considered invalid if there are more than 30 ? answers. Our own experience, however, has shown that with the above techniques few subjects should get more than 5 ? responses making this scale relatively meaningless. In practice, we will often omit even reporting the scale except in cases where the score is unusually high.

L (Lie) Scale

The L scale consists of 15 items of which a true answer would involve admitting a minor, but generally universal, fault. For example, one might have to admit that he or she does not read every editorial in the paper every day. Individuals trying to look especially good will often answer false to these items, causing the L scale score to raise. A high L scale score indicates that the person has not been wholly truthful in reporting symptoms and suggests a relative invalidity. In all cases, however, one must still look at the clinical profile. High L scale scores may accompany profiles which are diagnostically significant. The person may admit to some bizarre ideas and ways of adjusting, often because the person is not in touch enough with reality to recognize the items as bizarre. This, of course, has direct clinical relevance in understanding the individual.

High L scores may also indicate a person who is either highly moralistic or wishes to appear that way. In a valid profile such individuals tend to be conforming, uncreative, repressed (especially if there are high K and H scores), unaware of others, confused, generally without guilt, delusional (in psychiatric populations), and have strong beliefs of their own grandiosity. Such individuals may also be ministers, social reformers, perfectionists, and otherwise unusual individuals who do live the life they describe. In general, L scores greater than a T score of 60 can be considered elevated; scores about 70 are both rare and highly significant.

Low L scores (especially of 1 or 0 raw score) may indicate a person who is trying to present a negative picture, especially if associated with low K and high F scores. They may also be seen in unconventional normal people and in highly educated individuals trying to be "believable." Low L scores may also be associated with honesty, self-confidence, independence, and willingness to admit minor faults.

F Scale

The F scale consists of 64 items that were answered in the scored direction of this scale 10 percent of the time or less. Thus, endorsement of items on the F scale in the scorable direction involves the endorsement of bizarre and unusual items, including a significant number that are shared with the Schizophrenia and Paranoia scales. The F scale was designed to detect unusual or bizarre responding. A wide variety of individuals will get high F scores, ranging from the individual who answers randomly or answers everything true to the individual who is highly psychotic or otherwise disturbed.

In interpreting F scale scores, scores greater than a T score of 100 must be examined carefully as they may indicate an invalid profile. This may be due to an inability to read or understand the questions, random responding, or deliberate attempts to "fake bad." The attempts to fake bad generally involve individuals who have something to gain from a poor impression, such as the individual involved in a court case, the disability applicant, the person attempting to prove an insanity plea, or the patient who wants to use the hospital as a way to protect him or herself from life. If the above possibilities are not true, the alternate interpretation suggests an extremely psychotic individual with strong paranoid delusions, hallucinations, speech disorders, and extreme social withdrawal, which may or may not be associated with organicity.

F scores above 80 may indicate an individual who is answering all questions false, is malingering, is careless, is asking for help, or is clearly psychotic. This range, especially from 80 to 90, may frequently be seen during acute schizophrenic episodes or acute exacerbation of a chronic psychosis. It is rarely seen in individuals who do not upon interview appear to be grossly psychotic unless the profile is faked. For individuals clearly in trouble but not extremely psychotic, the F score may suggest a person who is desperate for help. (This should usually be accompanied by a high score on scale 7 as well.)

Scores between 70 and 80 are commonly seen in valid profiles from individuals with psychosis or who are diagnosed as borderline psychotics, especially if accompanied by high scores greater than 70 on Sc or Pa. This may also represent individuals who are very deviant in terms of political or religious attitudes or who are seen as opinionated, complex, restless, opportunistic, or affected. Antiauthority attitudes may be strong, as may be obsessive-compulsive behavior. These individuals may be very concrete and have suffered a serious brain injury affecting verbal responding. They may also be hostile, suspicious, and inappropriate. Signs of depersonalization can also be present.

Scores below 70 are rarely diagnozed as psychotic but may be diagnosed as borderline. Individuals with recent acute psychotic disturbances which are in remission may also get scores between 60 and 70. In a psychiatric setting, the F in this stage may indicate restlessness and agitation due to a recent acute situational disorder in a neurotic individual, or an extremely serious trauma (such as rape or the murder or death of a close relative) in a normal individual.

Scores between 50 and 70 may occasionally be associated with relatively intact paranoid psychosis or paranoid schizophrenics. These individuals will typically show no serious thought disorder but will have delusions that are characteristically reasonable and logical within themselves. These delusions will often be based on a single false assumption and built up from there into a perfectly reasonable delusional system that is difficult to break or place in doubt.

A low F score, below a T score of 60, will generally indicate a normal individual who functions well in most or all aspects of their life. The person may be socially conforming, fully normal, or have attempted to show a fake good profile (especially when the raw score is two or less and the K score is above or near 70). Normals with low F scores may be described as unassuming, sincere, honest, and calm. Such individuals are rarely social agitators and are usually happy or relaxed with their current life situation. The low F score in a person known to have serious problems but who is not faking may indicate an individual unable to confront the problems in their life.

The K Scale

The final validity scale is the K scale. The K scale was added to the MMPI in an attempt to detect more subtle instances of test bias than is measured by F or L. The K scale was also an attempt to provide a means of statistically correcting the clinical scales for these biasing tendencies. To determine the items on this scale, the profiles of psychiatric patients who look normal and normal patients who show psychiatric profiles were examined. The resulting K scale was intended to measure both biases against truthful answering (high K scores) and biases towards overly negative reporting (low K scores).

In general, high K scores are not associated with specific behaviors but rather a reluctance to admit symptoms. The high K responder may be trying to fake a good profile or may have responded false to all MMPI items (see Figures 4-1 and 4-2). Alternately, the high K responder may be shy, lack insight or awareness of problems, be hysterical, or very perfectionistic and conventional. High K scores in an obviously psychiatric profile may be strongly associated with a lack of awareness that the behavior of the person is different from the behavior of others.

Normal (average) K scores may suggest a generally normal balance and contact with reality if the remainder of the profile is consistent with such an interpretation. Overall, such individuals are characterized by a number of positive terms including independent, self-reliant, resourceful, versatile, clear thinking, and socially involved. When the remainder of the profile is not consistent with such an interpretation, however, these terms are likely to be misleading. For example, normal K scores are frequently found in acute psychiatric populations, in which case the score simply suggests no overt biasing in the answers to the MMPI.

Low K scores may be associated with faking bad profiles, suicidal ideation, homosexual concerns, and a generally negative orientation to the person's situation in life. The individual may be asking for help, either consciously or unconsciously. The patient may have little insight and be in a state of distress and suspicious of others. Low scorers are harsh in social interactions and may come across as cynical, awkward, and shallow.

K scale scores may be associated with education and age. Individuals who are young may take a more positive outlook towards life, minimizing or failing to recognize problems. Similarly, highly educated individuals may see problems as minor and unimportant. As a result, both of these groups may often produce exaggerated K scores, especially in the young, highly educated combination.

Determining Profile Invalidity

There is no clear difference between profiles that are invalid and those that indicate a number of important psychiatric conditions. As a result, the determination of profile invalidity can be difficult. The traditional method involving calling any profile with an F, K, or L score greater than a T score of 70 invalid, or invalidating any profile with more than 30 ? responses. While it is true that sticking to these rules will eliminate almost all invalid profiles, they will also throw out a large number of valid profiles. For example, F scores above 70 may indicate serious psychotic disorders, K scores above 70 may indicate a high level of defensiveness, while L scores above 70 may be associated with moralistic, rigid individuals.

An additional method of determining invalidity has been suggested by Gough (1950). He suggested taking the difference between the raw F and raw K scores (F-K). Gough indicated that a score greater than nine would mean that the individual was faking bad. Scores that were less than -9, on the other hand, would indicate a faking good profile. Carson (1969) suggested that the cutoffs should be at 11 rather than 9, while others have suggested alternate cutoffs for different populations. Unfortunately, the problems with this score are much the same as problems with the basic validity scales. Any rigid cutoff will generally exclude a number of valid cases as well. High F-K's may merely reflect individuals who are psychotic and severely disturbed, while low F-K's (negative) may reflect highly defensive, rigid individuals. Thus, while one can look at F-K much as one looks at the other validity scales, this still does not solve the problem of determining invalidity without losing valid results.

The first step in determining invalidity is for the clinician to be aware of and recognize typical response patterns associated with invalid profiles. Figures 4-1–4-9 present a wide variety of responses associated with random responding, all true responding, all false responding, faking good, and faking bad. As the reader can see, random response patterns generally create F scores above 100 and K and L scores above 50. This can be easily distinguished from a highly psychotic profile which would (generally) have lower scores on all three scales. The presence of a random profile can also be determined by observing the patient. If the profile is valid, the patient should be overtly and severely psychotic. Random profiles are also associated with patients who take the test in a quick and careless manner.

Fig. 4-1.   An example of a random profile. The heavy line is the plot for males, the dotted line for females.

Fig. 4-2.   A randomly generated profile. Note that in this figure and Figure 4-1 all validity scales are elevated above 50, as are all the clinical scales.

Fig. 4-3. Profile generated by all true answers. Solid line is male profile. Dotted line is female profile.

Fig. 4-4. Profile generated by all false answers. Solid line represents male profile while dotted line is female profile.

71

Fig. 4-5. Profile generated by alternating true and false answers. Solid line is male profile while dotted line is female profile.

Fig. 4-6. Profile generated by pattern of TTFF answers. Dotted line is female profile while solid line is male profile.

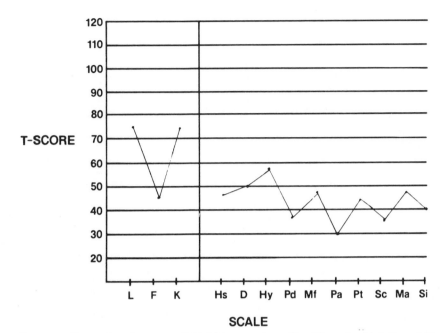

Fig. 4-7. Example of one possible faking good profile. Note the high L and K scores along with the low F score. The general low scores on all the clinical scales (except Hysteria) are also common to these profiles.

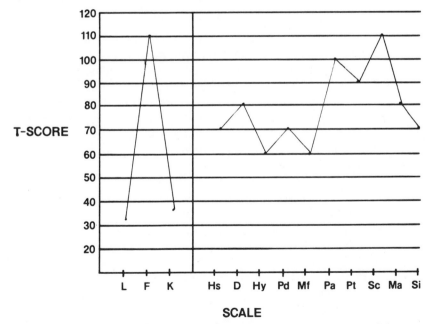

Fig. 4-8. Overt faking bad profile. Note the high F and very low K and L scores with the typical high points on scales Sc and Pa.

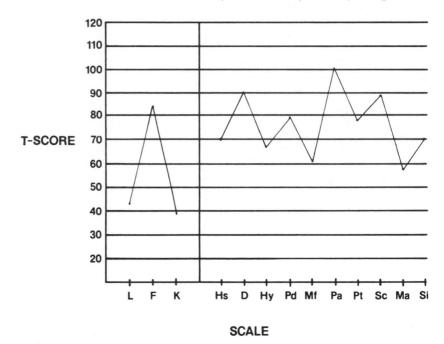

Fig. 4-9.   Malingering profile. This differs from the faking bad profile in its generally lower scores and the sawtoothed peaks on scales 2, 4, 6, and 8.

In determining the reason for a random profile, the clinician should interview the patient and confront them with the results if that is possible or request the patient to tell how they took the test. Random profiles may result from a lack of reading skills, which can be determined from a reading comprehension test (Chapter 3). Patterning may be seen in the answer sheet of the random responder. All true or all false profiles will often be generated, or the answers will be in a pattern such as two true, then two false, or some similar pattern. These patterns may often be detected by looking at the answer sheet.

Faking bad responses are similar to those seen in extremely severe psychotic disorders: F greater than 100, L and K less than 50. Typically, scales 6, 7, and 8 will be highest. Since this is such a severely psychotic profile, it is often easy to compare the patient's behavior to the psychotic, deteriorated behavior that would be expected. Faking good profiles are characterized by high K's and L's (greater than 70) and most clinical scales below 50. F scores will also be below 50, often with raw scores of two or less. In diagnosing both faking good and faking bad responses, the clinician should investigate to determine the motivation for such a response. In our practice, we have found it useful to discuss this with the patient and point out the advantages of taking the test honestly. While this will not always get the patient's cooperation, it has been successful in a significant number of cases.

Among the most difficult faking responses to pick up is the malingering profile. Such individuals do not try to show themselves as patently bad as those more overt faking bad profiles seen above. There will still be, however, an elevated F score (above 70 or 80) along with clinical peaks on scales 2, 4, 6, and 8 giving the profile a saw-toothed appearance. Since this is also a profile suggesting severe maladjustment, as well as the presence of psychosis, the matching of the patient's behavior against the profile and discussions with the patient can be useful in diagnosing this pattern (see Figure 4-11).

THE CLINICAL SCALES

There are ten basic clinical scales to the MMPI, although some clinicians exclude the Mf and Si scales. In evaluating the importance of each scale, several factors must be kept in mind. First, when we talk about high scores on a scale, the meaning is relative to the profile. Thus, a score which is both high (greater than 70) and high relative to all the other scales should be taken as much more significant than a high score that is only the fifth or sixth highest in the profile. Similarly, a score in the 60's might assume greater importance if it is the highest score of the profile, especially in an individual with a high K score. One must also be aware of the importance of the lowest score or scores in the profile, no matter what the actual elevation may be.

A second important factor is to recognize that several scales have a significant number of items that are repeated on a second scale. Thus, two scales like Hypochondriasis and Hysteria, will tend to move up or down together. The degree to which one is high and the other low often suggests specific interpretations important to the scale and pattern analysis.

Finally, the role of the validity scales must be considered. Interpretations should be adjusted according to whether a person minimizes problems, exaggerates them, or tends to be open and reasonable about the responses.

The material for the following descriptions and those of the validity scales come from a number of major sources including: Dahlstrom, Welsh, and Dahlstrom (1972, 1975); Drake and Oetting (1959); Osmon and Golden (1978); Golden, Sweet, and Osmon (1979); Good and Brantner (1974); Hathaway and Meehl (1951); Gilberstadt and Duker (1965); Boerger, Graham, and Lilly (1974); Marks and Seeman (1963); Welsh and Dahlstrom (1956); Graham (1977); and Hedlund (1977); as well as from the author's own clinical experience.

Scale 1 (Hs)

The Hypochondriasis scale serves as a measure of an individual's concern about somatic functions. High Hs scores are associated with abnormal concerns over bodily functions and vague hypochrondriacal complaints. Complaints by high scorers may include diarrhea, loss of appetite, insomnia, and general fatigue and depression. High scorers may be passive and tend to withdraw from others. Patients with true medical complaints may also tend to score higher on Hs, but scores over 65 in younger individuals and over 70 in older individuals almost always suggest a strong psychological component. In many people with high Hs scores, there are at least some real physical symptoms, ranging from the symptoms we all feel from day to day to more serious disorders like ruptured discs or diabetes which are exaggerated by the patient's psychological status. This is important to emphasize as all the complaints of the high Hs patients cannot be dismissed as psychosomatic.

High scorers on scale 1 are also likely to report general listlessness, psychomotor retardation, depression (often with a high score on scale 2 as well), anxiety, irritability, lack of self-confidence, ambivalence, lack of aggression with hostile feelings usually turned inward, and will often appear very defensive and unable to deal with negative emotions on any level. A high scale 1 accompanied by a significantly lower scale 2 suggests that only the general complaining and overconcern are present without the symptoms related to depression.

Low scores on scale 1 are common in young people and individuals who are free of somatic complaints and generally positive and optimistic about life. Such individuals may be described as sensitive, alert, cheerful, and sociable. Overall, this suggests that low 1 individuals tend to be free from most neurotic patterns and able to interact with others in an efficient and pleasant manner.

Scale 2 (D)

The depression scale is associated with depressed mood, a poor self-concept, suicidal thoughts, psychomotor retardation, mild anxiety and agitation. Somatic symptoms, loss of sleep, loss of appetite, are common in high scorers, especially if there are elevations on scales 1 and 7. Scale 2 is also correlated with feelings of helplessness, poor morale, dejection, distress, apathy, and a denial of positive feelings. Scale 2 scores are quite variable depending on an individual's mood when the test is taken.

High scale 2 individuals may report an inability to feel positive emotions. They will generally be very pessimistic about themselves and others, and express guilt over past behavior or thoughts. They may show symptoms of obsessive-compulsive disorders, especially when accompanied by a high score on scale 7. The high scorer will feel useless and attempt to withdraw from social contacts and business responsibilities, often spending excessive time sleeping. They will usually be ambivalent, especially if scores are above 80, and unable to make decisions even in minor matters. They will often be motivated to seek help, but offer little active cooperation. Individuals with chronic high 2 scores that interfere with daily life and cause serious somatic symptoms, such as a refusal to eat, often need treatment with antidepressive drugs. Patients with acute depressive episodes and without somatic scores (usually with high 7 scores) are more likely to recover on their own, as long as the remaining clinical scales are below 70.

Low scores on scale 2 are highly suggestive of a happy, relaxed individual who may show signs of high levels of activity depending on the height of scale 9. These individuals are cheerful and pleasant, at ease in social situations (also note the level of scale 0), responsible, clever, and likely to assume a leadership role. Combined with a rise on scale 4, they may also be impulsive, uninhibited, and have conflict with authority figures. These individuals generally do not have strong guilt feelings. A low point 2 (lowest score in the profile except for 5 and 0) in a profile with a high 8 and 9 can suggest a manic-depressive disorder, manic phase (see also the discussion of high point 29 patterns).

Scale 3 (Hy)

The Hysteria scale is a measure of the tendency to develop conversion problems, the substitution of somatic complaints for anxiety. The scale is also highly related to depressive symptoms such as psychomotor retardation, however. Scale 3 contains a number of items about physical complaints which it shares in common with Scale 1. As a result, a high score on Hy alone is not sufficient to suggest the presence of a hysterical disorder of either the conversion or the dissociative type, which may be characterized by amnesia, feelings of depersonalization, multiple personality, and the like. In some two point combinations (see next section on two point patterns involving scale 3), such individuals will tend to show a variety of somatic symptoms including headaches, stomach pains, backaches, and in women, disorders associated with the menstrual period. Such individuals will occasionally develop more dramatic symptoms such as psychogenic blindness, paralysis, or loss of sensation. These individuals are generally seen most often in hospitals or doctor's offices rather than psychiatric clinics, although a psychologist or psychiatrist may be called in to consult on the case after medical evaluations have failed to find significant physical correlates of the patient's complaints.

The presumed, underlying deficit in the high 3 individual is the inability to handle hostility and stress. Such individuals will appear to be very friendly, sociable, talkative, and enthusiastic. They will also be found to be egocentric, childish, immature, narcissistic, and lack psychological insight, however. Hysterical individuals will often act out sexually, often acting seductive towards physicians of the opposite sex, and may be promiscuous if there is a high point 34 combination. A low point 6 in these patients is very suggestive of severely repressed hostility which can come out in a cyclic manner in the form of temper tantrums or suicide threats and attempts. High point 3's are likely to have unhappy marriages, be resentful of anyone in authority (although pleasant to them in a face to face visit), and resentful of physicians and psychologists. A typical high 3 may tell each physician they see that they have had trouble with past doctors, but that the current doctor is obviously much smarter (more skillful, more attentive, knowledgeable, etc.) and things will go very well now. High 3's rarely have insight into their own behavior and resent suggestions that they have psychological problems. Scale 3 patients are often extremely repressed, as seen in concommitant high K and L scores.

Low Hy scores are associated with individuals who are conforming, unfriendly, suspicious, and have a narrow range of interests (especially if associated with significantly higher 6); low scorers may also be content with their life, realistic, and level-headed.

Scale 4 (Pd)

The psychopathic deviate scale was intended to measure asocial or antisocial tendencies in an individual. This can include lying, stealing, promiscuity, drug abuse, and a general disregard for social rules and conventions. High Pd patients may have assaultive thoughts, acting out behavior, hostility, irritability, and general antisocial ideas. In Freudian terms, these are individuals with little or no effective superego: they have been unable to incorporate the standards of society into their own consciences. High 4 individuals will often be rebellious, underachieving in school, have a history of acting out before age 15, be unable to form close relationships, have difficulties in marriage and at work, show poor judgment, act impulsively, and demonstrate narcissistic and egocentric tendencies. Such individuals under stress may turn to suicide gestures not out of real depression but as a way of getting revenge on others or manipulating them to support his or her own goals.

High 4's may seem highly sociable and interested in others, but this interest basically extends only to what can be gotten from the person. Goals may be short-termed and vary on impulse. High 4's may be intelligent, cynical, aggressive, and prone to worry, especially when not in control of a situation or the events directly affecting their lives.

On a more positive side, the more socialized high 4 individual may turn the aggressiveness, energetic, and sociable characteristics of the personality type to more positive goals, especially when a person's intelligence is high enough to control the more antisocial tendencies in the personality type. Such people make highly successful physicians, psychologists, salesmen, and other professionals who have to deal with people. It should be noted that one cannot diagnose the antisocial or dyssocial personality from this typology alone, but only on the basis of a history of antisocial activity.

Low 4's will generally be conforming, submissive to authority, passive, not competitive, moralistic, security conscious, uncreative, not interested in sex, and pliable. Such individuals are afraid of accepting responsibility for their own behavior and may have strong guilt feelings over minor infractions.

Scale 5 (Mf)

The Masculinity-Feminity Scale is the only MMPI scale scored differently for males and females and interpreted separately. The scale will be discussed separately for each sex.

In males, high scores on scale 5 indicate someone who may be confused about sexual identity and insecure in the masculine role. One important exception to this is the highly educated, culturally oriented male who values cognitive pursuits and creativity. Such individuals are creative, imaginative, individualistic, tolerant, and sensitive to the feelings of others. Thus, while high Mf scores in the male may suggest sexual confusion and even homosexuality, the examiner must be careful not to confuse this with the more positive traits suggested by the profile. Low scores in males, especially scores below 40, may suggest a man who sees himself as overly masculine, the traditional macho stereotype. Such individuals will place a strong emphasis on physical strength, aggressiveness, adventurousness, and thrill seeking. These individuals may be coarse and vulgar, and often have deep seated doubts about their own masculinity. The doubt of masculinity is most strongly seen in individuals with a macho image of themselves who very clearly do not fit that image. Alternately, low 5 males may lack insight, and be jolly, relaxed, and conforming.

In females, a high Mf score suggests the rejection of the typical feminine role. These women have strong interests in the so-called masculine areas of sports, work, and hobbies. These females may be aggressive, competitive, coarse, rough, outgoing, uninhibited, unemotional, and unfriendly. Such women may see themselves in active competition with men, attempting to show they are equal or better. A low 5 score in a female suggests a woman who describes herself in typical female stereotypes: she is passive, submissive, yielding, defers to males; and may have doubts about her femininity. These doubts may be strong in women professionals and women with high 4 or 6 codes, especially when associated with high 3 scores as well. Low scoring females may be sensitive, modest and idealistic or constricted, complaining, and self-pitying.

Scale 6 (Pa)

The paranoid scale suggests suspiciousness, and oversensitivity, and may indicate paranoid delusions when the score exceeds 70, especially in patients with high F and Sc scores as well. High scores on scale 6 are associated with formal thought disorders as well as depressive feelings, but without the feelings of guilt or responsibility which are typically projected onto others. High 6 patients may have strong sexual concerns and preoccupations. Delusions may be centered around threats of rape or homosexual rape either overtly or on a symbolic level.

Extreme elevations on Pa (greater than 75) are almost always associated with psychotic behavior in a valid profile. The individuals may have delusions of reference, grandeur, or persecution. Thinking disorders are almost always present (although in its incipient stages the paranoid delusions can exist without a thought disorder). Patients are often angry or fearful and may plot revenge on others. They may be dangerous to others or even to themselves as a result. (One patient, for example, jumped out of a second story window while escaping from imaginary pursuers.) Diagnoses of paranoid schizophrenia are most common in this group with occasional diagnosis of paranoid state.

High scores on 6 that are less than 75 are less associated with psychoticism unless there is a rise on Sc as well. These individuals are excessively sensitive, hostile, resentful, and eager to blame others for their own failures. They may be suspicious and guarded and lie in interviews, giving different stories to different investigators. They are rigid individuals and poor risks for psychotherapy.

Low and moderate Pa scores, in normal individuals, are generally associated with sensitive, trusting, energetic individuals who have a wide range of interests and values. Such individuals are found to be intelligent, poised, rational, and cooperative but may lack self-confidence or be submissive and prone to worry.

In psychiatric or maladjusted patients, a score in the range of 35 to 50 may suggest guardedness, self-centered behavior, high sensitivity, under-achievement, and undependability. These patients may feel little guilt (especially in association with a high 4). These individuals are unlikely to be psychotic, however.

Scores less than 35, especially in a psychiatric patient, may indicate someone who is overtly paranoid, delusional, defensive, and evasive. It is the defensive and evasive qualities which cause them to deny their symptomatology on the test and results in the extremely low Pa score. Extremely low scores in what appear to be normal individuals may suggest people unable to handle hostility or even face the fact that they have hostility towards others. Such individuals may be prone to temper tantrums as pressure build up because of their continuing denial and re-pression. The low 6 may often be associated with high K and high scores on scale 3.

Scale 7 (Pt)

The psychasthenia scale was devised to identify individuals with obsessive-compulsive traits or strong phobias: in other words, individuals with high levels of anxiety. High scores on Pt correlate with obsessive thinking (more so than compulsive behavior), strong feelings of anxiety or tension, depression (with frequent concommitant highs on scale 2), and with phobias of all kinds (the type depending on the experiences of the patient or the symbolic meaning of the specific phobia for that patient).

High scorers are seen as high-strung and jumpy and may show overt physiological signs of anxiety such as sweating. Because of the great ten-sion they are under, high 7 individuals will show difficulty in concentra-tion, thinking, planning, understanding, and recognizing environmental cues which could rationally reduce the anxiety state. High 7 patients are guilty, depressed, perfectionistic, and lack self-confidence. They may be overly organized, neat, orderly, and meticulous but lack creativity or in-genuity. They may be indecisive and vacillate, worrying over everything numerous times without reaching a decision of any kind.

High 7's may have physical problems, centering around the heart, intestines and stomach (such as ulcers), insomnia (because of obsessive thinking), tension headaches, and exhaustion. Such disorders as bronchial asthma may be brought about by anxiety in such individuals. High 7's need long-term psychotherapy as these are often life-long patterns: brief psychotherapy is ineffective or of short-term benefit. High 7's may use rationalization and intellectualization as defense mechanisms, making them hard to reach in therapy.

Low scores on scale 7 are associated with calm, capable, well adjusted individuals without neurotic tendencies (although they may show character or personality disorders). These individuals will generally be realistic and able to handle stress effectively. They may value success, recognition, and status.

Scale 8 (Sc)

Scale 8, Schizophrenia, is a measure of thought disorder in patients with psychiatric disorders. The scale correlates with such symptoms as unusual thought contact, psychosis, delusions, hallucinations, depersonalization, inappropriate affect, refusal to speak, peculiar posturing, peculiar mannerisms, bizarre behavior, bizarre dress, withdrawn behavior, dependent behavior, and emotional lability. It is also associated with poor memory, conceptual disorganization, disorientation, inability to concentrate, inability to understand proverbs, poor hygiene, and intellectual deterioration.

High 8 scores (above 100) are not usually produced by psychotic subjects but may indicate a random or faking bad profile. T scores of 80 and above are suggestive of extreme confusion that interferes with the test as well as the patient's life. Scores between 70 and 80 are associated with chronic schizophrenic conditions, while scores above 80 are more likely acute episodes or acute exacerbations. High scores on 8 (above 70) along with high scores on F (above 70) are nearly always associated with a current psychotic condition, while lower scores or high 8 scores without high F scores may be associated with a schizoid personality.

Individuals with schizoid personalities typically feel alienated from life. They have few friends, are isolated, feel misunderstood, and are rarely acceptable to others. They avoid situations that are new or bring them into emotional contact with others. The prognosis in psychotherapy for any high scores on schizophrenia is generally poor because of the typical chronicity of the disorder and the pervasiveness of the problem. Some help can be offered individuals with initial, acute psychotic breaks that are characterized by elevated scores on both scales 7 and 8, however (see the discussion for the 87 two point code). These individuals are generally best treated by a combination of psychotherapy and medication, especially in chronic disorders.

Low scores on Scale 8 are associated with mature, adjusted individuals who are described as well balanced, adaptable, and responsible. Such individuals may be cautious, practical, and conservative. They may avoid competitive situations, and be concerned about status and power.

Scale 9 (Ma)

Scale 9 measures the presence of hypomanic behavior, including such symptoms as overproductivity in thought and behavior, expansive (grandiose) self-concept, elevated mood, loud or excessive speech, impulsive acts, flights of ideas, increased motor activity, elation over sad things, and lability of mood. High Ma scores are also associated with psychotic symptoms such as confusion, delusions, suspiciousness, paranoid thoughts, depersonalization, poor memory, disorientation, and inability to concentrate. These symptoms are especially serious in patients with T scores over 80 and are often accompanied by high Sc scores as well. Hallucinations may also be present, especially as scores exceed 90. These high manic states are often associated with the manic phase of a manic-depressive disorder or with a schizo-affective disorder. These patients often respond to drug treatment with lithium while in the manic phase.

Individuals high on Scale 9 also tend to be friendly, sociable, and gregarious. They like to be around people, and will often joke and have a good sense of humor, unlike individuals with other forms of psychosis. The manic may also have periods where they are irritable, aggressive, and show strong paranoid delusions. The manic may make unrealistic plans for the future and claim to have high connections and power. The manic may also be reacting to a depressive episode in an attempt to deny a current depression by showing manic behavior. Such individuals may show the interesting elevated 29 pattern (see next section). Not surprisingly, these patients have fairly poor prognosis for psychotherapy and are unlikely to attend on a regular basis.

A low score on Scale 9 (especially below 40) indicates an individual with a low energy level. The person may be lethargic, listless, and report chronic fatigue. If not severely depressed, however, these individuals are described as reliable, sincere, modest, and overcontrolled. They may also be withdrawn (often showing a high Si and D score) and unpopular with others.

Scale 0 (Si)

The Social Introversion Scale attempts to measure the tendency of the individual to withdraw from others. The scale correlates both with the tendency to withdraw as well as with symptoms of depression: psychomotor retardation and low levels of activity. There is also a strong relationship to anxiety and phobia as well as preoccupations with bodily concerns. Thus, the scale has more significant diagnostic implications than simple withdrawal.

Individuals with high scores on Scale 0 are generally found to be socially introverted, although they may enjoy being with a single friend or a small group. Such individuals are not usually antisocial, but in more extreme forms, especially with a high 8, may show distinct schizoid qualities. High scorers are generally uncomfortable around members of the opposite sex, and lack self-confidence. They are hard to get to know and troubled by involvement with others, although they may be very sensitive to what others are thinking or doing. They are accepting of authority. They hide their feelings and have great difficulty expressing them to others. These individuals are serious, reliable, and dependable although they tend to be slow in personal tempo (associated with a low 9 score). They tend to be cautious and conservative, rarely finding original ways to do things. They enjoy work and personal achievement. They can experience periods of depression (with elevated D) and irritability and may appear moody.

A low score on this scale generally has more meaning than low scores on many of the other scales which simply reflect the absence of a pathological condition. Individuals with low 0's are sociable, extroverted, active, intelligent, confident, and interested in leadership. If the score is less than 40, they usually get along well with the opposite sex. Such individuals may also be childish, impulsive, self-indulgent, and show a strong tendency to form only superficial relationships, especially if there is a high score on 4. These latter individuals may also be manipulative, opportunistic, and arouse resentment in others.

TWO POINT CODES

Extensive MMPI research has examined the behavioral and diagnostic correlates of two point high codes in MMPI profiles. This research examines the relationship of the two highest scales on a given profile, excluding the validity scales, to MMPI interpretation. These codes have been found to be highly useful in the interpretation of the MMPI and are usually the starting point for an MMPI interpretation. As a rule, this research has ignored which of the two points is higher; profiles with scales 3 and 4 highest are regarded the same as profiles with scales 4 and 3 highest. In most cases it has not been found to matter which is highest. As a simple rule of thumb, however, if the difference between the two highest scales is greater than ten, the behavior of the individual tends to reflect the characteristics of the higher scale much more strongly than in profiles where the difference is less than ten.

Most profiles have one clear set of high points. There are, however, numerous profiles which do not. These include profiles where two or three scales have the same T score. Thus, a profile may have a scale 4 score of 70, a scale 3 score of 68, and a scale 6 score of 68. It is not possible to tell in this profile if there is a 43 or 46 high point. In these cases, both can be examined and used in the interpretation. A second important case occurs when several scales are quite close to one another. Thus, a profile may have scores of 75, 76, and 77 on scales 1, 2, and 3 respectively. While this profile has a clear high point pair (32), the difference between the scales is slight. Thus, one would also look at the meaning of the 31 and 21 profiles in interpreting this individual's scores. Finally, a profile may have a clear high point pair but might also have outstanding peaks in other parts of the profile. For example, a profile may have a clear 87 high point pair but also a secondary pair of high points on scales 1 and 3. In this case, the interpretation of both the 87 and 31 high points extends our understanding of the profile considerably. It is important, in this regard, to be observant and recognize certain high point pairs (to be discussed) that have important characterological or personality implications. In this manner, an acute condition can be interpreted (such as represented by the 87 high point) as well as an underlying personality disorder (represented by the 31 high point).

When multiple high point codes are interpreted in a single profile, the process is much the same as when the ten clinical scales are interpreted. The highest two point pair is given more weight than lower pairs if there are contradictions, and the overall descriptions are merged to form a psychologically meaningful constellation of behaviors and dynamics. This, of course, presupposes a knowledge of personality functions and of psychopathology by the' interpreter. The following pages describe the more common and more heavily researched two point codes. The reader will note that fewer codes are presented involving scales 5 and 0 as many researchers do not regard these as clinical scales. Profiles with high points on these scales should also be examined for high point pairs when these scales are excluded, as well as for the meaning of high scores on 0 and 5.

12/21

The individual with this profile is reporting significant somatic concerns along with depression. The somatic problems in this code can be the result of either organic or functional problems. Individuals with a 123 triple high point are generally hypochondriacal and have little basis for their pain. The raised 2 score is often related to a significant collapse of their defenses causing the onset of depression and anxiety along with more acute and severe somatic complaints. This profile, however, may also be seen in chronic pain patients who have an organic basis, but who have essentially given in to their pain and are exaggerating it considerably at the present time. The high point pair may also be seen in individuals who have undergone recent severe accidents, whose depression is acute and a reaction to the serious injuries incurred. In distinguishing these possibilities, it is necessary to know to what extent the patient's physical injuries can be objectively discerned, as well as history about the onset of the pain. In a recent study we completed on pain, we found the 12 pattern to be the average profile in an organically injured group; other research, however, has also reported the profile in psychosomatic groups.

Individuals with this profile do tend to exaggerate their physical problems beyond what is physically confirmable and often misinterpret normal pains or bodily functions. When the pain is functional, these individuals tend to be shy and withdrawn. When the pain is organic, they may be loud complainers and generally uninterested in others. Psychiatric patients with this profile may have histories of drug or alcohol abuse (usually justified as pain therapy), and are suspicious of any attempts to suggest otherwise. This is especially true in men with this profile who may see themslves as "macho" (low 5).

The most common diagnosis for these groups are hypochondriacal, anxiety, or depressive neurosis. The latter is most likely when the depressive symptoms are predominant, while anxiety neurosis is most likely when there is a 127 profile. These are rarely diagnosed as personality disorders, except when there is a 124, 126, or 1264 pattern suggesting passive-aggressive personality, dependent type with acute depression. Patients with 128 profiles and high F's may be diagnosed as schizophrenic (usually chronic undifferentiated type).

13/31

This profile is associated with the classical "conversion V" in which a 13 high point pair is accompanied by a lower scale 2 score. These individuals generally show a great deal of somatic complaining, and may be showing classical conversion hysteria although that is rare in this profile type. The pattern has also been found in numerous groups of chronic pain patients with known organic causes such as ruptured discs. These individuals generally do not show severe anxiety, the level varying with the height of the 2 scale. The higher the 2 the more likely the patient will be experiencing the stress and anxiety that they identify. In patients where the 2 is considerably lower, especially where it is the profile low point, the likelihood of conversion hysteria becomes significantly stronger. This may also be associated with an elevated 4 and low 5 scale in women (high 5 in men).

All 13/31 profile types, whether the pain is initially organic or functional, suffer from gross exaggeration of pain and a strong psychogenic factor. These patients tend to be superficial in relationships with others, and may lack skills with the opposite sex (scale 5 is often a clue in this direction as is scale 0). These individuals generally have considerable repressed hostility, often seen in a very low or relatively high 6. The very low 6 suggests a strong active repressive tendency which can cause extremely difficult problems with these patients, as overcontrolled individuals can release their hostility all at once in temper tantrums (especially if there is a high 4) or in suicide threats or attempts.

These patients are given a diagnosis of neurosis, usually hypochondriacal or hysterical, psychophysiological reaction, or described as chronic pain patients when there is a 132 pattern combined with a history of definitive organic injury.

14/41

Fourteen/forty-one patients tend to be rarely seen, but when seen present themselves as severely hypochondriacal. These symptoms may be highly manipulative in nature (reflecting the 4), but there are few if any signs of asocial behavior. These individuals may be extroverted (low 0) but are rarely skillful with the opposite sex (see scale 5). As with other individuals with peak 4's, there may be a history of alcoholism, poor work history, drug abuse, and poor marital history. These individuals are complainers and may be difficult to get along with. As are the 12 and 13 codes, they are highly resistant to psychotherapy. Diagnosis will generally be hypochondriacal neurosis with occasional additional diagnosis of a personality disorder depending on the constellation of the remaining scales.

18/81

When there is a high F score with this profile, these individuals are often diagnosed as schizophrenic. They have great trouble handling stress and anxiety, and may show clearly delusional thinking about bodily functions and bodily illness. They do not trust others and may appear paranoid, irrespective of the height of scale 6. These individuals may be confused and unable to concentrate. When the symptoms are less severe and the F score is in the normal range, the likely diagnosis is a hypochon-driacal or anxiety neurosis. The latter is more likely as scale 7 approaches the height of scales 1 and 8.

19/91

These individuals show a great deal of somatic complaining combined with an extroverted, verbal, and socially outgoing personality. The rise on scale 9 in these individuals tends to be a reaction to their basic personal-ity. Rather than give in to their dependent needs, the patient attempts to establish that he or she is independent and strong. This profile may have several other scales suggestive of a basically passive underlying personal-ity. These individuals expect a great deal from themselves, but their goals are unclear and often unrealistic. This profile can be seen in reaction to physical injury which limits an individual's capacity to cope and to achieve goals which were formerly possible. These patients can be diag-nosed as hypochondriacal, manic, or a combination of both. They may also be seen as passive-aggressive, especially with high 4 and low 6 scores.

23/32

These individuals report that they are fatigued, tired, weak, de-pressed, and anxious. They are often inadequate and unable to do things for themselves, relying instead on others to take care of them. Somatic symptoms are usually present but are often inconsistent and changing. The patients are generally found to be immature, childish, and have diffi-culty expressing their feelings. They may be insecure, socially in-adequate, and unable to deal with the opposite sex. It is important to observe the relative heights of the 5, 6, and 0 scales as this may reveal information about the patient's adjustment. A diagnosis of depressive neurosis is common, unless there are rises on both F and 8 suggesting psychotic depression. In cases of psychotic depression, one must also examine the personal history for the possibility of manic-depressive psychosis. Response to psychotherapy in these patients is poor.

24/42

Some have suggested that this profile represents the psychopath in trouble: the antisocial individual (scale 4) who is caught, usually by the law, and thus becomes depressed (scale 2). In other cases, these are chronically depressed people whose high 4's are associated with extreme hostility, either overt (high 6) or suppressed (low 6). These individuals generally have little regard for the rules of society or for working with a mental health professional. Their acting out behavior is deeply ingrained and may be expressed in crime, drug or alcohol abuse, and promiscuous sexual activity. When associated with high energy levels (9) and high overt hostility (6), these individuals may be extremely dangerous to others. When this profile is extremely elevated (near 90) the behavior may be overtly psychotic or prepsychotic, depending on the levels of the F and 8 scales. There is also a strong chance of manipulative suicides in the elevated profile. The interpreter must be careful at this point, however, as a 2468 pattern is also characteristic of malingering profiles.

While these individuals may express (and sometimes feel) guilt, their sincerity is limited. They will work to get themselves out of current difficulty but will return to their old patterns as soon as they are free. Consequently, they are poor risks in therapy. The clinician should especially beware of quick, overnight cures and promises to reform. In an acute hospital setting, these individuals may come across as friendly and sincere and can often manipulate staff into helping them out with their problems (which are often with the law). These individuals also tend to have poor marital and work histories and do not do well in school.

The 246 pattern may be associated with strong personality disorders (passive-aggressive or mixed antisocial and passive-aggressive), accompanied by acute depression. In these cases, scale 2 is often greatly elevated over scales 1 and 3. There are generally higher scores on 1 and 3 when the 2 component is more chronic. In addition, the integration and evaluation of the patient's history is important in making the chronic/ acute distinction. The history is best trusted when corroborated by a reliable source.

26/62

Patients with this profile show strong evidence of paranoid trends, sometimes to the point where the paranoid ideation is psychotic or prepsychotic. Psychotic profiles may be associated with raised scores on F and 8 as well as on 9 (see 69 patterns). Encapsulated paranoia, however, may show only an elevation in the 60's on the F or 6 scale. These individuals are often aggressive and sensitive to others as well as depressed. The depression is usually related to physical disorders (often real) whose cause is blamed on others. These individuals have difficulty with interpersonal relationships. Diagnosis can include depressive neurosis, passive-aggressive personality (especially in 624 combinations), paranoid state, or (incipient) paranoid schizophrenia. In rare instances, this can be associated with an involutional paranoid state.

27/72

This is one of the most common codes in psychiatric populations. These individuals are generally seen as depressed with additional symptoms of agitation, restlessness, and nervousness. The patients may show symptoms of neurasthenia (especially if combined with a 123 pattern) and report generalized weakness and fatigue. These individuals have a great need for recognition and are often depressed over their failures. They are rigid, compulsive, and perfectionistic. They often have a great deal of trouble handling hostility (which can be reflected in the scale 6 score) and appear to be passive-dependent (reflected in scales 3, 4, and 6). These patients are most likely to be diagnosed as depressive neurosis or anxiety neurosis, although a diagnosis of psychotic depression (with a rise on F) is possible as is manic-depressive psychosis (but only with a confirming history).

28/82

This code profile is common in psychiatric populations. Most of these patients complain of depression or anxiety, as well as sleep disturbance, confused thinking, and memory problems. They may present as physically ill or simply as seriously depressed. These are generally dependent and ineffective individuals who have difficulty expressing emotions openly. They do not get along with people as a result, and tend to be suspicious and wary of them. If both scales as well as F are above 70, the most likely diagnoses are psychotic depression, manic-depressive psychosis, involutional depression, or schizoaffective disorder. The latter diagnosis is most likely when the 8 peak predominates over the 2 by a significant amount. If this profile does not suggest psychosis, the diagnosis of schizoid personality with depression is possible as is depressive neurosis (287). These individuals are suicide risks and must be watched carefully.

29/92

The most predominant behaviors are usually manic in the 29 patient, although these may alternate with depressive episodes. The manic behavior serves to disguise the depression, making these individuals appear more intact than they actually are. If not overtly manic, these individuals will appear to be tense and restless. In younger individuals, this pattern may indicate someone who is unsure of their social role. In older individuals, this may be a reaction to physical disability or involutional depression. The high 9 serves as a denial mechanism in which the person avoids recognizing his or her limitations. This profile is reported by some in brain injured patients, but in our own samples did not appear to be particularly more prevalent than numerous other profile codes. The most common diagnosis in these cases is manic-depressive psychosis if both scales are elevated. Cyclothymic personality is occasionally diagnosed as well.

34/43

These patients are characterized by chronic and severe anger which they have great trouble expressing. Depending on the level of scale 6, they may or may not be able to clearly recognize this hostility and its source. If scale 4 is higher than 3, or the scales essentially equal (within five points), the individual is likely to have an explosive personality erupting in periodic temper tantrums. Individuals with this code are likely to develop a wide variety of medical disorders including headaches, menstrual problems, and other conversion or psychosomatic disorders. It is not unusual to see explosive periods alternate with somatic periods during which the patient is sociable, cooperative, and friendly. These individuals are usually hostile towards their families, and have histories of chronic marital problems. Antisocial acts, including savage crimes of violence, are not uncommon. Women with a 43 profile and a low 5 may be very seductive towards male therapists and are often sexually promiscuous. Suicide is a possibility as the result of an inwardly directed outburst or alcohol or drug intoxication. Diagnosis can include hysterical personality, passive-aggressive personality, explosive personality, or mixed personality disorder. Parents of these patients are often found to be alcoholic.

36/63

Individuals with this code may report somatic symptoms such as gastrointestinal difficulties as well as anxiety and nervousness. As in the 34 group, the problems arise from chronic and intense hostility towards family. These feelings are rarely recognized openly, however. These patients are rigid and highly rejecting of suggestions that their problems may be psychogenic. These individuals are self-centered and blame any conscious feelings of hostility on the behavior of others. They prefer to deny problems, however, rather than directly blame them on someone else. This pattern can lead to significant marital disharmony.

38/83

These individuals may report anxiety as well as feelings of depression. A large number of somatic complaints are possible. They show unusual thought patterns and strong repressive defenses. They often have delusions, poor concentration, and show significant social withdrawal. Delusions and other more bizarre behavior may not be readily apparent because of severe withdrawal and lack of cooperation, as well as an extreme loss of insight. These individuals are immature, dependent and unable to plan rationally for themselves. They are frequently diagnosed as schizophrenic, but occasionally seen as hysterical neurosis (especially if 8 and F are not above 70).

39/93

Patients with this profile are subject to considerable hostility, episodic attacks of acute anxiety, and medical complaints which appear overtly hysterical. The high 9 may be an attempt to cover up a basically dependent personality with an aggressive, arrogant, egocentric facade. The lack of insight is reflected in their belief that they are liked and admired by others, when in fact they may be seen quite critically. Periodic depressions are possible in these patients. Diagnoses include hysterical neurosis, anxiety neurosis, and passive-aggressive personality, aggressive type.

45/54

Individuals with this code type are likely to have significant troubles with sex role identification. Overt homosexuality or other sexual dysfunction is a strong possibility if both scales are above 70. Females with this code type are unusually aggressive, while males tend to be passive, dependent, and self-centered. These individuals are often nonconforming but rarely delinquent, although acting out is a possibility under stress or alcohol. Feelings of guilt or remorse are generally transient and rarely affect future behavior.

46/64

These individuals are generally passive-dependent, demanding a great deal from others but resenting any requests made of them. They are often depressed, irritable, withdrawn, and nervous. Significant repressed hostility is common, but acting out is possible if there is a high 9. Patients with 46 high points are generally self-centered, immature, and unable to form deep emotional involvements. Their needs for support and their extensive demands are insatiable. Consequently, little can be done to make them happy. As a result, marriage problems are common as are work problems. They deny problems in themselves, projecting them upon others. Likely diagnoses are paranoid schizophrenia, involutional paranoia (with 6 higher than 4 and both over 70) or passive-aggressive personality.

47/74

These individuals possess traits both of insensitivity to others (4) and a high tendency towards guilt over their behavior (7). They will frequently show cyclic behavior as a result, with periods of acting out alternating with periods of guilt and self-condemnation. During acting out periods, symptoms such as promiscuity and alcoholism are possible. While the subsequent guilt may be real, it does not prevent future episodes. During the guilt phase, there may be vague somatic complaints besides overt guilt and anxiety. This is a chronic pattern which does not change easily with any type of therapy. Antianxiety agents will often act to intensify the antisocial episodes. Diagnosis can be a combination of anxiety neurosis and psychopathic personality, despite the seeming contradiction in joining these disorders.

48/84

Patients with this profile are seen as odd and peculiar, often belonging to unusual religious or political movements. Their behavior can be erratic and unpredictable, and they may act out in antisocial ways. Such acts, however, are generally poorly planned and impulsive, and may be vicious. These individuals can be insecure, sexually perverse, obsessive, socially withdrawn, and isolated. When scale 8 is elevated, disorders of thinking, memory problems, confusion and other schizophrenic symptoms may be prominent. These individuals will generally be diagnosed schizophrenic and show strong paranoid delusions. If there are no signs of psychosis, the most likely diagnoses are schizoid personality, paranoid personality, or sociopathic personality. Borderline elevated profiles may indicate a prepsychotic pattern.

49/94

This profile is associated with a variety of antisocial behaviors. These patterns are often manic, irritable, violent, extroverted, manipulative, and energetic. They possess a marked disregard for social rules and conventions, and may commit any number of antisocial acts including confidence games, promiscuity, alcoholism, sexual perversion, rape, child abuse, assault, drug addiction, arson, freqeunt traffic violations, extortion, and a variety of white collar crimes. The patient with this profile is often impulsive, doing things with little or no forethought, unable to postpone desires, self-centered, unable to form close relationships except for manipulative purposes, immature, irresponsible, moody, resentful, and ambitious. They possess deep seated feelings of hostility and will act them out whenever it is possible. They may profess the desire to "go straight" when caught, but invariably return to earlier behavior patterns if given the opportunity. The most common diagnosis with this pattern is antisocial (or asocial) personality.

Among high school and college students, an elevated score needs to be in the 80's or 90's (rather than the 70's) for there to be significant concern. The rise in these individuals appears to be more related to a questioning of authroity and general rebellion against the establishment rather than specific antisocial acts. In diagnosis, it should be recognized that antisocial personality can be diagnosed only when they is a significant history of onset before age fifteen.

68/86

Individuals with this code are distrustful and lack self-confidence and self-esteem. They may withdraw from everyday life, show a flat affect, become apathetic, and show disorders of thinking and marked confusion. Hallucinations and delusions of a paranoid type are often present, and the individual is unable to maintain emotional ties with others. These people can lose contact with reality and withdraw into a fanstasy world. Cognitive deterioration may be present but it does not necessarily occur, especially in individuals younger than thirty. When scales 6 and 8 are elevated over 70 and the F scale is over 70, the diagnosis is almost invariably paranoid schizophrenia. Occasionally, in less elevated profiles, there will be a diagnosis of paranoid state or schizoid personality. In individuals in which the delusional material is encapsulated into specific, limited areas of the patient's life, a paranoid schizophrenia may exist without a significantly elevated profile. Chronic drug abuse (e.g., with amphetamines) or use of drugs like PCP may show this pattern until the drug effects wear off. Such profiles are usually markedly elevated in drug disroders. The 68 pattern may also be seen in thyroid disorders. Treatment for these individuals generally involves antipsychotic medication.

69/96

Individuals with this code type may show extreme anxiety or nervousness to the point of physiological signs like trembling. These individuals will generally withdraw into fantasy when threatened. They may appear overcontrolled at one time, with manic emotional undercontrol at other times. There are often strong impairments of conscious thought (associated with high 8 and F scales). Obsessional thinking is not uncommon. When combined with a high 8 and F, the diagnosis in these individuals is often paranoid schizophrenia or schizoaffective disorder if the manic symptoms appear more predominant. In cases where there is no overt thought confusion (lower 8), a diagnosis of manic-depressive psychosis is possible. These individuals often will respond to a combination of lithium and antipsychotic medication.

78/87

Patients with this profile are often highly agitated and upset. They typically lack defenses to handle stress in their environment; the profile sometimes represents a collapse of a previously stable defensive system. These patients are insecure, ambivalent, indecisive, confused, anxious, and socially inept. They are passive and have difficulty with mature heterosexual relationships. Obsessive-compulsive thinking may be present, as may psychotic symptoms such as confusion, hallucinations, or delusions. Guilt may be present as may depression and excessive fear. If these individuals drink or abuse drugs, it is often an attempt to cure their own disorders. A number of diagnostic possibilities are present depending on the complete configuration. Generally, 78 profiles are diagnosed as anxiety neurosis, although this profile may be the aftermath of an acute psychotic disorder which would be the primary diagnosis. (Often such individuals are not testable because of their agitation until the acute psychotic symptoms have passed.) In 87 profiles, the greater the distance between 8 and 7 and the higher the relative height of 8, the more likely the diagnosis is schizophrenia. The height of the 87 pattern compared to the rest of the profile is important in these cases. If the 87 pair is significantly elevated over the other scales, an acute psychotic disorder is probably present. If the entire profile is elevated, a chronic profile is suggested. In this profile and the 86 profile one must be aware of the possibility of random or faking bad profiles, however. In cases diagnosed acute neurotic or acute psychotic, there is also the possibility of schizoid or borderline personality which can be determined on a retesting after the acute symptoms have dissipated.

89/98

Individuals with this profile tend to be hyperactive, energetic, and emotionally labile. They are unrealistic, often having delusions of grandeur (with a rise in 6) about their role in life, contacts, importance, and so

on. They rarely have insight about their disorder and resent hospitalization. They demand a great deal of attention, and are seen as immature and
childish. They cannot form close social relationships, and a thought disorder may also be present. Diagnosis for these cases may include
schizophrenia or manic-depressive psychosis, depending on the relative
contributions of the thought and affective disorder. Diagnosis of schizo-
affective disorder, manic type are also possible. Often these individuals
must be treated with medication both for the psychosis and for the mania.
Antipsychotic medication is necessary when strong delusional or hal-
lucinatory material is present. Severity of the current disorder may be
seen in the height of the F scale.

SPECIAL DIAGNOSTIC CONSIDERATIONS

A number of major issues generally arise in the interpretation of an
MMPI profile. These issues include the prediction of suicide, the determination of whether a disorder is functional or organic, the chronicity or
acuteness of a profile, the presence of a psychotic or neurotic condition,
the prognosis for a patient in psychotherapy, the likelihood of acting out
behavior, and the likelihood of drug or alcohol addiction.

Chronic versus Acute Profiles

The acuteness of a profile may be inferred in several ways. Profiles
which have one scale or a two or three high point combination of scales,
such as 687 or 27, significantly above the level of the remaining scales,
have a greater likelihood of being acute profiles. Although there are no
formal cutoffs, differences between the raised scales and the rest of the
profile in the range of 15 to 20 T score points is generally indicative of an
acute profile, while differences of 10 to 15 points are often indicative of an
acute disorder. Another major measure is the average level of the profile.
The higher the average level of the entire profile, assuming it is valid, in a
pathological individual, the greater the degree of chronicity. It is possible,
it should be noted, to have a generally elevated profile, suggesting a
chronic disorder, with an acute rise on such scales as 68 suggesting a
current, acute exacerbation of the chronic condition.

Another major measure of chronicity is the slope of the profile. The
slope is determined by drawing a single straight line through the profile
which minimizes the deviation of the individual scales from that line.
(Statistically, this is the best fit regression line. In clinical cases, of
course, one estimates this by eye rather than calculating the correlation
between scale number and scale elevation.) Any line connecting the

Fig. 4-10. Examples of a neurotic and psychotic slope on an MMPI profile. The solid line represents a neurotic slope while the dotted line represents a psychotic slope.

scales at the same T value, a horizontal line, has a slope of 0. The greater a line deviates from being parallel with this line, the greater the slope. If the line is higher on the left side of the profile, not including the validity scales, then the scale is said to have a neurotic slope. If the line is higher on the right side of the profile, the line is said to have a psychotic slope. Examples are seen in Figure 4-10. The greater the slope, whether neurotic or psychotic, the greater the acuteness of the profile and the higher the degree of current acute disturbance for the patient from his or her baseline levels.

Psychotic or Neurotic Conditions

This can also be determined by several methods. In general, the two point codes as discussed before can be used to generate likely diagnoses, which in turn determine the psychotic or neurotic question. Neurotic conditions are generally characterized by high scores on scales 1, 2, 3, and 7, and are generally higher than elevations on scales 6, 8, and 9. The relative elevations of these scales determine the slope of the profile, as discussed above. Thus, the higher 1, 2, 3 scales cause a neurotic slope, while the higher 6, 8, 9 scales cause a psychotic slope. In cases where there are multiple scale elevations, the comparison between scales 7 and 8 are useful in establishing the presence or absence of psychosis. In general, if scale 7 is higher than 8, or within 5 T score points of 8, the condition is likely to be neurotic. If scale 8 is higher than scale 7 by ten points or more (and above 70), the condition is likely to be psychotic, especially if there is an elevation on F as well. The relative levels of cutoff points, it should be noted, depend on where one is working and who one is working with. For example, the current author has worked in hospitals where a psychiatric diagnosis of psychosis corresponded to elevation on the MMPI of 75 or more, while in another setting the psychiatrist was willing to diagnose as psychotic cases whose F was frequently between 60 and 70. There are also changes with the diagnostic system employed in a particular setting, some psychiatric criteria being more specific and rigorous than others.

A third method of diagnosing psychosis or neurosis, is the use of formulas which combine a variety of MMPI scores. For example, Goldberg (1965) suggested that one should use the following formula on the scale T scores: $L + Pa + Sc - Hy - Pt$. Using a cutoff of 45, Goldberg found that he could correctly classify 70 percent of his cases. This has been one of the more promising formulas, even its success is not at a significantly high level for daily work. (One could probably get 60 + percent accuracy simply by talking to the patient for five minutes. A diagnostic system needs to do significantly better than this.) It must be concluded that the clinician cannot allow a simple formula, no matter how attractive, decide such major questions. This must be done on the basis of all the information available to the diagnostician.

Functional or Organic

A major referral question is the request to discriminate physical disorders due to organic disease and those due to functional disorders. This research has fallen into two main areas: the differentiation of serious psychiatric disorders and organic brain disease, and the discrimination of medical symptoms due to conversion reactions and those due to organic injury or disease.

A number of researchers (e.g., Reitan, 1955) have demonstrated that brain injured patients have profiles suggestive of psychiatric pathology (significant elevations on F, Pa, Pt, Sc, Ma). More recent research (e.g., Osmon and Golden, 1978) has found that these elevations on the MMPI are related to the loss of speech skills rather than factors common to all brain injuries. Brain injured patients with only spatial or nonverbal skills loss are more likely to show normal profiles or elevations on K and Hy.

The presence of the elevations on the more pathological scales in a significant portion of the brain injured population makes it difficult to discriminate the brain injured group from many psychiatric groups, especially chronic schizophrenic patients.

In an attempt to deal with this problem, a number of investigators have attempted to devise scales or decision keys designed to discriminate brain injured and psychiatric patients (e.g., Hovey, 1964; Watson, 1971; Watson and Thomas, 1968; Russell, 1975; Shaw and Matthews, 1965). Although each of these scales has been supported in the introductory studies, none have stood up under cross validation at any level of accuracy higher than that of the Sc scale (the higher the Sc score, the more likely the person was schizophrenic rather than brain damaged). Even in carefully chosen populations, the Sc scale has not been more than 75 percent successful, however, a rate much too low for diagnostic purposes when one considers that 50 to 60 percent accuracy is chance level. The Sc scale is also a poor choice since its use assumes that one cannot be both brain damaged and psychotic, a phenomenon common in many disorders, especially left temporal lobe injuries (Golden, 1978). Overall, this research has not yet been encouraging on the ability of the MMPI to separate the brain damaged and schizophrenic groups. More reliance should be placed on tests directly measuring neuropsychological effects in investigating such diagnostic questions.

Similar attempts have been made to separate patients with pain and other medical symptoms from patients whose symptoms are due to functional disorders. As can be seen in the review of two point code types, many profiles associated with conversion reactions are also associated with chronic pain profiles in organically damaged patients. In the author's own experience, pure functional disorders are more likely to be seen in 13 patterns that have very low 2 values (2 is usually the lowest or next to lowest scale overall). Conversion patterns may occur within higher 2 scores, but they are often indistinguishable from the scores of the true organic patients. Conversion problems are also seen in 43 patterns, especially when there is a low point 5 or 6 in women and a low point 6 in men. Other 43 patients will also show conversion reactions but with significantly less consistency. It should be noted that conversion patients may also show numerous other patterns, especially on an acute basis. For example, if the conversion reaction fails to control stress in an individual's life, a 13 pattern may become a 12 or 21 or 23 pattern. Consequently, the presence of such patterns in the absence of medical evidence supporting a physical diagnosis should be taken as suggesting the possibility of conversion reaction.

Hanvik (1949, 1951) attempted to devise a scale for the identification of functional low back pain. Unfortunately, the additional research on this scale has been limited (Dahlstrom, 1954; Lewinsohn, 1965) and has not yet been convincing. In my own practice in a community general hospital, I found the Lb scale little better than chance. It is possible that the scale may be useful with some specialized populations, but use of the scale is cautioned unless validated in a specific population.

Suicide

A frequent referral question involves the likelihood of suicide. Although there are no definitive signs of the likelihood of suicide, there are a number of patterns and changes in profiles that suggest a higher likelihood of suicide.

One obvious indicator is the presence of severe depression. The greater the rise on scale 2, the greater the likelihood that the person is considering suicide. In individuals with acute depressions, the profile is most likely to be 27 or 72, as discussed in the section on high point codes. Prediction of suicide likelihood is influenced by the rise on other scales as well, high elevations on scales 4, 8, and 9 reflecting high energy levels and impulsiveness, for example. These individuals, as a result, are considered high suicide risks. Suicide is also likely, however, when an individual's depression begins to improve as this may reflect a decision to finally "end it all" which resolves the individual's ambivalence over what to do. Thus, an individual with repeated MMPI tests who shows a sudden drop in scale 2, or persons observed to be seriously depressed who show a low scale 2 subsequently, must be evaluated carefully for suicide ideation.

Particular attention should be paid to individuals with previous suicide attempts. Individuals with 24 or 28 profiles, being impulsive, are always high risks for further suicide attempts. The individual with a high 4 profile or 64 profile who attempts suicide is especially dangerous, as this may be an expression of revenge or an attempt to manipulate others. Once this type of an individual finds out that suicide threats allow them to control others, frequent attempts may ensue. As a rule, the nature of these attempts escalate with them in an attempt to get more information or to manipulate others (such as doctors) who, in the mind of the patient, may not be taking their attempts seriously enough. Because of this escalation factor, these manipulative suicides can often lead to death.

Prognosis in Psychotherapy

Barron (1953) attempted to devise the Ego Strength scale (Es) for the prediction of psychotherapy outcome in neurotics. Research on this scale has suggested that it basically measures an individual's fundamental adjustment to the world regardless of current situational difficulties. Thus, an individual with a high Es score is likely to be better adjusted and possess more cognitive resources for dealing with his or her problems. Such individuals are consequently much better risks for therapy, as well as for spontaneous recovery. Lower scores, on the other hand, suggest individuals with low tolerance for stress, low self-concept, and few resources available to them. These individuals tend to have less insight into their problems than high Es scorers. As a result, these individuals are less likely candidates for brief psychotherapy, although they may be candidates for long-term psychotherapy depending on their motivation and their intellectual resources. In general, the higher the individual's intellectual resources the better the chance the person will respond in verbal psychotherapies. The reader should note that these relationships will be altered for different populations or different therapies. As a result, such scales as Es need cross validation in the particular population one is working with.

Other factors enter into response to psychotherapy. Acute or neurotic disorders respond better, in general, than personality disorders or psychosis, although the latter may respond to proper medication plus appropriate therapy counseling and vocational or other training opportunities. Acute disorders, especially transient situational disorders, are by definition generally responsive to therapy and most likely to spontaneously recover. Extremely low or high 6 scores, even in nonpsychotic individuals, are often indicative of chronic hostilities which respond, if at all, only to long-term therapy.

Acting Out Behavior

As has been discussed earlier, elevations on scales 4, 6, 8, and 9 are highly characteristic of individuals with poor impulse controls. Thus, elevations on these profiles are often associated with a variety of assaultive behavior. Such profiles as 49, 469, 694, 468, 84, and so on, have often been associated with periodic or continual antisocial behavior including assaults on other individuals. As noted in the discussion of two point codes, the 43 profile may be associated with alternate hysterical and assaultive periods in both men and women. Although the relative elevation on scales 4 and 3 have been said to be related to the likelihood of such behavior, the probability of assault appears to be about the same for all 34 and 43 codes until 4 exceeds 3 by ten or more points. If 3 exceeds 4 by ten or more points, especially if 4 is at normal levels, the patient is much more likely to show hysterical behavior. Patients with 34/43 codes who do not show assaultive behavior, whether verbal or physical, should be considered potential risks for suicidal ("self-assaultive") behavior.

Alcohol and Drug Addiction

Alcohol and drug addiction are frequently encountered in all two point codes including scale 4. This addictive potential has been reported in numerous studies from a wide range of hospitals. Individuals with these scale profiles who are not currently using alcohol or drugs generally have a higher chance of showing such behavior later if placed under sufficient stress. In addition, individuals with psychotic profiles (84, 86, 89, 82, and 87) may turn to alcoholism in an attempt to medicate their own psychosis. Some drink to suppress strong feelings of anxiety and others to stop "voices" or other hallucinations and delusions. Alcoholism may be the presenting complaint in these individuals, but it is in fact secondary to the more serious psychotic disorders.

In addition to observations from the profile, a large number of studies have attempted to develop alcoholism scales. Most of these scales are not in general use, although one has received some widespread acceptance despite contradictory research data. The scale was developed by McAndrews (1965) as an attempt to develop an instrument that could differentiate alcoholics from other psychiatric populations. McAndrews's original study reports an accuracy of about 84 percent using a raw score cutoff of 24. Subsequent studies have varied from those finding strong support for the scale to those finding it essentially useless. The effects of the scale seem to differ depending on either the definition of alcoholism used, the base rate of alcoholism in the population studies, the relative proportion of primary alcoholics (with high 4 profiles) and secondary alcoholics (who initially drink as a psychiatric "treatment") and the type of population (including such parameters as sources of referral, age, sex, and psychiatric diagnoses).

ADVANTAGES AND DISADVANTAGES

As the preceeding discussion has outlined, the MMPI has a number of major advantages as a test of personality: it can be given as a screening device with little of the psychologist's time involved and can be scored easily and objectively; it is based on extensive research studies on numerous populations and for numerous problems, both major and minor and can be repeated when necessary without difficulty; and, most importantly, it has been shown to identify significant personality characteristics in psychiatric populations, to be useful in establishing psychiatric diagnoses, useful in identifying the underlying characteristics and dynamics in an individual, and useful in providing the information necessary to initiate and choose appropriate treatment strategies for a patient.

With this variety of advantages, one can often overlook the disadvantages of the technique. First, the test requires a certain level of reading ability and individual cooperation that is not present in all patients. In these populations, projective tests are generally more appropriate than the MMPI or other similar tests. Another positive feature of the MMPI leads to a significant problem. The objective format of the MMPI and the objective scoring have led to a proliferation of computer systems for scoring and interpreting the tests. These systems have led many clinicians to abandon their own interpretation of the test in favor of the computers' interpretations. More importantly, many individuals with little or no training with the MMPI have used these computer system's analysis as the "absolute truth," developing the attitude that a psychologist is not necessary to interpret the test. This has resulted in misuse of the MMPI to a serious degree which cannot be ignored. As stated before, the clinician is necessary if all of the factors involved in interpretation and the integration of interpretations are to be present. While one may choose to use a computer interpretation system, this approach is best used only as an adjunct to an individual interpretation system.

There is also a tendency for MMPI users to divorce the clinician from the patient. As stated before, interpretation of the MMPI may be done blind initially, but it is necessary to eventually integrate the test findings with the actual patient as he or she presents, as well as with the patient's history and other psychological characteristics. There is a strong need to avoid separating the clinician from the patient if maximum usefulness of the MMPI is to be achieved. Alternatively, we must recognize that the combination of the clinical interview, the judgment of the experienced clinician, and the MMPI offers a powerful and valuable approach to the psychological assessment of the individual.

CASE EXAMPLES

Case 1. Case 1, a 28-year-old female presented in Figure 4-11, is an example of a chronic paranoid schizophrenic as indicated by the elevations on 8, 6, and F. The profile also suggests a high score on hysteria, suggesting strong repressive defensives. Thus, although the patient has considerable hostility, she has little awareness of the problem, and projects the hostility onto auditory hallucinations and/or other individuals. The high 4 suggests impulsiveness in the patient, as well as a tendency towards manipulativeness. The patient is complaining of some fatigue and general physical disability (1), as well as indicating a strong tendency towards social withdrawal, isolationism, and depression (9, 2, 8). This description was confirmed by interview.

Case 2. Case 2, a 65-year-old male, presented in Figure 4-12, suggests at first glance a normal profile as no score is elevated above 70. The elevation of the F scale into the 60's, however, is suggestive of a possible intact paranoid, an

Fig. 4-11.   Results for Case 1.

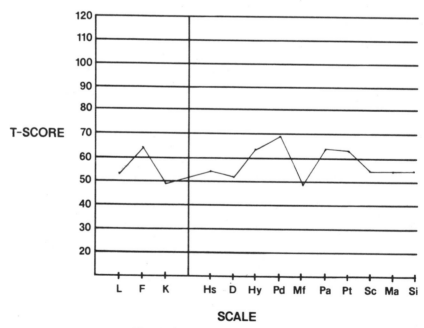

Fig. 4-12.   Results for Case 2.

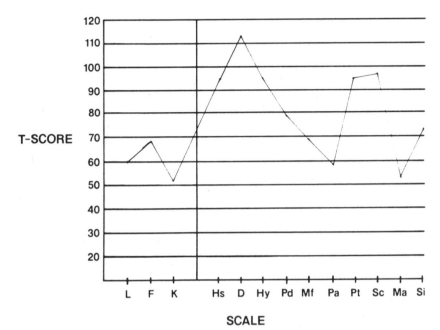

Fig. 4-13. Results for Case 3.

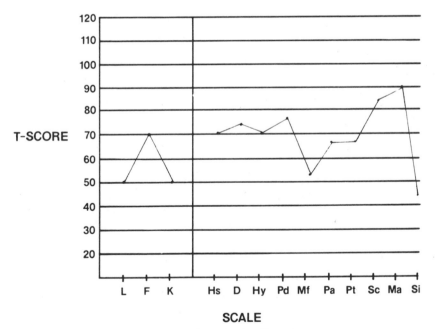

Fig. 4-14. Results for Case 4.

individual with a well encapsulated delusional system. In addition, the 46, 43, and 47 high point pairs are suggestive of impulsiveness, extensive anxiety, extensive hostility, and a possible passive-aggressive or paranoid personality. Such a person may represent a paranoid psychosis with a limited but significant delusional system, or a passive-aggressive personality which is seriously disturbed at the time of the testing. Interviews with the patient revealed an intelligent, 65-year-old man with an onset of an involutional paranoia. The patient believed he was in contact with space creatures who offered to take care of him, making it unnecessary for him to ever leave his apartment. No obvious signs of other thought disorder was present in the patient.

Case 3.   Case 3, presented in Figure 4-13 shows a markedly elevated 2 score (a T over 110) with extremely high scores on 1 and 3. In addition, there is a clear elevation of the 78 high point pair. The high 2 combined with the 78 elevation is highly suggestive of a reactive depression, In addition, the patient shows strong tendencies towards developing somatic complaints in the face of anxiety. The current situation, while acute, is probably an exacerbation of a previously unstable personality (anxiety neurosis, passive-aggressive) as normal individuals will rarely decompensate to this degree. The patient shows a strong tendency to withdraw from people, passivity, a denial of hostility and an extensive inability to deal with anger and hostility (common in individuals with a 6 as a low point or near low point).

Interviews with the patient revealed a passive, dependent individual in the hospital because of the death of his father. He was extremely depressed. His premorbid adjustment was characterized by efforts to allow others to take care of him because of diffuse and generally unreal physical problems.

Case 4.   Case 4, a 35-year-old male presented in Figure 4-14, has a clear 98 profile, along with an F score of 70 and elevations on scales 1, 2, 3, and 4, all of which were between T scores of 70 and 80. Individuals with the 98 profile tend to be hyperactive, emotionally labile, and often show delusions of grandeur. While the manic behavior is often accompanied by depression, the mania serving as a cover, the depression is rarely seen in the patient's behavior during manic episodes. Thus, the 1234 elevation on the MMPI is not accompanied by any clear depressive or hypochondriacal symptoms, although asocial behavior (as represented by scale 4) of an impulsive nature is quite likely. The patient is extremely extroverted and friendly, as is typical of this disorder, but likely has difficulty in forming meaningful close relationships. The F score and 8 score suggest some bizarre behavior, but this is limited and partially under control. In these patients, as noted previously, the bizarre behavior generally takes the form of delusions of grandeur and extremely elevated moods no matter what the situation. These individuals are prone to cyclic periods of depression when the more somatic and hysterical tendencies are clearer. Interviews with the patient confirm the impression gained from the MMPI. The patient carried a diagnosis of manic-depressive psychosis.

5
The Sixteen Personality Factors Questionnaire (16PF)

The 16PF is the end result of extensive factor analytic work by Raymond Cattell and his associates. Unlike the MMPI, the 16PF was designed to be a factorially pure test, each scale reflecting a basic aspect of personality structure. In addition, the 16PF was largely designed by working with normal rather than pathological populations. As a result, the 16PF places a much greater emphasis on day to day personality traits rather than containing the pathological focus seen in the MMPI.

The 16PF was not originally designed as a clinical instrument, and has seen little clinical use and research compared to the extensive clinical use and research available for the MMPI. There is an impressive amount of research literature on the 16PF, but it does not generally address the medical and psychiatric problems seen by many clinical psychologists. This state of affairs has begun to change in recent years, however. Several books have been published on the clinical or medical use of the MMPI and increasing clinical research with the 16PF is appearing in such journals as the *Journal of Consulting and Clinical Psychology* and the *Journal of Personality Assessment*. This growing literature, aimed at the clinician rather than the experimental personality theorist, indicates a valid and growing use for the 16PF in clinical practice.

PURPOSE

The purpose of the 16PF is to delineate the major personality factors in such a way as to allow the clinician to form a broad picture of the individual's personality functioning. It does not seek to recognize severe pathology or specific diagnostic entities, but rather concentrates on deviations in the personality characteristic of the normal individual. It also allows for a more extensive evaluation of the tendencies in individuals classified as "normal," enabling the clinician to gain a more effective picture of the client's weaknesses and strengths, even in the absence of pathology of any kind.

ADMINISTRATION

The 16PF is relatively simple to administer. There are five forms of the test, each presented in a paper booklet. Forms A and B have 187 items and are used with adult patients and are most frequently given in clinical practice. Forms C and D represent shorter forms of A and B, but are not recommended for clinical use. Form E is used with individuals with a low reading level, usually below the sixth grade level. Each question on the test is multiple choice and has three possible answers (a, b, c) which vary depending on the question.

The test may be taken individually or in a group. The patient answers each question on a computer answer sheet. The answer sheets can be scored by computer (if the proper pencil is used) or by hand. Although many prefer computer scoring services because of the convenience, our own tests are scored by hand since this takes little time and provides instant feedback rather than the delay of using an outside scoring service. Hand scoring employs templates which can be bought for each form of the 16PF.

After the raw scores for each scale have been determined, these are translated into sten scores. Sten scores have a mean of 5.5 and a standard deviation of two. The highest score possible is ten and the lowest score possible is one. As a result of this scoring system, scores may vary only 2.25 standard deviations in either direction for a total variation of only 4.5 standard deviations. Some of the MMPI scales, on the other hand, can vary over eight standard deviations.

Overall scoring is available for 16 standard scales (discussed below). In addition, Karson and O'Dell (1976) report the development of several scales which serve the same purpose as the MMPI validity scales. Two of these scales are the faking bad and motivational distortion scales (faking good). The items on the faking bad scale (and answers indicating a scorable response) are: 14(a), 38(a), 42(c), 51(b), 52(c), 55(c), 68(c), 80(a), 89(c), 117(a), 119(a), 123(a), 143(a), 176(c), and 182(c). For the motivational distortion (faking good) scale, the scorable answers are: 7(c), 24(c), 61(c), 62(a), 81(a), 97(a), 111(a), 114(c), 123(c), 130(a), 133(c), 149(c), 173(a), 174(c), and 184(a). These items are taken from Winder, O'Dell, and Karson (1975).

A third supplementary scale is the Random scale (O'Dell, 1971). This scale includes answers which very rarely occur in normal protocols or answers which are very rarely omitted. One point is given for each answer of: **A** to items 38, 54, 77, 78, 80, 93, 102, 118, 119, 121, and 143; **B** to items 12, 20, 23, 51, 52, 66, 87, 91, 109, and 127; and **C** to items 4 and 73. One point is also scored if any of the following answers are omitted: 1(a), 2(a), 28(b), 29(a), 53(b), 112(a), 116(c), and 128(b). For each of these supplementary scales, there is no key provided with the 16PF. Keys must be made by the user. These validity scores are not translated into sten scores.

After the basic scale scores have been calculated, second order factor scores can be calculated. These scores represent more basic tendencies which underlie two or more of the basic scales. These scores are calculated automatically by the computer, or can be done by hand by employing formulas in the 16PF handbook (Cattell, Eber, and Talsuoka, 1970).

INTERPRETATION

Validity Scales

The Motivational Distortion scale (MD) and the Faking Bad scale (FB) both use cutoffs of six. Any score above this point indicates faking good in the case of the Motivational Distortion Scale, while a score above six on Faking Bad suggests that the patient has been faking bad. Winder, O'Dell, and Karson (1975) report a high rate of accuracy for these scales: MD picks up 85 percent of the faking good profiles while misidentifying only 10 percent of the normal profiles. FB identifies 94 percent of the faking bad profiles while misidentifying none of the honestly answered profiles. For the Random Scale, a score of five or greater suggests randomness. This scale is able to identify about 90 percent of the random files while misclassifying only about 6 percent of the nonrandom records.

As was the case of the MMPI, there is no need to throw out a protocol with a high score on any of the validity scales (except Random). Tendencies to answer in a faking good or faking bad direction can be used to modify interpretations of profiles presented by patients, as well as have clinical significance. For example, as we saw in the MMPI chapter, faking good can be associated with strong repressive and hysterical tendencies, while faking bad may be associated with a cry for help or a person strongly divorced from reality.

Clinical Scales

Several important factors must be recognized when interpreting the 16PF scores. First, although standard interpretations are provided for scores, one must be careful not to simply string together the appropriate adjectives for an individual. Otherwise, one ends up with a diagnosis which describes the same person as hostile and friendly, tense, calm and other equally unusual combinations. These cases require careful integration of the full profile to account for possible contradictions. Although such blatant cases of contradiction are rare, more subtle cases, such as one anxiety indicator being up and another down, are more common. These cases also require careful evaluation to determine the aspects of anxiety or other dimensions important to the case.

The 16 scales of the 16PF are indicated by letters or letter number combinations: A, B, C, E, F, G, H, I, L, M, N, O. Q1, Q2, Q3, and Q4. The following discussions of each scale are drawn from several primary sources: Cattell (1957); Cattell (1973); Cattell, Eber, and Tatsuoka (1970); Cattell and Warburton (1967); and Krug (1977). The Karson and O'Dell book must be regarded, at present, as the single most useful clinical reference on the 16PF, while the Cattell, Eber, and Tatsuoka (1970) reference includes the basic material on the 16PF, including references to much of Cattell's earlier work.

Scale A

Scale A is theoretically a measure of warmth. As with the other scales of the 16PF, Cattell has attempted to describe the difference between high and low scores in terms of dichotomies such as reserved, detached, aloof, stiff, critical, rigid, cold, and prone to sulk (low score) versus good natured, warmhearted, outgoing, softhearted, trustful, and attentive to people (high score). Low A scores are generally associated with what are seen as negative traits—hostility, egotism, and suspiciousness; many of the negative traits associated with paranoid schizophrenia (although the scale does not measure such a pathological dimension). Cattell associates the concept of flat affect with low scores, while high scores are more emotionally expressive. High scores can be associated with manic type states in extreme cases.

High A scorers generally like to be around people, especially if other scales are consistent with this interpretation. Thier adjustment is likely to be troublesome if forced into a position where they are not allowed contact with others. Low scorers, on the other hand, may find contact with others to be anxiety provoking or even painful. As noted above, frankly schizoid symptoms are possible in these individuals. It is important that extremely low scores on A be considered seriously by the clinician.

Scale B

The second scale is a measure of intelligence. In this respect, it differs considerably from the other scales on the 16PF. Low scores on scale B are associated with low mental capacity, poor judgment, lower morale, less perserverance, and less ability to work with abstract problems. High B scores are associated with high intelligence, ability to work with abstract ideas, good judgement, good morale, and preserverance. Users should note that 16PF norms are available for different populations. Thus, IQ is figured in comparison to others in the same reference group, rather than the population as a whole. Since this is also a very short scale, the reliability of the IQ is questionable.

Poor scores on scale B may be associated with anxiety, inability to concentrate, as well as poor intelligence. Scale B may also be used to modify interpretations on other scales: for example a person with scores indicating manipulativeness would be looked at considerably differently if the person had a low score on B (suggesting that the attempts at manipulation are likely very concrete and not too subtle) or a high score on B (suggesting the possibility of a shrewd, active, subtle manipulator of others).

Scale C

Scale C is described by Cattell as a measure of ego strength. Low scores on the scale are suggestive of an inability to handle frustration, a general emotional lability, an evasion of responsibility, and a tendency to worry and give up. High scores are associated with emotional maturity, general lack of anxiety, and an ability to deal with frustrating or difficult situations. As might be surmised from this description, scale C plays a prominent role in many psychiatric disorders. Low scores on scale C suggest a general inability to deal with stress (or faking bad), as well as a poor prognosis in psychotherapy because of a tendency to avoid difficult situations and a lack of resources on an emotional level. Similarly, high scorers on scale C, if seen for psychiatric problems, are likely experiencing temporary, situational difficulties rather than long-term personality problems.

Scale E

Scale E is suggested as being a measure of dominance. Low scores on the scale are associated with submissiveness, obedience, conventionality, docility, and dependence. High scores are associated with dominance, aggressiveness, hostility, rebelliousness, and independence. Low E scores may be related to excessive passivity, and can be associated with passive-dependent problems. Such individuals may also serve as "doormats" to others, even to the point of being the scapegoat in a pathological family situation. High E scores are not likely to be pathological, but it can be a serious sign in connection with other scale elevations that suggest a sociopathic personality or a tendency towards emotional outbursts.

Scale F

This scale is a measure of impulsivity. Low F scores are associated with seriousness, introspective behavior, the presence of inner values, and a generally slow or cautious approach to problems. High F scores are associated with enthusiasm, cheerfulness, quickness, alertness, impulsiveness and a tendency to be very talkative and group involved. Low F individuals are described by Cattell as being dull, depressed, anxious, suspicious, and rigid. While it is not actually an indication of depression, low F's are frequently seen in association with depressive states. High F's reflect impulsivity, extraversion (although self centered, according to Karson and O'Dell), originality, and adaptability. Karson and O'Dell suggest that in extreme cases high F scores may be associated with manic phases of emotional disorders. As with other similar measures, F scores tend to decrease with age, reaching a stable level in the person's 30s.

Scale G

Scale G is a measure of group conformity. Low scores suggest a tendency to be fickle, frivolous, self-indulgent, undependable, and generally unconcerned about group standards or morals. High G scores are associated with strong superegos, responsibility, conscientiousness, moral correctness, and a strong sense of duty. The items on scale G are similar to those of the MMPI L scale. Hence, high scorers are either excessively rigid and moralistic or are answering in a faking good direction. These scores may also be associated with strong repression and a tendency towards conversion hysteria, an important consideration in a medically referred population.

Low G scores, on the other hand, may suggest a tendency towards admitting faults or faking bad. It may also be associated with a lack of superego, the classic definition of the sociopathic or antisocial personality. If combined with indications suggesting acting out, this scale could indicate a tendency towards crime, drug abuse, and the other disorders associated with the MMPI 49 profile.

Scale H

Scale H represents the concept of boldness. Low H scores are associated with shyness, restraint, sensitivity to threat, emotional cautiousness, and unfriendliness. High H scores are associated with adventurousness, extroversion, social boldness, interest in the opposite sex, responsiveness, impulsivity, and a general insensitivity to danger signs.

Cattell has associated low H scores with tendencies towards schizoid personality (as do low scores on scale A). Combined with other traits indicative of schizophrenia, low scores on this scale can be a significant warning sign. Cattell has described the low H as shy, hostile, withdrawn, and cold; all aspects of the schizoid or frankly schizophrenic individual. High H scores do not have the significance of low H scores, but can be a problem in a patient whose adventurousness is not matched by socially appropriate skills and intelligence.

Scale I

Scale I is a measure of emotional sensitivity. A low score is associated with tough mindedness, self-reliance, lack of sentimentality, cynicism, logic, practicality, and lack of hypochondriasis. High I scores are associated with emotional sensitivity, insecurity, dependence, imaginativeness (in inner life and conversation), attention-seeking behavior, and hypochondriasis. Karson and Pool (1957) found a close relationship between this scale and the Mf scale of the MMPI, reflecting the kind of cultural interests people have and their reactions to hostility.

This factor is not closely associated with pathology as is true of the MMPI Mf scale. Low scores involve some repression of emotionality but this is not pathological unless one is in situations which demand emotional sensitivity. The high I persons may be somewhat more sensitive to stress because of their emotional sensitivity, which can be a problem in some situations demanding logical, rational decisions no matter what the human factors in the situation are.

Scale L

Scale L is a measure of suspiciousness. Low scorers on L may be characterized as trusting, nonhostile, permissive, tolerant, and generally uncritical. High L scorers are likely to be jealous, dogmatic, suspicious, frustrated, domineering, and irritable. If carried to the extreme, high L scorers may show distinct signs of paranoia. Thus, high scores on this scale combined with high scores suggesting schizoid behavior should be indications for more extensive evaluation.

Low L people are trusting and nonsuspicious, according to their self-description. In general, this score is looked upon as an indication of health. As we saw in the MMPI, however, extremely low Paranoia scores may be associated with intense suspiciousness and denial. Similarly, extremely low scores on L, if found in profiles with strong indicators of pathology, must not always be taken at face value.

High L scores, at the very least, suggest an individual who is probably very difficult to get along with in everyday situations. These patients typically project their negative feelings onto others, as well as appearing hostile and sullen themselves. One should be careful to remember, however, that this scale does not get into the more delusional, hostile material that characterizes MMPI Paranoia scores over 70. Thus, high scorers may be normal people who are simply high on suspiciousness and who may be functioning quite well otherwise, or they may be overt paranoid schizophrenics. Hence, the lack of items at more pathological ranges makes it impossible to discriminate on the basis of the test result alone.

Scale M

This scale is a measure of imagination. Low scorers are generally described as conventional, practical, objective, conservative, and not overly imaginative or farseeing. High scorers, on the other hand, are imaginative, interested in art and philosopy, fanciful, subjective, and unconventional. This scale is not a major measure of psychopathology.

Individuals with low scores are generally suited to jobs with many practical, realistic demands and will generally perform better in these situations than high M individuals. These individuals are generally seen as tough minded, especially with a high score on I as well. High scorers will do better in jobs requiring imagination and artistic skills. Karson (1959) found that anxiety neurotics tend to score higher on M (reflecting general worry over basic, philosophical ideas) than psychosomatic individuals, whose concerns and worries are more practical and concrete.

Scale N

Scale N is a measure of shrewdness. Low scores on scale N are suggestive of genuineness, spontaneity, vagueness, a lack of self-insight, simple tastes, passivity, and a blind trust in human nature. High scores on scale N suggest social awareness, a calculating mind, emotional detachment, worldliness, ambition, and alertness to cutting corners and taking advantage of situations. Scale N significantly correlates with the Hysteria scale of the MMPI.

Karson and O'Dell classify this scale as one of the least useful on the 16PF. They note that it can be important in the right context. Indications of high N along with rebelliousness and intelligence, for example, suggests an individual for whom a superior would do well to watch. In addition, it would not be rare for the sociopath to show high N scores, but rare for them to show low N scores.

Scale O

Scale O is a measure of guilt proneness. Low O scores are suggestive of an untroubled, adequate individual, who is likely to be self-confident, cheerful, internally controlled, and likely to act when it is necessary. The high O scorer, however, is an apprehensive, insecure and troubled individual who is likely to be anxious, depressed, sensitive to the disapproval and approval of others, hypochondriacal, phobic, and lonely. Clearly, this scale is of immense importance in the clinical analysis of the 16PF, although it is generally considered only a minor scale in Cattell's theoretical system. Low scores on O may be associated with weak superego controls while high scores on O suggest overly dominating superego controls. Thus, deviations in both directions can suggest psychopathology.

High O scores may be a measure of both anxiety and depression. As would be expected from this description of symptoms, high O scores can either be chronic or reactive to environmental events. Chronic high O scorers do not respond well to psychotherapy, as a rule, and are better off with directive counseling aimed at eliminating the behaviors that cause them guilt and depression. Low O scores may be associated with sociopathic personalities, or intense denial patterns in which the person is unable to face his or her guilt and anxiety.

Scale Q1

Scale Q1 is a measure of rebelliousness. Low scores are associated with conservatism, while high scores are associated with radicalism, a tendency to be experimenting, liberal, analytical, and free thinking. Extreme Q1 scores may be associated with radicalism and an inability to accept authority, a trait commonly seen in the sociopathic patient. Such individuals are difficult to have as subordinates. Low Q1 individuals tend to be respecting of tradition and unwilling to change the way things are done. This is pathological only in situations where nontraditional change is needed to work out serious life problems.

Scale Q2

Scale Q2 is a measure of self-sufficiency. Low scorers are apt to be group dependent, frequent joiners, and good followers. High scorers are likely to be self-sufficient individuals, who prefer depending on their own resources and their own judgements. Clearly, this is also an alternate measure of introversion-extroversion, with the introversion being a healthier, more creative type of effort. The scale does not indicate pathology by itself, although it can be part of a general extroverted or introverted style (see the section on second order factors).

Scale Q3

Scale Q3 has been characterized as a measure of the ability to bind anxiety. Low scorers are characterized by a lack of control, a carelessness with respect to social rules, and a tendency to follow one's own urges. High scorers are controlled, socially precise, compulsive, and possess strong will power. The high Q3 individual thinks before acting and does not let emotional upset disturb routine. Such individuals are dependable, well controlled, and good workers. High Q3 scores are associated with good mental health, although taken to extremes it can indicate extreme obsessive-compulsive behavior.

Low Q3 scores are associated with overreactivity. They are not able to handle stress productively, and have difficulty in large organizations in which responsibility is an important factor. If a low Q3 is found in the presence of other anxiety indicators, there is strong reason to suspect that the person is currently in emotional trouble, often of a serious nature.

Scale Q4

Scale Q4 is a measure of free floating anxiety and tension. Low scores are associated with low tension, low anxiety, a relaxed and tranquil approach to life, and a general lack of frustration. High scorers on Q4 are characterized by tension, frustration, and a generally highly anxious approach to problems. This scale is the single best indicator of neurotic anxiety on the 16PF. High scores can be associated with a person with extreme problems, a cry for help, or a faking bad profile. One should also recognize that this scale is subject to daily fluctuations depending on the current status of the individual. The score may also be low in individuals who have bound their anxiety into a medical symptom or into obsessive or compulsive behavior. Q4 has a .75 correlation with the MMPI Psychasthenia scale, and consequently should be taken very seriously whenever it is elevated. When the scale does not fit in with the rest of the profile, it is better to discuss the scale with the patients rather than ignore it (Karson and O'Dell, 1976).

SECOND ORDER FACTORS

Second order factors attempt to identify basic symptoms underlying the 16 primary scales on the 16PF; they represent broader and more basic trends in personality than do individual scale scores. As a result, they can be very important in a more generalized clinical impression of the patient. A number of second order factors can be identified on the 16PF, but Karson and O'Dell suggest that five factors have basic relevance to the clinician. The order of the factors represents their size in the factor analytic studies which derived them. As a consequence, the first factors are more significant to behavior than the later factors.

Factor I

Factor I is the measure of extroversion-introversion, a finding consistent with other theories of personality. A person who scores high on this factor is typically high on scales A (warmth), F (impulsivity), H (boldness), and low on Q2 (self-sufficiency). The opposite profile is characteristic of the patient with low extroversion (introversion). Intermediate scores, as well as moderate deviations from the mean in either direction, can be achieved by manipulating the scores of these four scales. In some of these cases, one or more of the scales may be in the wrong direction.

Profiles suggesting a high level of introversion should be evaluated carefully, as introversion is associated with depression, neurotic disorders, and schizophrenia. This is especially serious when sten scores are greater than eight or less than three (this is true of all the 16PF factors). High extroversion scores are not considered as pathological as our society tends to reward such behavior. Extreme extroversion scales, however, may be seen in manic-depressive disorders (manic phase), in sociopathic disorders, in normal people who are successful salesmen, as well as psychologists and physicians.

Factor II

Factor II is the second-order measure of anxiety. The major scales which contribute to this scale are Q4 (free floating anxiety), O (guilt proneness), C (ego strength), L (suspiciousness), and Q3 (ability to bind anxiety). High anxiety scores are associated with low scores on C and Q3, with high scores on L, O, and Q4. Each of the scales contributing to the anxiety factor are easily faked; as a consequence, it is necessary to interpret this scale only after consideration of the validity scales.

High scores on this scale are associated with significant psychological problems (unless the profile is the result of faking bad, which can be a call for help or a deliberate malingering or falsification for some external gain.) In general, the level of scores on scale C (ego strength) is important in determining chronicity: high scores (good ego strength) are associated with acute disorders which respond well to treatment, while low scores suggest chronic anxiety and anxiety related problems that are less responsive to treatment.

In profiles with general anxiety indicators up and ego strength down, therapy leading to a reduction of environmental stress (by changing the patient's environment), as well as appropriate medication, is more effective than traditional psychotherapy. Attempting to force such individuals to be more self-sufficient will generally cause the patient to stagnate or even get worse as the requisite psychological skills are not there. In one of our patients (with a high intelligence score) we were able to reduce stress by transferring the patient into an academic/research setting with little pressure (except intellectual which was all the patient could handle). In this environment, the patient was able to make positive contributions though still requiring frequent directive therapy and close follow-up.

Factor III

Cattell has named this factor "tough poise." An individual high on this factor is low on A (warmth), I (emotional sensitivity), and M (imagination). These are people who are not easily swayed by feelings. Low scorers are more likely to be swayed by their emotions and reactions to personal factors in a situation. While this has some relevance to job selection (where this trait may act as a hindrance or advantage, depending on the setting), the factor does not appear to be important in most clinical situations. Extremely low scores in a person with emotional problems, however, may suggest an unusual degree of repression or an avoidance of people to reduce interpersonal stress.

Factor IV

This factor is a measure of independence. High scores on the factor are associated with high scores on scales E (dominance), L (suspiciousness), M (imagination), Q1 (rebelliousness), and Q2 (self-sufficiency). Cattell suggests that individuals high on this scale are a law unto themselves. This does not necessarily indicate hostility towards others, although this is possible when seen in a patient with other pathological signs.

Factor V

Sociopathy is the title of this final factor. The primary scales loading on this factor are high scores on G (group conformity) and high scores on Q3 (ability to bind anxiety). On one end, the scores on this factor suggest conformity, rigidity, and lack of spontaneity while low scores are associated with freedom and lack of restraint. Extremely low scores are associated with sociopathic tendencies; an important question in many clinical examinations.

GENERAL INTERPRETIVE STRATEGIES

In interpreting a 16PF profile, the clinician should be alert to those patterns which signal high anxiety, sociopathy, or extroversion/ introversion. Beyond this, interpretation begins with those scales that are the most significantly deviated from 5.5, especially scores of nine, ten, one or two which are indicative of extreme tendencies in one direction or the other. From this, one works to those scales significantly different but not as extreme (7, 8, 3, 4). Scores of five or six are normal and rarely need comment (unless pathology in the area has been suggested by another scale or by the referred source.)

In this way, an initial description may be generated. In the inexperienced user, some points of the interpretation may conflict or be vague. Thus, one must review the profile and interpretations to correct for these tendencies based on the profile as a whole. One should be especially attentive to scales which disagree with the major profile interpretation as these can offer valuable modifications.

The validity scales should also be closely considered in making interpretations. This takes some clinical experience with known cases in an individual population, as the general validity of these scales has not been fully validated. Indeed, the validity scales and the effects of distortion by patients are the weakest part of the 16PF. While some users have suggested that such scales are not necessary as patients rarely distort on the 16PF (see Krug, 1977), the present author has found that such manipulation is common in medical populations suspected of psychiatric disorders.

A final caution on the 16PF is not to confuse extreme scores on this test with extreme scores on the MMPI. Extreme scores on the 16PF between and including scores two and nine are all within the normal two standard deviations from the population mean. Variant normal people and extremely pathological individuals may thus get similar scores on a single scale, although it would be rare for a normal individual to come up with extremely pathological patterns (except when in acute distress).

As a result, the 16PF is generally inadequate to fully diagnose a pathological condition. In those cases where such a condition is suggested, follow up testing with the MMPI and other instruments described in this book is advised. We rarely use the 16PF to give a definitive diagnosis but rather emphasize its use as a description of the individual's personality processes.

CASE EXAMPLES

Case 1. The most outstanding scores in case 1 (Table 5-5), a 37-year-old male, are scores of nine on L, ten on O, ten on Q4, one on C, and two on Q3. Overall, this is a pattern consistent with a very high level of anxiety in a fairly intelligent (B) individual. The anxiety seems to be the basic and only problem in the profile. This individual is probably neurotic, as there are no clear signs of a more psychotic disorder based on the patient's scores on A, G, I, and Q2. Further testing would be in order to determine the exact nature of the disorder and whether it was acute or chronic. (The individual was suffering from an acute anxiety disorder because of recently losing a job held for 15 years.)

Case 2. Case 2 (see Table 5-5) is a highly intelligent (B), dominant (E), suspicious (1), self-sufficient (S2), calm (Q4), and aloof individual (A). This profile is

Table 5-5
Case Profiles

Scale	Case 1	Case 2	Case 3	Case 4
A (Warmth)	5	2	10	2
B (Intelligence)	8	10	8	3
C (Ego Strength)	1	7	7	4
E (Dominance)	4	10	6	4
F (Impulsivity)	4	8	9	1
G (Group Conformity)	6	3	4	3
H (Boldness)	4	7	9	2
I (Tender-minded)	7	3	4	5
L (Suspicious)	9	10	6	8
M (Imagination)	5	7	5	6
N (Shrewd)	6	8	7	4
O (Guilt)	10	3	5	7
Q1 (Rebellious)	5	8	6	7
Q2 (Self-sufficient)	6	9	1	10
Q3 (Compulsive)	2	6	6	5
Q4 (Anxiety)	10	2	5	8

characteristic of individuals who are sociopathic. They are often able to manipulate people, because of their high intelligence and their general disregard for the feelings of others. These individuals do not respond well to psychotherapy, and are prone to involvement in confidence games, violence (of a well planned type), and other antisocial behavior. On the other hand, this type of individual could be a highly successful professional with a reputation for competence, organization, and intelligence. It is important in these profiles to get a good history to allow one to discriminate between these possibilities.

Cases 3 and 4.   These cases, the first of a 28 year-old-male and the second a 31 year-old-male, are included to show the differential profiles of an extrovert and an introvert. The first profile is of an individual who is warm, intelligent, outgoing, impulsive, and who prefers group situations to being alone. Such an individual may be at one extreme of normal, although the present case was taken from an individual with a diagnosis of manic-depressive disorder. The second profile represents an individual of low intelligence, who is aloof, shows schizoid tendencies, is very controlled, lacks boldness, is very self-sufficient and quite anxious. Again, this can represent one normal extreme in some cases, but was taken from the case of an individual with a schizoid personality disorder who was not actively psychotic.

These latter two cases emphasize the importance of carefully evaluating extreme profiles for possible signs which must be investigated through history or other diagnostic instruments.

6
Benton Visual Retention Test

The Visual Retention Test was originally devised by Benton (1945) as a measure of neuropsychological function. The test is commonly called the Benton Visual Retention Test, or referred to simply as the Benton. The test assesses visual construction skills, visual memory, and visual perception. Since its introduction, the test has become a major measure of neuropsychological function and is in wide use throughout the country.

ADMINISTRATION

There are three sets of ten cards for the Benton Visual Retention Test, each of which constitutes an equivalent form (form C, form D, form E). Each set of cards has two designs with only one figure on it, while the remaining eight designs have three figures which differ in size. Each set of cards can be administered in one of four ways.

Administration A

The first administration technique begins with giving the patient ten blank sheets of paper which are 5½" x 8½" in size, the exact size of the cards the designs are drawn upon. The patient is also given a pencil with an eraser. Then the subject is instructed to study each of the cards presented to him or her for ten seconds, after which the patient is asked to draw the design from memory just as it is on the page. Unlike the Bender,

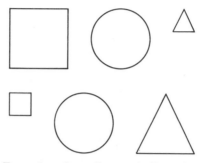

Fig. 6-1.   Examples of two figures similar to items from the
Benton.

the design book is placed at an angle of about 60° to the horizontal in order
to facilitate viewing by the patient.

If the subject begins to draw before ten seconds and the withdrawal
of the picture, the patient should be told that although the current picture
may be easy, others will be harder and we wish the patient to get used to
studying the picture for ten seconds. Before the third card, the first with
three designs (see example in Figure 6-1), the patient is reminded not to
forget to reproduce everything in the design. If the subject fails to reproduce all figures in design 3, then these instructions are repeated for design
4. During any administration, the subject is permitted to erase or correct.
The examiner does not routinely reassure the patient about the quality of
his or her performance, but may do so if the patient asks. All drawings are
done on a fresh sheet of paper so that there is only one drawing per page.

Administration B

The same instructions are followed, except the patient is only allowed five seconds to memorize the figures.

Administration C

The patient is given paper and pencil as in A, but this time told he or
she will be shown the card on which there are one or more figures which
should be copied as exactly as possible. The card is left in the patient's
view and removed only after the drawing has been completed. These instructions are repeated if the subject requests any additional instructions.
Slow patients may be urged to work a little faster, especially if maximal
effort is not being put forth by the patient. In all other respects, this administration is identical to Administration A.

Administration D

This is administered the same as A, except the patient is told he will see the card for ten seconds, and after a wait of 15 seconds, will then be allowed to draw the design from memory. Unlike the initial administration, the patient is only given one sheet of paper at a time and only at the end of each 15 second delay period. Comments before designs 3 and 4 are the same as above. If the patient attempts to begin a conversation during the waiting period, the examiner should suggest they concentrate on remembering the design. Benton notes that some patients may sketch the design during the waiting period with their fingers. This is allowed as long as no visual record is left on the patient's "sketch."

SCORING

There are two scoring systems used for the Benton: The first system, number of correct answers, is the easiest to use and most appropriate for individuals using the Benton as a quick screening test. The second system, number and type of errors, is somewhat more complex and difficult to learn. This system is best used when a detailed anlaysis of the patient's performance is desired.

Number correct

In this system, the patient's drawings are each scored as 1 (correct) or 0 (wrong). Any error in a drawing makes the entire design earn a score of 0. Benton presents clear instructions for identifying errors which make this system quick and efficient. Possible scores range from 0 to 10. Number correct can be determined for all administrations, using the same criteria.

Number of errors

In any design with less than perfect performance, the patient has made one or more errors which may be coded according to a system devised by Benton. The error score for any one figure can vary considerably depending on the patient's performance. As a result, error scores show more variance than the number of correct reproductions score. The error score is not more efficient in identifying the presence of brain dysfunction, but can be considerably more useful in analyzing the nature of a dysfunction.

Benton identifies six categories of errors: omissions, distortions, perseverations, rotations, misplacements, and size errors. Each of these categories will be discussed separately.

Omissions refer to leaving out any figure, or the drawing of only one or more lines which have no resemblance to the missing figure. If the subject leaves a space for the figure or places a line in the proper place, this indicates that the person remembers a figure was included, while the failure to leave a place or state the figure was there suggests that the person either failed to perceive or immediately forgot the figure in its entirety. If the error occurs in designs 1 and 2 (which have only one figure), the error is scored as *M*. If a major (large) figure is forgotten in designs 3 through 10, the scoring is *MR* or *ML*, depending on whether the figure was on the left or right. If the subject fails to indicate that a figure was omitted in some way, the scoring is *MR!* or *ML!*. If a peripheral figure is forgotten, the scoring is *PR* or *PL* (R and L always referring to location). If a figure is added which is not scorable as a distortion or perseveration (see below), the error is coded *Add*.

Distortions represent inaccurate drawings of figures in the design. If the error is made on cards 1 or 2, the scoring is *SM*. On the other cards, the scoring is *SMR* or *SML* when a major figure is involved or *SPR* or *SPL* when a peripheral figure is involved. This system is used only when the distortion involves simple substitution (e.g., circle for square). In all other cases where fragmentation, mutliple reproduction, or misplacement of an internal detail occurs, the *S* in the scoring is replaced by *I*.

Perseverations involve substituting or adding a figure from the previous design into the current design. Perseverations are also scored if an inappropriate figure is placed from one design to the next and then on to further designs (e.g., a square from card 3 could be carried forward to cards 4, 5, and 6). Perseveration also occurs when one figure in a design is drawn identical to a major figure in the same design. Benton notes that perseveration is never scored along with an *Add* or substitution error for the same figure, nor can a rotation be scored for the perseverated figure. Misplacement or size errors, however, may be scored. Scoring symbols for this class include *PerM* (perseveration on design 2 from design 1), *PerMR* and *PerML* for major figures, and *PerPR* and *PerPL* for peripheral figures.

Rotations are scored for rotating the figure more than 24° from the way it is drawn. They are scored for the degree of rotation present. Rotations are scored as 180°, 90°, or 45°. The single exception is when a figure is rotated to rest on a side rather than an angle. This is scored as St. Other rotations are scored as 180M, 90M, and 45M for the first two designs; 180MR, 180ML, 90MR, 90ML, 45MR, StMR, and StML for rotated figures; and the same with *P* substituted for *M* for peripheral figures. For figures with mirror image transformations (Mir) is added after the rotation code (such as 90MR(Mir)).

Misplacements are errors in the spatial relationships of the figure within a design. If the position of the two major figures are exchanged, this is coded *Rev*. The failure to show an overlap between overlapping figures is coded *NOv*. Showing overlap between two nonoverlapping figures is coded *Ov*. If an overlap should be present, but occurs at the wrong place the error is coded *WOv*. If a right peripheral figure is placed to the left of, between, above, or below the major figures, this is coded *MisPR;* the same problem with a left peripheral figure is coded *MisPL*. Displacement of a peripheral figure upwards or downwards is coded *UPR* or *UPL* for upward problems or *DPR* or *DPL* for downward errors.

Size errors deal with problems in the size of the figures. If the right major figure is less than 3/5 of the height of the left major figure, the error is coded *SzMR* while the opposite problem is coded *SzML*. If the peripheral figure is greater than 3/5 of the larger major figure, the error is coded *SzPR* or *SzPL*.

There are 27 fundamental errors possible overall, with the remaining codes referring to the involvement of peripheral or major figures and the location on the right or left. Benton estimates that up to four or five errors may be present in a single design, while up to 24 may be found in a poor protocol: While higher scores are theoretically possible, they rarely occur. Although the error system is more complicated than the correct number system, it is generally easy to score with experience and familiarity with the symbols.

Several additional rules are important when using the error system. First, if an error can possibly be scored as a rotation or distortion, the error is classified as a rotation. Only one misplacement error can be scored for a single feature of the design. For example, one cannot score a misplacement for a right peripheral figure and an upward displacement of the same right peripheral figure at the same time. When a perseveration is scored, a substitutive, additive, or rotational error should not be scored for the same figure. Misplacement or size errors can be scored however. If a peripheral figure is displaced relative to one major figure but not the other, no misplacement of the peripheral figure should be scored.

Normative data

One of the strengths of the Benton is its normative data. Adult norms are provided for forms A and B which take into account both IQ and age. Norms are given for both errors and number correct. Form B norms are derived by subtracting one point from the form A norms. Similar normative data is presented for form C, although users of the manual will find these norms on page 75 rather than in the manual's norm section. Norms are also available for an eight-item version of form C; however, such a version saves only about one minute, making its use rather questionable since some diagnostic power is lost. No norms are currently available for form D.

DISCRIMINATIVE VALIDITY

Benton emphasizes in the manual the role of such factors as motivation, depression, autistic preoccupation, poor motor skills, and faking on the test results. It is important that such possibilities be examined and test interpretation be suitably cautious if any of these conditions is likely to interfere. This is an important part in the interpretation of any test results.

Benton suggests that the best measure of organicity is the deviation of the patient's score from his or her expected score. For the number correct score, a value two or more points below expectation was seen in 69 percent of the organic group and only 16 percent of the normal group. A value three points below expected was seen in 57 percent of the organic group and only 4 percent of the control group, making such a score a likely indication of brain damage in an otherwise normal individual. Using error scores, nearly identical results were obtained. Benton notes that the accuracy of the test will change with the location, severity, and chronicity of the injury. Like other visual-construction tests, the Benton is most sensitive to diffuse injuries and right hemisphere lesions.

Other studies have reported results of the same magnitude. The hit rates for the test have generally been in the range of 80 to 90 percent for controls and 60 to 70 percent for organic patients (Brilliant and Gynther, 1963; L'Abate, Friedman, Vogler, and Chusid, 1963; Sterne, 1969, 1973; Von Kerekjarto, 1961; Cronholm and Schalling, 1963; Zwann, De Vries, and Van Dijk-Bleker, 1967; and Crochelet, 1970).

Of important interest in examining the Benton is the performance of psychiatric patients. Neurotic patients are generally able to perform at normal levels and present no diagnostic problems when the possibility of organicity is being studied. Schizophrenic patients do show significant deficits on the Benton when compared with normal controls, however (Nikols, 1963). An examination of the performance of schizophrenics reveals a wide range of behavior, apparently related to motivation and the degree of cognitive dysfunction. Despite this, the Benton appears to be better than the Bender or Memory for Designs in the discrimination of brain damaged and schizophrenic patients (see next chapter). Benton noted that in addition to the differences in the standard scoring, schizophrenics give more truly bizarre responses than organic patients without emotional disturbance. Thus, the presence of bizarre responses indicates a schizophrenic process. The reader is cautioned to remember that one may be both brain damaged and schizophrenic, however.

Variable performance is also seen in depressed patients, the degree of deficit varying with the severity of the depression and the ability of the examiner to motivate the patient. Depressed patients will generally do poorly on these tasks requiring motor skills. As a consequence, interpretation should be cautious except, of course, when the performance is in the normal range.

Benton (1974) also addresses the question of simulators. A series of studies by Benton and Spreen (1961a, 1961b) compared the performance of deliberate malingerers with brain damaged patient performance. They found that simulators scored significantly less well than the organic patients who generally score within five points of their expected level on the number of correct measure. Simulators also showed more distortion errors and tended to demonstrate fewer omissions, perseverations, and size errors. Simulators may also be noted by comparing their test performance to the skills in nontest interactions, especially if one is allowed to observe them in an inpatient setting.

Qualitative considerations

Research on the Benton has suggested that three kinds of errors are more likely in brain damaged rather than normal populations. The first is the omission of a peripheral figure, especially without any indication by the patient that he or she is aware that such a figure exists. Benton states that this is even more significant after the patient has been exposed to several designs, each with a peripheral figure. This finding can be associated with a reduction of visual field width associated with parieto-occipital lesions. An important problem is the unilateral omission of figures, usually on the left side. This phenomenon, called unilateral neglect, is often associated with right hemisphere lesions, especially those in the posterior areas of the hemisphere.

Rotations are common in brain injured patients, but are also seen in normals. In normals, however, the errors tend to be stabilizing errors in which a figure, drawn to sit on an angle, is rotated so it sits on a flat side. The presence of other types of rotational errors are thus likely to be more discriminating.

Size errors are also relatively more common in brain injured patients. Normals may vary their figures in size, but do get the basic relationships among the major and peripheral figures correct. The brain injured patient, however, may fail to do this, and show striking enlargements or shrinkages of specific items.

Good performance

As is true with other tests of brain dysfunction, a good score does not rule out the possibility of a brain lesion. As noted earlier, some 30 percent of all brain injured patients will be missed by the Benton. In general, these are more likely to be left hemisphere or frontal lesions rather than lesions in the right parietal area. Even lesions in the right parietal area, if there has been significant time for recovery, may present with few or no deficits however. Thus, good performance must be interpreted to mean that there is no evidence for a brain lesion although one may still be present. Because of this situation, it is better to use the Benton in conjunction with alternate tests of brain function which are more sensitive to those areas which the Benton is not likely to pick up.

ADVANTAGES AND DISADVANTAGES

The primary advantage of the Benton is the availability of well normed alternate forms which can be administered in several different ways. Thus, a patient can be given both forms A and C in order to directly investigate a possible nonverbal memory problem without confounding the analysis with such variables as the person's current drawing level. The presence of alternate forms allows the test to be repeated without the patient remembering the figures from a previous administration. In addition, the Benton is as effective or more effective than other drawing tests (with or without a memory component) in discriminating among normal, brain damaged, and psychiatric patients (Benton, 1974; Watson, 1968).

There are few strong disadvantages to the Benton. It is appropriate for a wide range of ages, and has been shown to be useful in a wide range of circumstances. Its main deficit has been the tendency of some to use the Benton in an inappropriate manner. This usually involves using the test as a final arbiter of the presence of organicity rather than as part of a more comprehensive screen.

CLINICAL EXAMPLES

Examples of the clinical use of the Benton are included in the examples at the end of Chapter 8.

7
The Bender-Gestalt

The Visual-Motor Gestalt test devised by Bender (1938), more commonly
known as the Bender-Gestalt or simply the Bender, has been a major instrument used by the clinical psychologist over the past quarter century.
It is a test that arouses strong feelings on the part of both supporters and
opponents. The former have sometimes seen it as a test which could reflect intellectual skills, organicity, and personality traits, and the latter,
who decry the teaching of the test to new graduate students, see it as a
prime example of sloppy, unscientific clinical practice (probably second
only to the Rorschach). It continues to be used as both an objective and
projective test by many clinicians, although its use has declined with the
increasing popularity of such tests as the Halstead-Reitan (for organicity)
and MMPI (for personality interpretations). Despite this, however,
the Bender continues to play a significant role in modern clinical assessment.

The test was originally devised as a measure of visual-perceptual
skills based on the Gestalt theories of Koffka, Wertheimer, and Kohler,
the leaders of the Berlin school of gestalt psychology. In her original
monograph, Bender presented examples of the test's use in diagnosing
brain damage, psychiatric disorders, mental retardation, and malingering.
Since its inception, the test has inspired extensive research and clinical
use. This work has resulted in a wide variety of administration
techniques, scoring and interpretation systems (including many that are
highly idosyncratic), and uses in many populations. Extensive research
has been both positive and negative, offering support to nearly any position one wishes to adopt in the use of the Bender.

PURPOSE

The major purpose of the Bender-Gestalt as an objective test is the detection of brain dysfunction. This area has been the major source of much of the extensive Bender research. The Bender has also been used as a way to estimate intelligence, but it is less effective in such a role than the WAIS or the other intelligence tests discussed previously. As a projective test, the Bender has been used as a largerly nonverbal measure of personality. The way in which the Bender is interpreted projectively is a controversial topic with no one method accepted entirely by most users. The most popular system of projective interpretation is outlined in Hutt (1969).

Administration

Nearly all systems of Bender administration use the nine figures suggested by Bender (1938) as originally presented or as slightly modified by Hutt (1969). The figures on the Bender are reproduced in Figure 7-1, at about 25 percent of the size they are presented to subjects in the testing situation. Each figure is on a card about the size of a large index card.

The wording and actual administration details differ considerably among examiners depending on personal convictions and the systems they were taught. Some general considerations can be stated, however. The patient should have several sharpened pencils available (usually standard No. 2) and at least one sheet of white paper. Examiners differ on the number of pages of paper allowed: some feel only one (or two) should be allowed so that the subject has to plan ahead and use the space on the page intelligently. Others suggest that a pile of paper should be made available, so that the behavior of the patient in regard to number of pages, number of designs per page, size of figures, and the like may vary more considerably. This is especially useful when one wishes to test a projective hypothesis, while the first administration technique is more useful when one is examining for organicity.

For all techniques, the patient is then told something like this: "I have nine cards here, each with a design on it. I want you to copy the design on each card as exactly as you can on the page before you." Then the cards are presented to the subject one at a time with the figure placed directly in front of the patient. (In most systems, the patient is not allowed to rotate the figure in any way, nor to rotate the writing page except for the minor rotation most individuals use for writing and drawing.) Any additional questions from the patient about any aspect of the task should be answered: "Just draw the figures on the cards as exactly as you can." These instructions can be modified to be more ambiguous if desired. For example, say "I want you to copy what is on each card" rather than

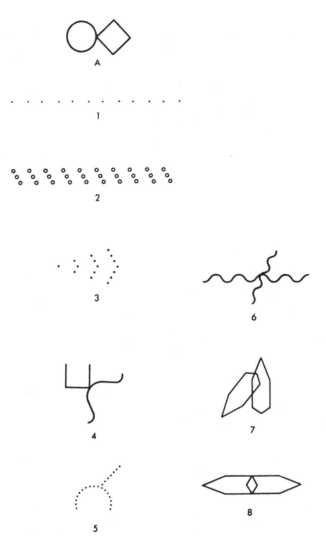

Fig. 7-1.   Bender figures (reduced to present here). Repro-
duced by permission of the publisher and author from Hutt,
M. L., *The Hutt Adaptation of the Bender-Gestalt*. New
York, Grune and Stratton, 1977.

mention the word design. On the other hand, they can be made more
specific: "I want you to copy the figures exactly as they are on the card;
the same size, the same shape, and the same number of figures."

   Other administration techniques are available as well. Many clinicians use unstandardized memory techniques, in which the subject is
shown the card and then asked to draw the picture after the stimulus is

withdrawn. The present author, however, feels that such techniques are best used with tests like the Benton Visual Retention Test (see last chapter) which were specifically designed for memory presentations.

A more interesting revision of the Bender has been presented by Canter (1976). Canter employs what he terms a background interference procedure. This test requires the subject to first draw the Bender figures on a single sheet of clean white paper as described above. Then, a second administration is given in which the subject must draw the figures again on a sheet of paper covered by wavy lines. This technique assesses the relative skills of the person to draw the figures both with and without interference from the wavy lines.

SCORING

Scoring systems abound for the Bender-Gestalt. An informal survey of clinicians made by the author reveals that most clinicians do not use any system in its entirety, but rather employ an intuitive combination of several systems. The major problem in such systems is the lack of any evidence establishing validity as well as the inability to teach the system to others, since the system is more often based on clinical intuition rather than hard and fast rules. Hutt (1968) has defended a more clinical interpretation of the Bender, suggesting that formal systems may lose much of the major information included in the patient's test performance.

Bender (1938) did not originally propose a system of scoring, but rather relied on qualitative analysis. Pascal and Suttell (1951) presented an early diagnostic system which is still in wide use. The system was intended to measure the amount of disturbance of brain function in the patient, whether the disturbance was due to brain injury or psychiatric disorder. The authors assigned each important deviant response on each card a value. When the deviant response was present, the patient's score was increased by the value of the item. Overall, 106 scorable characteristics were identified in this system, ranging from 10 to 13 for each figure (excluding the first practice figure), as well as seven variables relating to the performance as a whole. The system includes such errors as rotations, substituting angles for curves, substituting curves for angles, producing distorted or lopsided drawings, tremor, erasures, drawing over previously completed lines, and other similar errors. This system appears to be generally successful at differentiating normals and neurotics from significant brain injuries or psychiatric disorders, although mildly impaired or recovered persons may not be diagnosed accurately.

The scoring system developed by Hain (1964) views the Bender performance as a whole. Hain has identified 15 categories each with a specific weight. Any instance of an error in a category results in the person being assigned points for that category. Four point categories include perseveration (repetition), rotation or reversal, and concretism. Three point errors included added angles, separation of lines, overlap, and distortion. Two point categories are embellishments and partial rotations. One point errors can include omission of a figure or line, abbreviation of designs one or two (involving the rows of dots), separation of figures, erasure, failure to attain closure, and lacking the point of contact between the circle and the square in figure A. In his original study, Hain, reported that 80 percent of his normals scored below six points, while 80 percent of the brain injured patients scored above five points.

Hutt (1969) has presented a 26 factor scale to measure the degree of psychopathology in a profile. This system, like Hutt's, evaluates the performance of the figures as a whole. Factor 1, sequence, investigates the placement of the figures. Figures are normally placed either from left to right or top to bottom. Each time a figure is not placed below or to the right of the previous figure, the patient's sequence score increases by one.

The second factor is the position of the first figure. Any placement within 1 inch of any edge is scored as abnormal. Factor 3 is the use of space. This relates to the closeness of each figure to the succeeding figure. Basically, Hutt outlines normal distances between figures which relate to the size of each figure. Designs that are placed too close or too far apart are scored as abnormal. Factor 4, use of space II, refers to the size of the designs. Normal limits for the width and height of each design are given by Hutt. A drawing is judged as compressed if either of the dimensions is too small, and expanded if either is too large.

The fifth factor is collision, the running together or overlap between any two figures. Scoring is based on the frequency of such collisions. Factor 6, use of margin, refers to placement of any figure within ½ inch of the margin on seven or more figures. Factor 7 involves 90° rotation of the drawing paper for any figures. The score depends on the frequency of such rotations of the paper. Factor 8, shift in the position of the stimulus card, refers to rotation of the design card 90°.

Factor 9 is concerned with overall decrease or increase in size of the designs. An overall increase occurs when five figures are expanded; an overall decrease occurs when five figures are compressed. Factor 10, progressive increase or decrease in size, involves a progressively larger expansion over at least six figures or a progressively greater compression over at least six figures. Factor 11 is an isolated increase or decrease in size. This can refer to a single figure in which one part is one third larger or smaller than the other parts. Among figures, this refers to a figure which is one fourth larger or smaller than the other figures.

Factor 12, closure difficulty, involves problems in joining or closing within a figure. This may be reflected in two parts separated by a gap when they should be touching, the failure of two sides of a figure to join, or overlap in which the drawn line overshoots the junction point between two lines. Factor 13, crossing difficulty, refers to figures six and seven. It is indicated by redrawings, sketching, erasing or other problems at the point of contact between the figures. Factor 14, curvature difficulty, involves obvious changes in the curves in Figures four, five, and six. This can occur by replacing a curve with a straight line, exaggerating the curve or decreasing it, or increasing the number of curves.

Factor 15, change in angulation, refers to an increase or decrease in the size of an angle by more than 15°. Scoring depends on the frequency of these errors. Factor 16, perceptual rotation, refers to the rotation of any figure when the test card and test paper are in the normal position. Factor 17, retrogression, is the substitution of an immature drawing for a more mature figure. Hutt suggests that the substitution of loops for well formed circles, the substitution of dashes for dots, and the substitution of dots for circles are specific examples of this behavior. The error must occur at least twice in a single figure to be scored. The total score is the number of times this criterion is met.

Factor 18, simplification, refers to the substitution of a simpler for a more difficult figure. Reducing the number of curves in figure six, for example. Factor 19, fragmentation, involves the essential destruction of the gestalt, such as failure to complete the figure, gross separation of the parts, or failure of the figures to resemble the actual design. Factor 20, overlapping, refers to problems in overlapping figures which should not overlap (such as Figure A) or problems in maintaining the overlap when it should be there (Figure 7). Factor 21 involves elaboration or doodling, including additional lines or curves, extensions of figures by addition of new figures. Factor 22, perseveration, occurs when a subject includes elements from a previous design or repeats a figure beyond the number required in a design.

Factor 23, redrawing of the total figure, refers to a second attempt to reproduce a figure after partially finishing or crossing out an earlier attempt. Factor 24, deviation in direction of movement, involves moving in directions which are unusual while drawing a figure. The usual movement directions are left to right, top to bottom, or counterclockwise when drawing circles or other closed figures. One exception to this is left-handed individuals. Factor 25 is similar to Factor 24 in that it involves inconsistency in movement of direction. This involves a shift in directions from one figure to the next.

Factor 26 is concerned with line quality. Hutt identifies six types of lines: excessively heavy, excessively heavy with poor coordination, excessively faint, excessively faint with poor coordination, poor coordination alone, sketchiness and irregularities in the line. Sketching involves retouching of lines or joinings that result in a poorly reproduced figure. In addition to these factors, Hutt recognizes that other scoring dimensions are possible, such as those suggested by other systems.

A final important system has been developed by Koppitz (1963, 1975). This system is primarily a developmental system, appropriate for the analysis of children's Benders and not usually used with adult subjects. The Koppitz system defines certain possible errors throughout the figures which can be scored. Total scores can be compared to age norms to determine if a child is operating at, below, or above normal age expectations. All adults should show essentially perfect scores within the Koppitz system.

CLINICAL INTERPRETATION

Clinical interpretation of the Bender may be approached at two levels. In the first level, the scoring systems are used to produce total scores which are used to discriminate between various diagnostic groups: in general, these systems stress differentiation between brain damaged patients and non-brain damaged controls, ranging from psychiatric to normal patients. On the second level, one interprets the research findings on each factor in a system similar to that of Hutt's, using each factor to suggest possible hypotheses which can be integrated with one another and compared to other test data, interview results, and historical data. This information can be further extended by examining each figure for specific signs which may be present.

Discriminative Validity

The results from the different scoring systems are remarkably similar in terms of discriminative validity. Studies supporting the use of the Bender as a diagnostic tool for brain damage have generally reported discriminative rates ranging from 70 to 90 precent (e.g., Brilliant and Gynther, 1963; Bruhn and Reid, 1975; Goldberg, 1974; Hain, 1964; Levine and Feirstein, 1972; McGuire, 1960; Orme, 1962; Tymchuk, 1974). There are, however, a number of problems in interpreting these studies. First, the nature of the organic groups in terms of severity is unclear: in general, the more severe the organicity the better the discrimination. Secondly, control groups are rarely appropriate. The most meaningful group would be one consisting of possible neurological patients who are eventually found to have no disorder. Such groups have been rarely used unfortunately. When these factors are taken into account, some general conclusions can be reached. In a general population the Bender is about 70 to 80 percent accurate in discriminating brain injured and normal or mixed psychiatric patients; the rate increases in more severe brain injured groups and less impaired control groups irrespective of the system of scoring employed. This rate is consistent with the accuracies of most other single tests attempting to make this discrimination.

The Bender's poorest performance occurs when trying to discriminate chronic schizophrenic patients from milder forms of brain injury; a finding common to most tests (Golden, 1978). Results will often be at chance levels (50 percent) in these populations. The test results suggest that the Bender may be used as a basic screening instrument, but it is not, by itself, an adequate measure for determining the presence or absence of organicity. A common test battery used by clinicians is the combination of the Bender and the WAIS, using both to discriminate brain damage. It is common to find a great deal of redundancy between the Bender and Block Design, however, making this combination somewhat inefficient in the analysis of organicity.

Of interest in the most recent literature has been a series of studies on the Canter Background Interference Procedure. After summarizing the literature on the procedure, Canter (1976), has found the procedure to add about 15 percent accuracy to that of the Bender, placing it in the 80 to 90 percent range; an excellent result for any single test of brain dysfunction. The accuracy was achieved by scoring the normally given Bender and the interference Bender using a modification of the Pascal-Suttel system. The normal score was then subtracted from the interference Bender using a modification of the Pascal-Suttel system. The normal score was then subtracted from the interference score. The larger the difference, the greater the likelihood of brain damage. As noted above, the difference score has been able to consistently achieve results in the 80 to 90 percent range. This form has not been studied as extensively as the general Bender, and it is not certain that these results will stand up to extensive cross-validation. If they do, however, this form of the Bender should become a major test in the assessment of organicity.

Factor Interpretation

The extensive work represented in Hutt's (1969) book on the Bender is an excellent example of the organic and personality interpretations that can be made from the Bender. While not exhaustive, the system includes most major categories of errors and surveys most of the dynamic and organic hypothesis which may relate to the patient's performance. As a result, familiarity with the system is useful even if one adopts an alternate approach to the use of the Bender.

Factor 1, sequence, may reflect several dimensions of psychopathology. Compulsive individuals will be very precise in how they lay out the figures, while highly anxious or impulsive patients will show highly irregular sequences. Irregular sequence may generally be seen in any highly confused, disorganized individual. Factor 2, position of the first drawing, is also indicative of abnormal personality, especially if the person selects the lower corners of the page to put the first drawing. Factors 3 and 4, use of space, may relate to hostility if there is an excessive amount of space suppressed. Constricted use of space is related to a tendency to withdraw and possibly to schizoid tendencies. If both tendencies are present, a possibility of ambivalence is suggested.

Factor 5, collision, may relate to neurological dysfunction, especially if there is evidence that poor motor control is causing the collisions. This phenomenon does not occur in normals and generally indicates the need for psychotherapy in a non-neurological population. Factor 6, use of the margin, is suggestive of anxiety. Hutt theorizes that excessive use of the margin allows the subject to us an external support (the edge of the paper) to help control anxiety. In organic brain dysfunction, the use may indicate a need for supports and reference points, while paranoids may be expressing considerable fear and suspicion. High Factor 6 scores occur rarely, if ever, in normal populations. Factor 7, shift in paper position, reflects overt or covert oppositional tendencies in the patient.

Factor 8, shift in stimulus card position, is similar in meaning to Factor 7 according to Hutt. Factor 9, overall increase or decrease in size, represents the manifestation of anxiety in the test situation. Increases may be associated with inadequacy and poor self-concepts, while decreases are associated with intense anxiety. In certain subcortical neurological diseases, most notably Parkinson's Disease, severe decrease may be associated with attempts to limit the motor functions required for writing. Tremor is often seen in these drawings as well. Factor 10, progressive increase or decrease, may be associated with irritability and impulsiveness if there is a progressive increase. If there is a progressive decrease, there is a tendency to withdraw and be depressed, as well as the possibility of psychosomatic complaints. Hutt notes that this is a weak factor and should not be given excessive weightings in a clinical analysis.

Factor 11, isolated increase or decrease in size, is significant clinically but may have idiosyncratic meanings, usually reflecting disturbed emotional functioning in an area for which the patient has little conscious insight. Idiosyncratic possibilities include the association of circles with females, diamonds with males, or the figures with sexuality in general. A reduction in size for any part would indicate an attempt at regression. while increase may represent a compensatory defense against sexual stimuli. In order to further isolate such data, Hutt regularly employs two projective stages to his testing. After the drawings are complete, the patient is asked to elaborate on the figures in any way which makes the figures more pleasing. The subject is then asked to give his or her associations to the drawings and the elaborations, much as is done with the Rorschach.

Factor 12, closure difficulty, may represent a difficulty in interpersonal relationships. It may be related to emotional fearfulness, or a general emotional disturbance in the patient. This can also be related to organic brain dysfunction, especially in the right hemisphere. Factor 13, crossing difficulty, is related by Hutt to psychological blocking and such symptoms as indecisiveness, compulsive doubting, and phobias. Factor 14, curvature difficulty, is a highly sensitive indicator of emotional disturbance. Increases represent overly active emotions, while decreases represent the opposite. Factor 15, change in angulation, reflects affective control. Increases indicate that there is a decreased affective level in the patient, while decreased angulation (towards more acute angles) is related to increased affective states. This problem may be related to organic brain dysfunction or mental retardation as well.

Factor 16, perceptual rotation, is frequently found in the records of organic patients or patients who are overtly psychotic. As such, their presence in adults must be taken as indications of severe dysfunction. Although relatively more frequent in organics and mental retardates, the sign is not exclusively associated with these conditions since it is also seen in those psychiatric conditions in which there are significant disruptions of ego functions. Factor 17, retrogression, is the result of strong and chronic defenses against trauma resulting from a failure in ego functions. This sign is seen in some schizophrenics who have a significantly disorganized personality, as well as others with severe deterioration of personality, such as significant or highly acute brain disorders.

Factor 18, simplification, may reflect a variety of conditions. This can include deliberate attempts not to work at the task because of oppositional tendencies or an attempt to malinger. Simplification can also be seen in cases of disrupted ego function in which the individual is not able to handle the more complex designs. Factor 19, fragmentation, is associated with inabilities to abstract and categorize, and is almost always indicative of profound disturbance (although this can be either acute or chronic in nature). In organic brain dysfunction, this behavior is seen most often in injuries to the right parietal-occipital areas of the brain. In adults, this factor is *always* indicative of some kind of serious problem.

Factor 20, overlapping difficulty, is generally associated with brain dysfunction, either of a diffuse nature or involving the right hemisphere alone. Factor 21, elaboration or doodling, is indicative of ego dysfunction in all cases where the elaboration or doodling significantly distorts the design. This can reflect a loss of ego control, and can be seen in psychosis, mental retardation, and organic brain damage.

Factor 22, perseveration, can reflect a rigid cognitive set or a motor impairment of the frontal lobe areas of the brain's dominant hemisphere. Both types of perseveration are seen in organic brain dysfunction, with motor repetition (e.g., drawing a circle over and over) indicating a lesion in the middle frontal lobes (the premotor area) and perseveration of a prior figure suggesting damage to the anterior frontal (prefrontal) lobe. If no organic brain damage is present, severe perseveration is usually associated with deteriorated schizophrenics.

Factor 23, redrawing of the entire figure, is related to an overly critical attitude on the part of the patient or the absence of advance planning and consideration of the design. Hutt cautions that this should occur at least twice before being seen as significant. Factor 24, deviation in direction of movement, may suggest some oppositional tendencies, especially when clockwise rather than counterclockwise movements are used to draw circles or similar figures. Factor 25, inconsistency in direction of movement, can indicate a psychotic block because of the personal meaning of a given design to the patient. Factor 26, line quality, is significant in a number of conditions. Motor incoordination is associated with brain dysfunction, while heavy lines reflect emotional disturbance or anxiety. Tremors are associated with brain damage, usually involving subcortical centers such as the basal ganglia or cerebellum, although intense anxiety or side effects of such drugs as the phenothiazines may also produce tremors. The latter drug effect is especially important for psychologists in hospital settings.

Specific Item Interpretations

In addition to the more general overall scores and the factors suggested above, the clinician may also interpret the performance of the patient on specific designs. These are generally similar to the overall considerations, but there are specific problems to look for in each design which are particularly applicable.

Figure A is one of the most frequent figures to show rotations in organic brain disorders. The errors on A are especially significant because of the simplicity of the figure. Psychoanalytic theorists have been especially interested in the combination of the circle (female) and diamond (male). Increases in one as compared to the other may suggest sexual problems related to male or female characteristics. Hammer (1955) has suggested that overlap between the figures may indicate virility strivings. Gross distortion in this simple figure is generally associated with significant psychosis or organic brain dysfunction.

In Figure 1, any general difficulty has been associated with some kind of pathology in the adult. Dashes substituted for the dots may indicate aggression (including delinquency), lack of impulse control, or organicity. An inability to produce a horizontal line may be caused by right hemisphere brain dysfunction or by depression (downward slope) or denial (upward slope). Circles instead of dots suggest regression and poor impulse control. Perseveration (continuing the line of dots) suggests organicity, while only a few dots may indicate carelessness or lack of cooperation if the person is not psychotic or brain injured.

Figure 2, is also one of the easier items to reproduce. If the figure as drawn represents an arc, there are strong suggestions of egocentrism. Substitution of musical notes suggests psychosis or organic brain syndrome, as does perseveration. Irregular slope or shifting can be associated with extremely poor ego function or strong mood lability.

Figure 3, has been given numerous dynamic interpretations. Troubles with the figure have been associated with sexual problems. Compulsive care in reproduction may indicate anal fixations. Flattening or rounding of the point may indicate difficulty handling aggression, while reduced size, or preoccupations with details may indicate a fear of emotional expression. Substitution of circles or dashes may suggest significant ego dysfunction as seen in brain damage or psychosis.

Figure 4, when rotated, is generally indicative of brain damage or psychosis. Enlargement of the square is associated with neuroses, while a lack of closure may suggest schizoid symptoms or more severe disorders. An extra loop suggests impulsivity, while flattening of the loop suggests a flattened affect. The separation of the two figures suggests hesitancy, self-doubt and, usually, anxiety.

Figure 5, if drawn with an unusually long straight line, is suggestive of a need to emphasize masculinity. Drawing the line through the half circle may indicate immaturity or a feeling of being overwhelmed. Obsessive-compulsiveness may be associated with counting the dots, even to the point of worrying about the number of dots rather than the shape of the design. Rotation, substitution of circles or dashes for the dots, substitution of lines for dots, or squaring of the hoop may be associated with organicity or psychoses.

Figure 6, when drawn with sharp angles rather than sinusoidal curves, suggests aggression and possible organicity. Incorrect placement of the crossing may indicate instability, or, if the upper curve is left mostly above the horizontal curve, denial. Decreasing size of the curves indicates flat affect or a neurotic condition. Drawing the figure as a face or adding a dot for an eye suggests paranoid delusions. Excessive erasure indicates ambivalence or lack of self-assuredness, while perseveration suggests brain damage. Drawing straight lines suggests aggression, and problems with femininity in women. Reduction in overall size suggests intellectualization, while exaggeration of curves suggests over emotionality. Two "U" shaped curves substituted for two crossing curves may indicate fearfulness and interpersonal problems.

Figure 7, if performed correctly, generally contradicts organicity involving the right hemisphere, although other forms of brain dysfunction may still exist. Difficulties with the angles have often been associated with brain dysfunction, as have closure problems, difficulties in sizing, and rotation over 45°. Problems in closure may relate to interpersonal difficulties, as may difficulty with overlapping. Problems related to the general phallic shape of the figure may imply sexual dysfunction or over concern.

Figure 8, when correctly produced, also argues against significant right hemisphere dysfunction. Problems with the angles may be associated with brain dysfunction or regression of the ego back to early childhood states (the figure requires a mental age of about 11 years). Overlapping of the figures has been associated with homosexuality or other emotional disturbances. Elongation of the figures points, or their elimination, may be associated with sexual problems, particularly with castration fears. Rotation is generally indicative of organicity or psychoses.

Interpretive Strategies

As described above, there are a number of interpretive strategies one can use with the Bender. In each case, the conclusions generated by each method are only tentative. The information from specific scoring systems, the scoring factors, or the separate designs must be integrated to form a picture of the individual. Initial hypothesis indicated by only one or two signs are generally rejected in favor of those symptoms which are the most pervasive and, thus, most likely characteristic of the individual. The process is very much like that described for the MMPI in this regard. It is especially necessary to weight evidence from other tests when deciding the difference between emotional conditions and those suggesting organic brain dysfunction since there is considerable overlap in the signs relevant to each group.

Except for more simple discriminations (no impairment versus some kind of impairment), the use of the Bender requires extensive experience in both scoring and interpretation. As it represents a cross between objective and projective tests, the user must decide which approach (or combination) is appropriate to the setting in which the test is employed, and then follow appropriate interpretive strategies and validity checks to evaluate such a system. As will be described later, the Bender is best used to generate and confirm hypothesis in coordination with other tests and clinical interviews.

ADVANTAGES AND DISADVANTAGES

Supporters of the Bender outline a number of important advantages for the test (Hutt, 1969). These advantages include: (1) It can be used as a buffer or warm-up test as it is not threatening to most patients and may be enjoyable to many; (2) It is useful as a supplementary technique which provides a good source of nonverbal material more reliable than many other projective techniques; (3) It provides information otherwise difficult to obtain from uneducated or culturally deprived individuals; (4) It is a useful measure of emotional states when the person otherwise denies problems; (5) It is sensitive to malingering; (6) It is useful as an adjunctive technique in the diagnosis of brain damage; (7) It is useful in discriminating borderline psychotic disorders; and (8) It is a useful research tool.

There are also significant disadvantages to the Bender. First, when used alone, it has tended to be over-interpreted, with clinicians accepting possibly hypotheses as certainties without adequate verifying information. The ease and speed in which the test is given can reinforce this tendency in situations where a quick evaluation is needed. It is necessary as a result, to emphasize that the test must be used as part of a test battery including a complete clinical interview and evaluation rather than as a single test. Used in conjunction with such tests as the MMPI and various measures of organic brain dysfunction, it can add a great deal to a battery in terms of possible hypotheses and in confirming or contradicting the results of other tests. Its short administration time makes it an excellent test in this role.

A second problem is the lack of an accepted and verified manner of interpreting the test. This leaves a great deal up to clinical judgement and experience and allows for extensive disagreements among "experts." As there is no clear evidence supporting any one system, the new clinician usually begins with a system favored by his or her supervisors and ends up with one which often takes a little from many systems. While this can result in a highly workable system, it can also serve to give continued support to unprovable hypotheses and clinical superstitions. It also makes it very difficult to change the mind of the interpreter, since, under these conditions, each clinical research study uses a different administration, different instructions, and different methods of analyses.

CLINICAL EXAMPLES

The use of the Bender as part of a neuropsychological battery is illustrated in the cases at the end of Chapter 8.

8
Neuropsychological Tests

Neuropsychological testing represents a major segment of the assessment work done by psychologists. Two of the major and most commonly used tests for brain dysfunction, the Benton and the Bender, have already been discussed. There are hundreds of tests beyond these which are used by some psychologists for the diagnosis of organicity however. In her recent book on neuropsychological assessment, for example, Lezak (1976) presents a test index which covers seven pages of small print.

In this chapter, we shall examine those tests which are used with some frequency by clinicians, though not as frequently as the other tests presented in this volume. The chapter will also examine tests for which there has not been a great deal of use but which the current literature suggests can be of significant value to the clinician. Finally, the chapter will consider the issue of neuropsychological test batteries.

TOKEN TEST

The Token Test is a simple, easy-to-administer test using a minimum of material. It is intended to assess speech functions, and is, consequently, much more sensitive to left hemisphere damage. The test requires about a fourth grade education, and is usually easy for the normal individual. (Its use in psychiatric populations has been limited, however, and it is likely that poorer "normal" performance would be found in such groups.) The test has been found sensitive to aphasic disorders which are not apparent upon observation of the patient.

Administration

The test requires 20 tokens, varying in shape (circle, rectangle), size (small, large), and color (red, yellow, green, blue, and white), so that every possible combination is represented. The sets are normally made out of plastic but could be made out of other material as well. The test has 62 commands, each of which requires the manipulation of, or attention to, one or more of the shapes. For example, one may ask "Touch the green rectangle." In more complex items, the person might be instructed to "Put the red rectangle under the red circle." The complexity of the statement the individual can reliably respond to is quickly established in this way. If an item is missed initially, it is repeated. If correct the second time, the individual gets full credit for the item. A shorter 39 item version of the test was developed by Spreen and Benton (1969) working from Boller and Vignolo's (1966) original items.

Discriminative Validity

The test is able to discriminate aphasics from normals about 90 percent of the time (Boller, 1968; Hartje, Kerstechensteiner, Poeck, and Orgass, 1973; Orgass and Poeck, 1966). As noted above, however, there are no clear indications of the test's effectiveress when given to a psychiatric population. This fact currently limits the use of the test in many neuropsychological settings. Within this limitation, the test can be an extremely useful addition to any screening battery investigating the possibility of organic defecit.

PURDUE PEGBOARD

The Purdue Pegboard, published as a test of fine motor skills by Science Research Associates, has been shown to be an extremely useful, quick test of neuropsychological function. The test allows the clinician to assess right and left hand motor function, an area in which deficits commonly occur in brain injuries. Motor function is an especially valuable area to assess since specific deficits in the right hand can usually be localized to the left hemisphere and specific deficits in the left hand to the right hemisphere. Since the test is short, averaging under five minutes, it can fit easily into a larger test battery.

Administration

The patient is given a long pegboard with two rows for pegs. The examiner then requires the patient to begin by placing the pegs in with the left hand, then the right hand, and finally both hands. The subject is given

30 seconds for each trial. The patients score is the number of pegs placed in each trial.

Discriminative Validity

A series of studies (Costa and Vaughan, 1962; Costa, Vaughan, Levita, and Farber, 1963; Fernald, Fernald, and Rines, 1966) have revealed generally good hit rates for the test when comparing normal and brain injured patients. Brain damage was generally represented by scores below 13 on the right hand, 11 on the left hand, and 10 for both hands. The cutoff points are reduced to ten on both the left and right hands and eight on both hands for patients over 60. Overall accuracy averages about 80 percent for the test. Significantly poor performances are seen with psychiatric populations, however; Fernald, Fernald, and Rines (1966) reported only a 34 percent hit rate in a psychiatric group. Our experience has not been so negative, as we have found that psychiatric patients can be motivated to do better. Test results must be interpreted with caution in such patients, however, especially those showing psychomotor retardation. Specific deficits in one hand as compared to the other is a much more reliable sign in such patients. A right hand score equal to or less than the left hand score, for example, is generally indicative of a left hemisphere problem, while a left hand score 25 to 30 percent below the right hand score suggests right hemisphere dysfunction. As with the Token Test, this is an excellent addition to a screening battery for organic function when the test's limitations are considered.

STROOP COLOR AND WORD TEST

Several recent publications have demonstrated the usefulness of the Stroop Color and Word Test in the diagnosis of brain damage. The Stroop has been found to have several advantages: it is easy to give and easy to score; it is sensitive to most brain injuries, but especially sensitive to frontal lobe injuries, which are often difficult to detect by neuropsychological tests; and the Stroop takes less than five minutes to administer.

Administration and Materials

The Stroop test consists of three 8½ by 11 pages. Each page consists of five columns of 20 items. Each item on page one is one of these words: Red, Green, or Blue. The words are repeated in a largely random order. Page two consists of 100 items, as does page one, but each item is the sequence XXXX. On this page, each XXXX is printed in red, green, or blue ink. Page three consists of the words on page one printed in the colors on page two, with the limitation that a word and the color it is printed in may not match. Thus the word Red may appear in blue or green ink, Green in red or blue ink, and Blue in red or green ink.

The instructions for the test are simple (Golden, 1978). On page one, the subject is instructed to read down each column as quickly as possible, pronouncing the words presented there. On page two, the instructions are the same but the subject is told to name the color of the XXXXs. On page three, the subject is instructed to name the color of the ink the word is printed in rather than the word itself. The subject is given 45 seconds on each page. The score is the number of items correctly finished within the time limit on each page. These are converted into T scores using tables in the test manual.

Discriminative Validity

Golden (1976) found that the Stroop could reliably differentiate between normal, psychiatric, and brain damaged patients. Specifically, on page two, normal patients tended to complete 70 to 90 items, while psychiatric patients completed 60 to 80 items, and brain damaged patients generally scored below 60. The three scores of the Stroop can be used to localize a lesion as well: good scores on pages one and two, along with a poor score on page three, is indicative of frontal injuries, especially to the left hemisphere. Right hemisphere injuries are characterized by normal scores on page one with depressed scores on pages two and three. Left hemisphere (nonfrontal) injuries are characterized by poor scores on all three pages of the Stroop (Golden, 1978; Perret, 1974).

The Stroop score is also useful in the diagnosis of dyslexia. Specifically, equal scores on pages two and three are never seen in literate adults. Thus, if page three is within 10 percent of page two, there is a high possibility of dyslexia as this implies that the normal interference problem (the words interfering with color naming) has not occurred, and that there is a lack of word reading responses.

The Stroop is an excellent addition to other screening batteries because of its speed and the usefulness of the test in diagnosing lateralized and frontal injuries.

MEMORY FOR DESIGNS TEST

The Memory for Designs Test (Graham and Kendall, 1960) consists of 15 designs which must be reproduced from memory. The test is similar to the Benton in this sense. The Memory for Designs, however, does not have a copy phase as does the Benton and the figures are considerably simpler as well.

Administration

Each design is shown to the patient for ten seconds. The patient is then asked to reproduce it on a single sheet of paper. The scoring system is relatively simple: designs completely forgotten or reproduced with one error or less are scored 0; two or more errors without loss of the essential design is scored 1; loss of the essential design is scored 2; and rotations or reversals are scored 3. The total score is the sum of the individual scores. Scores in the range 0 to 4 are scored normal (one could get this by forgetting all the designs completely); scores 5 to 11 are considered borderline; and scores 12 and above are considered organic.

Discriminative Validity

The scoring system of the Memory for Designs, since it does not penalize lapses in memory, is closely related to the Bender scoring systems (McIver, McLaren, and Phillip, 1973). The discriminative rates for the test are, as a result, highly similar to those yielded by the Bender. Brilliant and Gynther (1963) reported hit rates of 88 percent for psychiatric controls and 63 percent for the organic group. Other studies have presented results basically in the 70s (Grundvig, Ajax, and Needham, 1970, 1973; McManis, 1974; Shearn, Berry, and Fitzgibbons, 1974). Watson (1968) reported problems with differentiating chronic psychiatric from brain damaged patients with the Memory for Designs.

Although the Memory for Designs appears accurate in basic discriminations, it does not yield the rich clinical material that the Bender and Benton can. The test does not take significantly less time, nor does it have as well established norms as the Benton for the memory components. Although some prefer the test over the others presented, the current author does not see, as a consequence, that it is superior to those tests. There appears to be no clear reason, other than personal preference, for substituting the Memory for Designs for either test.

WECHSLER MEMORY TEST

This test, developed by Wechsler (1945), is an attempt to measure both verbal and nonverbal components of memory. Its importance lies in the general lack of tests able to yield a comprehensive assessment of memory. Since memory function is frequently impaired in brain damage, many have included this test as part of an organic test battery.

Administration

The Wechsler Memory Test consists of six subtests. The first two subtests, Orientation and Memory, are measures of basic memory for such things as date (year, month, day), knowledge of the current president, governor, mayor, and where the patient is. There are some problems with these measures: mass transportation is currently so available that patients travel extensively on their own, often moving from state to state. Consequently, they may not know who's the state's governor is or who the city's mayor is. This is also difficult for the rural patient transferred to the big city hospital. The current author, for example, has worked in hospitals that received patients from four different states. With these questions, one can substitute and ask for the mayor of the patient's city or governor of the patient's state (if the psychologist knows the correct answer). One can also simply give credit for these questions without using them. One point is given for each correct answer.

The third subtest, Mental Control, asks the subject to count, to add, and to repeat the alphabet within specific time limits. Scoring is based on time and accuracy. The Logical Memory subtest requires the subject to listen to two paragraphs individually and repeat from each the details they can remember. One point is given for each detail remembered. The total correct for both paragraphs is divided by two.

The fifth subtest is Digit Span, a test basically equivalent to WAIS Digit Span. This version does not have a three digit trial for Forward Memory or a two digit trial for Backward Memory, however. Scoring is the same as in the WAIS Digit Span. The Visual Reproduction subtest is a measure of visual memory. Points are assigned for each detail remembered, as described by Wechsler (1945). The final subtest, Associate Learning, asks the subject to memorize ten word pairs, six of which are defined as easy and four which are defined as hard. The list is read to the subject three times, and followed by a recitation of the first words which the subject must follow with the other half of the pair. On each recall trial, the examiner notes the number of correct easy pairs and the number of correct hard pairs. At the end of the test, a total easy item and total hard item score is reached. The total score for the test is one half of the easy item score plus the hard item score.

After all scores are calculated, the scores for each subtest are summed. A factor for age, growing as the individual gets older, is added to this to yield a total score. This score can be turned into a Memory Quotient (MQ) with a mean of 100 and a standard deviation of 15 (equivalent to WAIS IQ) using tables given by Wechsler (1945). Additional normative data is available from Hulicka (1966). This includes normative data for each subtest as well as the overall scores (except for test two).

Discriminative Validity

Despite the importance of memory fucntions in neuropsychological disorders, the research on the Wechsler Memory Scale has been disappointing. Many researchers have found the test unable to differentiate between organic and psychiatric patients (Cohen, 1950) or between organic and normal patients (Parker, 1957). Bachrach and Mintz (1974) found the design test alone to be a successful discriminator, while Kljajic (1975) found evidence to support the use of Digit Span, Associate Learning, Information, and Orientation. Holland (1974) and Howard (1950) found the paired associates learning test to be useful.

One problem with the test is that several of the subtests are likely to be insensitive to brain damage. Tests of Orientation and Information and Mental Control, specifically, are rarely affected by brain damage except in the most severe cases. In addition, while specific left hemisphere injuries may affect some of the verbal tests (although many of the Paired Associates items are so easy that memory is often not required), the design test would not be heavily affected. In right hemisphere injuries, the test would show little overall deficit as impairment on only the Design subtest would be expected. Thus, some severe to moderate left hemisphere injuries might lower scores on several subtests, while patients with right hemisphere injuries would show essentially normal total scores. It is not surprising, then, that the test does poorly in making discriminations when overall scores are tested.

It would appear that the best use of the Wechsler Memory would not be in calculating MQ's, but in comparing subtests to one another. For example, a comparison of Associate Learning, Logical Memory, and Digit Span to Design Memory might be useful in establishing possible differences between the right and left hemisphere, an important aspect of many evaluations (see next chapter). In addition, specific deficits on any one subtest may be useful in determining the nature of problems interfering with the patients social or neurological functioning.

Advantages and Disadvantages

The major advantage of the Wechsler Memory Scale is its status as the only clinical measure of memory functions in general use. Its use has been continued on this basis despite its limitations. There appears to be no test likely to take its place as a comprehensive battery at present, although there is a general memory test presented with the Luria Neuropsychological Battery that may be of value to the clinician (see Chapter 10).

HOOPER VISUAL ORGANIZATION TEST

The Hooper Visual Organization Test, commonly referred to as the Hooper, was designed to be an objectively scored test which could discriminate between brain damaged patients and patients with functional disorders. Hooper states that a visual organization test was chosen for this purpose because such tasks are sensitive to brain dysfunction and relatively independent of language and intelligence.

Administration

The Hooper may be given as an individual or group test. The test consists of 30 items, each of which presents the drawing of a simple object cut into pieces and mixed up. The task of the patient is to visually organize the pieces and name the object. It closely resembles the Object Assembly Test except for the additional demand of Object Assembly on motor construction skills.

The patient is shown the 30 pictures singly. The patient can write down his answer in a booklet or this can be done by the examiner. There is no time limit on items, although after one minute subjects are usually prompted to guess. The manual for the test lists acceptable answers for full credit and, in the case of some items, half credit. The examiner may give credit for alternate answers at his or her discretion, however.

Interpretation and Validity

Hooper classified scores in the following manner: no impairment is indicated by scores between 25 and 30; mild impairment is represented by scores of 20 to 24.5 and is seen in mild organic disorders, severe emotional disturbance, or schizophrenia; moderate impairment includes scores from 10.0 to 19.5 and is seen in cases of organic brain syndrome, as well as schizophrenics whose performance can be recognized by neologistic or bizarre responses; scores below 10.0 represent severe impairment and are seen in severe organic or schizophrenic disorders which can again be discriminated by the qualitative aspects of the record.

Hooper describes four classes or errors that are useful in making a qualitative analysis. In isolate responses the patient reacts to a concrete aspect of one piece rather than making the abstract integration. This response is seen in both organics and severe schizophrenics. Perseveration is using a response appropriate for an earlier item. This response is characteristic of schizophrenics but has been seen in organics as well. The final category is neologistic responses in which the patient forms words with no meaning to the examiner, such as "Megaloon."

Discriminative Validity

Hooper presents one study which received 100 percent accuracy in a schizophrenic group (not including chronics) and 79 percent accuracy in an organic group using a cutoff of 20. A second study by the author in a state hospital produced less significant results: 64 percent in a chronic brain syndrome group versus 78 and 67 percent in two chronic schizophrenic groups. Neurotics and patients with personality disorders, however, were able to do the test without difficulty. Lezak (1976) concluded that many brain damaged individuals can complete the Hooper without difficulty. The Hooper may not always indicate the presence of brain damage as a consequence. Poor scores may not indicate brain damage, although they do indicate disruption in the patient's thought processes.

Advantages and Disadvantages

Our own experience has indicated that the Hooper is not very sensitive to many localized forms of brain injury. The good results come, instead, from populations with diagnosis of chronic organic brain syndromes. Thus, if one is looking for less obvious lesions, the Hooper would not be the test of choice.

The Hooper could be useful however, in discriminating the reason for poor Object Assembly performance if one needs to discriminate between visual and visual-motor skills. It can also be used as part of a screening battery that does not include other visual-discrimination tests.

OTHER NEUROPSYCHOLOGICAL TESTS

A number of other individual tests discussed in this book can be and are used for neuropsychological evaluation. These include the WAIS subtests (as discussed in Chapter 1), the Shipley-Hartford and Raven's Matrices (Chapter 2), achievement tests (Chapter 3), personality tests (Chapter 4), the Bender (Chapter 6), the Benton (Chapter 7), the individual subtests of the Halstead-Reitan (Chapter 9), and the individual subtests and items from the Luria Neuropsychological Exam (Chapter 10). These tests are discussed in the indicated chapters.

TEST BATTERIES

The current literature supports the premise in this chapter that no one test of organicity is sufficient for the diagnosis of an organic disorder. Nor has any one combination of tests received widespread support as "the" best battery. Several important considerations can, however, be described for an organic test battery.

Screening Batteries

Most psychologists who test for organicity do so as a screening of a patient population to identify individuals who need further testing or who should be referred to a neurological consultant. Such batteries, since they are given to large numbers of persons, must be relatively short. A second type of screening battery, done on a smaller group of referred patients, is able to be somewhat longer (since fewer people are tested) and needs to be more discriminating (since all the patients referred would be expected to have some signs of neurological problems).

For both types of batteries, it is important to put together a set of tests that are not overlapping. Giving the Benton, the Bender, and the Memory for Designs, for example, would be little better than giving only one of them since they each tap the same skills and generally identify the same patients. A better battery might be the Stroop Color and Word Test, the Canter Background Procedure, and the Token Test. These three tests cover a wide range of skills and are likely to show brain damage in almost any area of the brain. Similar batteries may be chosen from among the many tests available for diagnosing brain dysfunction.

Longer batteries can be more efficient in screening than shorter batteries. A longer battery might include the three tests described above plus the Purdue Pegboard (as a motor measure), the Seashore Rythm Test (a measure of nonverbal auditory skills discussed in the next chapter), and the Speech Perception Test (a verbal auditory procedure discussed in the next chapter). Such a battery would take about an hour to administer.

Golden (1976) suggested a battery consisting of four WAIS subtests —Object Assembly, Block Design, Similarities, and Digit Symbol—along with the Stroop Color and Word Test, Speech Perception, the Rhythm Test, and the Aphasia Test (see next chapter). He found the battery to have an accuracy of about 90 percent. Optimally, the battery took about 1½ hours to administer.

These batteries, of course, are not the only ones possible. One should be careful to evaluate the usefulness of any set of tests chosen, however, as all combinations will not work as well, even when they appear to be logically sound.

Extended Diagnostic Batteries

In addition to screening for brain dysfunction, psychologists are also engaged in the detailed description of the deficits due to a brain injury, as well as localizing of brain injury and identifying its nature and extent.

Such decisions require extensive test batteries. These batteries can be individualized, designed for each patient depending on the goals of the evaluation.

When this technique is used, a great deal of weight is placed on the clinical judgement of the examiner who must select the proper tests or risk misidentifying the nature of the patient's problems. Such batteries are also more difficult to interpret since the relationships of the tests in the battery may not be known except on a theoretical basis.

The alternate method of putting a battery together is to use a comprehensive standard battery. Such batteries generally include measure for all significant neuropsychological skills—intelligence, perceptual motor, auditory, tactile, and visual skills, verbal skills, nonverbal skills, and basic motor skills (see Golden, 1978). Two batteries, differing greatly in construction but with the aim of fulfilling these conditions, are discussed in the two following chapters.

CASE EXAMPLES

Case 1.   Case 1 was originally seen on a medicine ward for a variety of complaints including headache, fatigue, depression, and general listlessness. The patient, a 35-year-old male, was uncooperative and displayed a number of bizarre symptoms. A psychiatric consultation was requested as a result. The psychiatrist, in turn, suggested psychological testing for an organic brain syndrome.

The patient was given the tests listed in Table 8-1 with the results indicated in the table. On four subtests from the WAIS, the patient performed normally on two verbal tests (Similarities, Vocabulary) while showing extensive impairment on two performance tests (Block Design, Picture Arrangement). The Picture Arrangement score was especially significant as it was substantially below all the other scores, a finding common in right frontal injuries. On the Reitan-Indiana Aphasia Test (discussed more completely in the next chapter), the patient showed no deficits, except for an inability to draw a cross. The patient's performance on the Token Test was normal. On the Stroop Color and Word Test, the patient showed normal performance for word reading, and was slightly impaired on color naming, and substantially impaired on the interference page. The patient's Memory for Designs fell within the borderline range.

Overall, the pattern of deficits clearly suggested brain damage which was probably worse in the right hemisphere and most likely involved the frontal areas. Neurological procedures were later able to identify a previously unsuspected hematoma (sac of blood exerting pressure on the brain) primarily over the right frontal area but involving the left frontal as well. The patient's "psychiatric" symptoms were due to the effects of the brain dysfunction.

Case 2.   Case 2, a 37-year-old man with a history of significant alcoholism, was screened for possible organic damage. As can be seen in Table 8-2, the patient was able to do the copy phase of the Benton (administration C) without error, but

Table 8-1

Results for Case 1

Similarities	12 (scale score)
Vocabulary	10 (scale score)
Block Design	7 (scale score)
Picture Arrangement	3 (scale score)
Aphasia Test	1 (errors)
Memory for Designs	6 (points)
Stroop Test:	
Word	95 (items)
Color	63 (items)
Interference	15 (items)

Table 8-2

Results for Case 2

Benton Visual Retention Test			
Administration C:	0 errors	10 correct	
Administration A:	5 errors	6 correct	
Purdue Pegboard			
Right	11		
Left	11		
Bender-Gestalt			
Borderline			
Stroop Color and Word Test			
Word	96		
Color	76		
Interference	26		

Table 8-3

Results for Case 3

Wechsler Adult Intelligence Scale	
Performance IQ	82
Verbal IQ	109
Full-scale IQ	97
Purdue Pegboard	
Right	15
Left	6
Benton	
(see Figures 2 and 3)	
Memory for Designs	
4 errors (see Figure 8-1)	
Wechsler Memory Scale	
74 (MQ)	

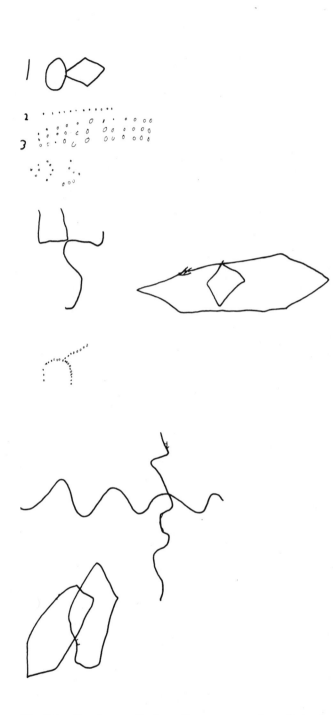

Fig. 8-1.   Bender results from the case example under regular administration.

missed four of the ten designs on Administration A with a total of five errors, suggesting some impairment of memory function. By age and intelligence (which was normal), the patient would be expected to get eight right on the memory administration. Thus the subject performed at a level of −2 below his expected score, a borderline finding seen in both brain impairment and normals a significant percentage of the time.

Fig. 8-2.   Bender results from the case example taken under background interference conditions. Note the substantially greater impairment in the drawings in this example, as well as the "hugging" to the edge of the paper in both examples. These reproductions should be compared to the actual figures presented in the Bender chapter.

The patient showed some impairment on the Purdue Pegboard, scoring equally well with the right and left hands. We should expect the right hand to do better generally. On the Bender, the patient scored at a low normal level, close to the cutoff score of the Pascal and Suttel (1951) system. Finally, the patient scored normally on the Stroop test, on both the Word and Color pages, but showed significant losses on the Color-Word score.

Overall, the data seems to suggest someone functioning at a borderline level with some indications of minimal frontal atrophy, especially in the left hemisphere and possibly in the right as suggested by the Purdue Pegboard, the Stroop, and the borderline Benton. As one can see, had only some of these tests been given, conclusions for the patient may have been significantly different, an important consideration in putting together a screening battery. In this patient, later CAT scan results suggested minimal frontal atrophy consistent with the test results.

Case 3.   Case 3, a 31-year-old male, was seen for evaluation three years following a brain injury suffered in an automobile accident. The patient earned the test scores reported in Table 8-3. As can be seen, the patients performance IQ is significantly below his verbal IQ (27 points). No subtests were particularly impaired compared to the others except for a score of four on the Digit Symbol.

The patient was given several visual-motor tests. The Memory for Designs (Figure 8-3) was awarded a score of four (in the normal range). The Bender (Figure 8-1) showed a significant number of dysfunctions, as did the Bender taken with background interference (Figure 8-2). (The reader should compare the reproduced

Fig. 8-3.   Memory for designs performance of same subject as the Bender performances. This was given a normal diagnosis using the Memory for Designs criteria. Note evidence of tremor.

figures to those in Chapter 6.) Note the heavy use of the margin as a point of reference and the general poor drawing skills. There are also extensive overlap errors, especially on the interference Bender.

The patient also showed severe memory disruption (MQ of 74) compared to the expected MQ which should have been equal to the patient's overall IQ. Finally, on the Purdue Pegboard the patient achieved very poorly with the left hand. These results clearly point to an overall widespread impairment of the right hemisphere of the brain.

9
The Halstead-Reitan Neuropsychological Battery

The Halstead-Reitan Neuropsychological Test Battery began with the work of Ward Halstead in 1935 at the University of Chicago. Halstead exhaustively studied the behavior of brain injured patients, developing and discarding hundreds of tests in the process. The results of his initial investigations were published in his 1947 book *Brain and Intelligence: A Quantitative Study of the Frontal Lobes*. In this book, Halstead introduced some of the tests which have become an integral part of the neuropsychological battery.

Subsequent to the publication of the book, one of Halstead's students, Dr. Ralph Reitan, established a neuropsychology laboratory at the University of Indiana Medical Center. Beginning in 1951, Reitan established a test battery designed to measure a broad range of abilities. He only included tests thought to be valid indicators of brain dysfunction. The major goal of this test battery was the development of a variety of principles of inference which would allow the diagnosis of the individual subject (Reitan, undated).

Reitan began with Halstead's basic battery and supplemented it with a number of additional tests in order to broaden the scope of the battery. Over the past 25 years, Reitan has published a number of important studies which validated or modified the battery. This initial work of Halstead and Reitan has led to the adoption of the battery across this country and around the world. Its acceptance has been illustrated by the numerous studies appearing in major psychological and medical journals on the validity of the battery, and the popularity of workshops in the use of the Halstead-Reitan presented by Reitan and others.

PURPOSE OF THE NEUROPSYCHOLOGICAL EXAMINATION

Smith (1975) has suggested four major purposes for the neuro-psychological battery: (1) To be an aid in neurodiagnosis; (2) To establish baselines to measure future performance; (3) To make prognostic statements about clients; and (4) To aid in planning rehabilitation.

Neurodiagnosis

As an aid in neurodiagnosis, the neuropsychological examination can be useful in confirming a neurological diagnosis. There exists a number of neurological conditions where a diagnosis is questionable. Such cases include patients where there is a question between a neurological cause (e.g., head trauma) and a functional disorder (e.g., schizophrenia). In other cases, there are questions of the origin of learning disabilities.

Baseline

Neuropsychological testing is useful to examine the effects of treatments affecting brain function. Given before treatment has commenced —whether it is drug treatment, surgery, or educational intervention —later testing can establish any improvement or subsequent decline.

Prognosis

Neuropsychological tests can aid in estimating the degree of recovery a patient is likely to show. Although this area has not been investigated as fully as is necessary, initial research results suggest that neuropsychological tests can be a valuable aid (Meier, 1974). This information would be especially useful in counseling clients and family in planning rehabilitation programs, and in using limited rehabilitation resources.

Rehabilitation

It has become increasingly recognized that a primary purpose of neuropsychological testing is the planning and evaluation of rehabilitation programs for brain injured patients (Golden, 1978). Luria (1963) has suggested that an extensive neuropsychological examination is necessary to identify the nature and scope of a brain injury behaviorally. With such information, rehabilitation programs may be designed which treat directly the major deficits of the patient.

As described by Luria (1963, 1966) and Golden (1978), the process of rehabilitation planning closely parallels the process of neurodiagnosis by neuropsychological tests. Our knowledge of the effectiveness and use of these techniques is limited as yet, but the initial data suggests good potential for such techniques (Gudeman, Golden, and Craine, 1978).

APPARATUS, ADMINISTRATION AND SCORING

The Halstead-Reitan Neuropsychological Battery consists of a number of independent tests. Unlike most of the other tests included in this volume, the exact procedures which make up the battery differ somewhat among neuropsychological laboratories. Most users of the battery include the following tests, however: (1) Wechsler Adult Intelligence Scale (or its earlier form, the Wechsler-Bellevue); (2) Minnesota Multiphasic Personality Test; (3) Halstead Category Test; (4) Speech-Sounds Perception Test; (5) Seashore Rhythm Test; (6) Tactual Performance Test; (7) Trail Making Test; (8) Reitan-Klove Sensory-Perceptual Examination; (9) Reitan-Indiana Aphasia Examination; (10) Lateral Dominance Examination; and the (11) Halstead Finger Tapping Test. The Wechsler Adult Intelligence Scale and the Minnesota Multiphasic Personality Inventory are discussed elsewhere in this volume. The remaining tests will be reviewed individually here.

Halstead Category Test

The Halstead Category Test was designed to measure an individual's capacity to deduce general principles from experience with specific items. The test consists of 208 slides, each of which suggests a number from one to four. When subjects are shown a slide, they must decide what number the slide suggests by attempting to guess the principle represented by the slide. For example, the first slide contains the Roman numeral "I." Almost all subjects deduce that this slide suggests the number one. After the subjects decide on an answer, they press one of four levers numbered from one to four. If the subject has guessed the correct answer, the pressing of the correct level causes a pleasant door chime to ring, reinforcing their guess of the underlying principle. If the subject's guess is incorrect, the pressing of the lever is followed by a loud, disagreeable buzzer. This indicates the subject must utilize a different underlying principle in order to get the correct answer.

The test consists of seven different subtests, each with its own underlying principle. For example, the first group of items suggests the correct answer by presenting the Roman numerals I, II, III, and IV. In the second set, the correct answer is determined by the number of items on the page.

If two circles were shown, for example, the correct answer would be two. In the third set, four items are always presented. One of the items is unique in some manner, however. The correct answer for this set is the position of the unique item. So if the unique item is the third figure, the correct response would be three.

The items for the Category Test are presented on a small viewing screen contained in a projection box. Because this apparatus is somewhat clumsy, different investigators have devised alternate ways of presenting the items. There is no alternate method which is generally accepted at present.

At the beginning of the test administration, the subject is told that items will be presented which suggest a number from one to four. The subject is told that the bell indicates a correct choice, while the buzzer indicates an incorrect choice. Finally, they are told that there is one principle which runs through each subtest that they must deduce. At the beginning of each subtest, the subject is again told that there is a principle which they must deduce, and which may be the same or different from the principles underlying the other subtests. Before the last subtest, the subject is told that the answer to the item is the same as the answer when the subject previously saw the slide.

The most serious administrative problem with the Category Test is the length of the procedure. Although a normal patient might finish the test within an hour, a brain injured patient may take two hours or more. Despite the Category Test's value in making diagnostic decisions, this extreme length makes many clinicians reluctant to use it. The length may also cause severe fatigue in a patient; answering may become random or a subject may sometimes be unwilling or unable to finish.

Fatigue during the test may be lessened by giving the subject breaks between subtests, although this may adversely affect performance on subtest seven because of the increased time the subject must remember the items. This technique may also increase the length of the testing session considerably. A second method to control fatigue is to employ a short form of the test which uses fewer items. At present, however, there is no short form of the test which has been shown to be equivalent to the longer form for interpretation purposes.

A third alternative is to limit the length of the test to a set time period. We have found that the prorated score after one hour of testing correlates highly ($r = .85$) with the overall score achieved by the subject. This procedure has the effect of eliminating the more difficult, later items for the subjects unable to complete them accurately. This technique does as well as the longer test in disiriminating among brain injured, schizophrenic, and normal patients, although it does tend to underestimate the number of errors which will be made by severely brain injured patients.

It is useful in some cases to employ a testing the limits procedure. Here, the subject unable to do the test initially has the items repeated along with hints and suggestions that might lead the subject to the correct principle. Such a procedure sometimes illuminates the qualitative problems that the patient may have.

The score for the Category Test is the number of items missed. If all items are not completed, the total score is prorated by the formula:

$$\frac{\text{Number of Errors}}{\text{Number of Items Attempted}} \times 208$$

SPEECH-SOUNDS PERCEPTION TEST

The test, one of Halstead's original examinations, consists of six sets of ten items. For each item, the subject hears a nonsense word (e.g., feep) which must be matched with one of four written alternatives (e.g., teep, feep, feek, teek). All the nonsense words are formed by adding a consonant before and after the vowel "ee." Thus the discrimination made is between different consonant sounds.

The test is administered by telling clients that they will hear nonsense words that must each be matched against their written equivalent. Three sample items are presented on the tape which correspond to the first three items of the first set. If the subjects successfully match the sample items, the test is then given by playing the tape. If the subjects fail to understand the instructions, they are repeated. After the test items have begun, the examiner has no role as all items are presented by the tape.

The score for the Speech-Sounds Perception Test is the number of errors made out of 60 items. Inspection of the items missed is sometimes useful as an aid in determining specific speech sounds which give the patient more difficulty.

SEASHORE RHYTHM TEST

The Seashore Rhythm Test was taken by Halstead from the Seashore Battery of Musical Abilities. The test consists of 30 items, each of which is a pair of rhythmic patterns presented by tape. The client must indicate whether the two patterns in each item are the same or different. This is indicated by having the subject place an "S" or "D" in the appropriate space on the answer sheet.

The test is administered by telling the clients that they will hear two rhythmic patterns, one after the other. The client is told that it is necessary to tell if the patterns are the same or different. Following this, the sample items are presented. After the samples, the client is told to write "S" or "D" as appropriate. The examiner also writes "S = Same" and "D = Different" on the answer sheet to avoid misunderstandings. If the subject understands the directions, the tape is started and the 30 items presented.

Once the test has begun, it cannot be stopped even if a subject should become confused because of the speed at which the items are presented. This procedure makes the test more sensitive to brain damage, but it also interferes with interpretation as poor performance may be due to an inability to pay attention or work at a normal speed rather than an inability to remember and match rhythmic patterns. If this appears to be the case, it is often informative to repeat the items slowly by stopping the tape recorder. This procedure allows a more detailed analysis of the results. The score for the test is the number of items missed under the normal administration.

TACTUAL PERFORMANCE TEST

The Tactual Performance Test is a modification by Halstead of a standard Goodard-Sequin formboard. The formboard consists of a board with ten spaces removed, each corresponding to a wooden geometric figure. In the standard formboard task, the subject attempts to place each geometric shape into the corresponding cutout. In this modification, the formboard is placed on a base which holds it at a 45° angle to the horizontal. The subject is required to do the test blindfolded, in addition. Many of the skills demanded by the Tactual Performance Test are, consequently, quite different from those required by the standard, visual formboard test.

Since no visual skills are to be used in this test, it is imperative that the subject never be allowed to see the board or the geometric shapes. The subject, consequently, must be fully blindfolded before any test apparatus is shown. It is extremely important to insure that the subject is not able to see in any direction.

After the subject is blindfolded, the board and blocks are placed directly before the subject. The examiner then tells the subject the task that is to be done and shows the subject the outline of the board. Then the subject is allowed to begin the test. Three trials are run: dominant hand only, nondominant hand only, and both hands together. Throughout the examination, the examiner keeps the shapes directly before the subject.

A number of problems may arise in the course of the three trials. First, subjects may attempt to use both hands during the single board trials. Whenever this occurs, the subject should be immediately stopped from using the extra hand. In some cases, this may require the examiner to hold the alternate hand in the patient's lap.

A second problem is the wandering of the subject from the board to the base supporting the board or the table. When this occurs, the subject should be told and stopped. Similarly, subjects may be on the board but ignoring a whole section such as the upper third. In these situations, the subject should be told to feel the whole board so that this error may be corrected.

There may also be problems with blocks already placed. The most common problem occurs when a subject accidentally knocks out a block which has already been correctly placed. In these cases, the examiner should replace the block for the subject and tell the subject that this is being done. A rarer problem is the client who forces a block into the wrong hole. This is difficult to do, but not impossible if a subject persists. In these cases, the examiner should have the subject feel the block and the space, explaining that they are not the same. The examiner is not to explain *why* they are not the same, however.

Problems may also develop with subjects who are fearful of being blindfolded. This is more common in settings where psychiatric as well as organic clients are seen. This problem may be handled by shortening the time period for each trial (see below) and allowing the subject to remove the blindfold between trials. When this is done the examiner must ensure that the subject does not see the board or blocks. In some patients, even these measures may be ineffective and it will be impossible to test a subject while blindfolded. These subjects can be tested without the blindfold, although the interpretation of the results under this condition is greatly altered.

A similar kind of problem occurs with the patient who cannot work for long periods of time or gets dizzy after being blindfolded for several minutes. In each case, the examiner may respond by shortening the length of each trial or providing rest periods. If such rest periods are provided within a trial, it is necessary to note this on the protocol and take it into consideration during the interpretation.

If a subject is unable to use one hand at all, all three trials should be given using only the good hand. As might be expected, this procedure also considerably affects interpretability of the results.

The final problem is the length of each trial. As can be seen above, there are specific problems which limit the time during which a patient can be tested. In addition to those considerations, there are subjects who would take 30 minutes or more on each trial if allowed. This is an inordinate amount of time to spend on a single trial within a test battery. Reitan (undated) suggests that 15 minutes is a reasonable cutoff in most cases, although in some, where the subject tires easily or becomes frustrated, he suggests a time limit of ten minutes. Russell, Neuringer, and Goldstein (1970) have suggested a general time limit of ten minutes for each trial.

We have found that the ten minute limit yields as much information as the fifteen minute time limit, as well as saving a significant amount of testing time. For subjects unable to work ten minutes, one should attempt to get at least a five minute sample. The shorter the time period, however, the less reliable the results produced.

After the three trials have been completed, the blocks and board are put away and the subject's blindfold removed. The subject is then given a clean sheet of paper and instructed to draw an outline of the board and to then draw each of the shapes as close to the spot where it actually was. After this phase of the test, the examiner shuold examine the sheet. If any of the shapes are not clear, or if the subject is unable to draw, the subject can indicate by verbal description and pointing what a shape is and where it goes. There is no penalty for poor drawings if the subject can indicate the shape and position in these alternate methods.

Several scores are generated for the Tactual Performance Test. First, there are three time scores, one for each trial. These are totaled together to yield a total time score. Two additional scores are derived from the drawings after the test: one for Memory, a point being given for each correct shape remembered, and one for Location, a point for each correct shape placed in a correct position.

Trail Making Test

The Trail Making Test consists of two parts (part A and part B). Each part consists of 25 circles distributed randomly on an 8½ x 11 inch piece of white paper. In part A, there is a number, from 1 to 25, written inside each circle. In part B, there is either a number, from 1 to 13, or a letter, from A to L, written inside each circle.

Before beginning part A, the client is shown a sample page that has seven circles on it, each numbered between one and seven. The client is given a pencil and told to connect the circles, beginning at number one to the circle labelled number two and then to the circle labelled three and to continue until the end is reached. The client is also told to work as quickly as possible. If the subject completes the sample correctly, the test page is presented and completed.

If the subject fails to complete the sample correctly, the errors are explained. For example, one might say, "You did not complete the circles in order. You are to go from one to two to three rather than one to two to four." If the subject cannot complete the sample even after explanation, the subject should be guided through the correct sequence. Then, the subject is allowed to try alone. This process can be repeated until the subject successfully completes the sample or until it becomes clear that the subject is unable to complete the test.

When the actual test for part A begins, the instructions are repeated and are followed by the command to begin. The client is watched closely by the examiner. Any time a mistake is made, this is immediately told to the patient who is then allowed to continue from the point where the error was made. For example, the examiner might say, "You skipped a number," or "You failed to draw your line all the way to the last circle." The test is completed when the client correctly reaches the last circle. The score for the test is the time in seconds between the examiner saying "begin" and the client correctly reaching the last circle.

After part A is completed, the subject is given the sample from part B. The client is told to connect the circles by going from one to A to two to B, doing first a number, then a letter, then a number again. The subject is then allowed to do the sample. If it is correctly performed, the examiner presents the test page. If an error is made, the examiner follows the same procedures described for part A.

Except for the change in basic tasks, the test for part B is conducted exactly as the test for part A. Scoring for both parts is identical as well. In some cases, the examiner will find the subject unable to complete a section of the test (usually part B). In these cases, the subject can be stopped after 300 seconds.

Reitan-Klove Sensory Perceptual Exam

This examination consists of a number of separate procedures designed to measure sensory function.

The first test is for tactile imperception. The subject's hands are placed palm down on a table, and the examiner touches the right and left hand using a random sequence. The subject must report which hand is touched. During these trials, the examiner determines the pressure needed to get a consistent, accurate response from the subject.

The method of reporting may be changed if the subject cannot say "right" or "left" reliably. For example, subjects could raise the hand that was touched, or they could point to the word "right" or "left" after opening their eyes. The method of reporting is not important as long as only tactile input can be used by the client.

Some subjects are uanble to keep their eyes closed, especially those with right hemisphere injuries (Fisher, 1956). These subjects may be blindfolded, or their arms hidden from them behind a curtain or through a board. Again, the method is not important as long as the subject is denied visual feedback.

After these initial procedures, the subject is then touched on the left hand alone, right hand alone, or both hands together in a random order. Each type of touch should be repeated four times. The purpose of this procedure is to see if the subject can report the touch on both hands simultaneously. The failure to do so is a suppression. Suppressions are rare but of important diagnostic value. If the apparent suppression is due to a failure to sense the touch on one side because of inadequate pressure, however, the interpretation of the suppression changes considerably. Consequently, it is important to correctly use the pressure determined in the initial phase of the examination.

Additional suppressions can be determined for the right hand/left face combination and the left hand/right face combination. This is done by repeating the procedures used for the right and left hands discussed above.

A similar procedure may be used with auditory stimuli. The patients are told to keep their eyes closed and the examiner stands behind them. The examiner tells the subject that he or she will make a noise in the right ear (touching it) or the left ear (touching it). The subject must report in which ear the noise is made. The examiner makes the noise by rubbing two fingers together. The examiner determines the necessary level of loudness, and then alternates the four left, right, and simultaneous trials as was done for the tactile stimuli.

To determine suppressions for visual stimuli, the subject must fixate on the examiner's nose. If the subject cannot do so consistently, items can be presented only when the subject is fixating; this must be determined on a trial by trial basis by the examiner.

The visual trials are conducted by having the examiner sit three feet in front of the sitting client. The examiner extends her or his hands, and tells the subject it will be necessary to identify whether the hand on the (patient's) right or the (patient's) left is imoved. Then the sequences used for the tactile and auditory procedures are employed. The procedures are administered three times with the examiner's hands above eye level, examiner's hands at eye level, and the examiner's hands below eye level.

Patients will have a loss in peripheral vision in some cases. Examiners must then reduce the distance between their hands so the subject is able to report unilateral stimuli on both sides accurately. Some subjects may have a complete loss of one visual field (homonymous hemianopsia) which makes it impossible to test for suppressions, or partial loss in the upper and lower visual field on one side (upper or lower quadrantanopsia). In cases of partial loss, either above or below eye level, trials are omitted depending on the locus of the loss.

In all testing for suppressions, irrespective of the modality, the client is never told there may be bilateral stimulation, although most subjects soon realize this. In some cases, suppressions may appear to occur because the subject is not paying attention or gets confused. It is useful, in these cases, to redo the trials for that procedure to insure the reliability of the results (Goldstein, 1974). For all suppression procedures, scores are the number of suppressions separately recorded for left and right. If more than four trials are given, this is indicated.

After completing the suppression procedure, the examiner begins the Finger Agnosia procedure. This tests the ability of the subject to identify which finger is touched by the examiner. In this test, subjects close their eyes, or are prevented from seeing their hands in an alternate manner. The fingers of the subject's hands (first right, then left) are then touched four times each in a random order.

The subject reports by saying the name of the finger touched (i.e., thumb, forefinger, middle finger) or a number assigned to the finger (one through five). The system of naming or numbering the finger is determined before the procedure, and should reflect a method the subject prefers. If a subject cannot use a verbal response, the subject might respond by raising the appropriate finger or touching it with the other hand. Scoring is the number of errors out of 20 (five fingers × four) trials.

The next procedure is fingertip number writing. The examiner writes numbers (three, four, five, or six) on the subject's hands which the subject must identify. The examiner begins the procedure by writing the numbers three, four, five, and six on the subject's palm and identifying each number. If the subject requests, the examiner can modify how the numbers are written. Then the subjects close their eyes (or use any of the other procedures discussed above for limiting visual information) and the examiner writes numbers on each finger of the right hand, proceeding from the thumb to the little finger. This is repeated four times. The number to be written at each trial is given on the scoring form. The procedure is then repeated for the left hand. The score for each hand is the number of errors out of 20 trials.

In the coin recognition procedure, the examiner places a penny, nickel, and a dime into the subject's right hand and then left hand. The subject must identify the coin by touch alone, and is not allowed to rub it on other objects or do anything except feel the coin. If the subject is able to identify coins in one hand alone, the examiner places a coin in each hand simultaneously, either two pennies, two nickels, or two dimes. The subject is not told the coins are the same. The score is the number of errors made for each hand.

The Tactile Form Recognition Test uses four shapes cut out of plastic: a square, triangle, circle, and cross. These shapes are available to place in the patient's hand, and are also mounted at the top of a board with a hole in it. The subjects alternately place their right and left hands through the hole. The examiner then places a plastic shape in the subject's hand. The subject feels the shape and points to the correct shape mounted on the board with the other (free) hand. Subjects first place their right hand through the board. All four shapes are placed in the subject's hand, one at a time. The order of presentation of the shapes is given on the scoring forms. The procedure is then repeated with the left hand, right hand again, and the left hand again. Two scores are determined: the number of errors for each hand and time measures. Time measures for each item are calculated by measuring the time from placement of the shape in the palm of the subject's hand and the subject's answer. These times are summed to get a total right hand, and left hand time.

Aphasia Screening Test

This test consists of a survey of the major forms of aphasia. A booklet of items, containing pictures and words to be recognized or read, is necessary to administer the test. The test requires the subject to (a) name objects; (b) spell words; (c) draw shapes, including a Greek cross; (d) read letters and numbers; (e) read words; (f) read sentences; (g) write words; (h) pronounce words; (i) write sentences; (j) explain concepts; (k) do arithmetic, on paper and in one's head; (l) discriminate body parts; and (m) tell right from left. Items must be presented exactly as described in the manual, and any deviations from the correct answer is counted as an error.

Two systems of scoring exist. In the first, the score is the number of items in which there is an error. In the second, a weighted scoring system is used. More points are scored for items seen as more significant. The weights for each item are presented in Russell, Neuringer, and Goldstein (1970).

Lateral Dominance Exam

This is a set of procedures attempting to establish the hand, eye, and foot dominance of the individual and the relative functioning of the right and left hands.

The first items on the test determine the subject's ability to follow the test's instructions. The subject is asked to do such things as "show me your right hand." The next section attempts to determine the subject's hand dominance. The subject is asked to demonstrate how to do seven things such as "throw a ball." The examiner notes which hand the subject uses. The subject is asked to write his or her name, the examiner noting the hand used and the time it takes. The subject is then asked to write their name using the other hand, and the time to do this is also recorded.

The subject is then asked to show how he or she would look through a toy telescope or shoot a toy rifle. The examiner notes the eye used in the first item, and the shoulder used in the second. The subject is then asked to show how a bug would be stepped on and a football kicked. The examiner notes the leg used.

The next procedure is the Miles ABC Test of Ocular Dominance. The subject must look through V-shaped scopes at various items. The subject does now know that only one eye can look through the scope at a time. The examiner holds the stimulus items directly below his or her eyes; the subject looks through the scope and the examiner determines the eye used. Ten trials are given. The score is the number of trials in which the right eye is used and the number of trials in which the left eye is used.

The final procedure is grip strength. This requires a dynamometer, preferably one which can be adjusted to the size of the patient's hands. Subjects take the dynamometer in their hands. The hand is extended downward, and the subject instructed to squeeze as hard as possible. Two trials are given for each hand. If the two trials differ by more than five kilograms (11 pounds), additional trials are given until two trials within five kilograms are available. These two trials do not have to be consecutive. The final score for each hand is the average of the two trials selected.

Halstead Finger Tapping Test

The Tapping Test uses a counter with an arm that is mounted on a flat board. The arm can be pressed down by the subject's index finger, and then returns to its original position. The subject is told to place his whole hand on the board with their index finger on the arm of the counter. The examiner instructs subjects to tap the key down, allow it to return and then tap it down again as quickly as possible. The proper method is demonstrated by the examiner.

The subject is then given five ten second trials with each hand, starting with the preferred hand. The subject is given a rest after the third trial. Additional rest periods may be included if the subject appears fatigued.

The scores on each hand must be within five taps to be acceptable. If this is not the case, additional trails are given until five trials within five taps are obtained. This is usually achieved within eight trials. The final score are the averages of the five trials selected for each hand.

One major problem in this test is the tendency of some subjects to move the whole hand or arm instead of just the index finger. In these cases the subject should be informed of the failure to follow instructions, and the trial begun over again. In those few cases where the subject is unable to tap with the hand and arm immobilized, the examiner must attempt to get as close an approximation as possible. Since these subjects generally do quite badly even with the nonstandardized administration, this does not actually affect the interpretation of the results significantly.

Category Test

The Category Test has been found to be the most sensitive test in the Halstead-Reitan to the presence of brain dysfunction. Numerous studies have found that the test is highly effective in differentiating brain injured and normal subjects. Wheeler, Burke and Reitan (1963) found that the test was able to achieve a hit rate of nearly 90 percent. The optimal cutoff point for the test has been found to lie between 50 and 51 errors (Halstead, 1947).

Impairment in the Category Test may reflect a number of underlying deficits in the ability to sustain attention, remember past performance, learn from reward and punishment, concentrate, evaluate past performance, analyze visually presented material, understand spatial relationships, and flexibility to handle a complex, changing problem. It is this complexity of skills demanded by the test that makes it sensitive to brain impairment of all kinds.

It can be difficult to identify the specific reasons for poor performance on the Category Test in an individual subject. In many cases, the reasons are multiple and impossible to separate. In other cases, comparison of Category performance with performance on other tests in the battery can yield information on the underlying deficits. For example, if tests of visual-spatial performance are normal, this can be ruled out as a cause of the deficit. If visual-spatial deficits are prominent, and Category test performance is impaired on the subtests demanding strong spatial skills (subtests five and six), this can be regarded as a major cause of the deficit.

In cases where the Category Test is impaired while most other tests show normal performance, the deficit is generally in the patient's ability to evaluate their own performance, to learn from the combination of missed and accurately guessed items, and to form hypothesis relating feedback to the items. These are generally abilities associated with the frontal lobes (especially in the left hemisphere). Consequently, significantly impaired Category performance with otherwise generally normal performance may indicate the presence of a frontal lobe disorder. When the Category Test and other tests show impairment, this may indicate lesions almost anywhere in the cerebral hemisphere.

The same features that make the Category Test highly sensitive to brain injury make the test sensitive to many forms of thought disorder, especially schizophrenia. Several studies have found the test (and the battery as a whole) unable to differentiate chronic schizophrenics and organics. Other studies, however, have supported the ability of the Category Test and the Halstead-Battery to differentiate schizophrenics and organics.

The studies finding negative results usually used populations made up of chronic, long-term schizophrenics on medication which affected their ability to perform on the Category Test. The more successful studies generally used more acute populations and controlled for the effects of medication and motivation in a schizophrenic population. Even in these cases, however, the accuracy of the Category Test is reduced. For example, Golden (1978) found that is was necessary to raise the cutoff point for the Category Test from 51 to 64 errors when using an acute schizophrenic control group. The hit rate for the Category Test was consequently reduced to 70 percent.

A second factor in the poor performance of some non-brain injured subjects is the close correlation between the Category Test results and age and IQ. Logue and Allen (1971) found a correlation of .71 with IQ, for example. In clinical practice, it is important to take these factors into account when interpreting the meaning of a score on the Category Test.

Speech Sounds Perception Test

The Speech Sounds Perception Test measures the ability of a subject to discriminate speech sounds and match them to their written representation. Thus, subjects must have the ability to hear and code speech into phonemes, to match phonemes to their alphabetic equivalents, and to find the appropriate answer and underline it. Disability in any of these areas can affect performance adversely.

Halstead (1947) suggested that the test might be a measure of interference, as he found that subjects missed the second phoneme in an item much more often thàn the first. The first phoneme, he suggested, interferes with the second. Such a view, however, would predict that performance would worsen over the course of the test as interference built up from succeeding items. Golden and Anderson (1977), however, found that the opposite occurs: performance improves as the test proceeds.

Wheeler, Burke and Reitan (1963) found the Rhythm test 75 percent accurate overall. Unlike speech sounds, rhythm is more effective in discriminating brain injured patients (82 percent) than normal controls (72 percent). As is common in tests highly sensitive to brain injury, the hit rates are considerably reduced when a psychiatric control group is used. Golden (1977) reported an overall hit rate of 70 percent using an acute psychiatric control group. The optimal cutoff point for the Rhythm Test is between four and five errors.

Tactual Performance Test

The Tactual Performance Test is highly sensitive to the presence of brain injury because of the complex pattern of skills demanded. The test requires adequate motor control in both the right and left arm, as well as kinesthetic and proprioceptive feedback which enables subjects to locate and move their arms in space without visual feedback. In addition to these basic skills, the subject must also be able to plan a logical and efficient approach to the test in order to place the blocks quickly. Finally, the Location and Memory scores place great demands on incidental and spatial memory. The test is effective because most brain injuries involve impairment to one or more of these many abilities.

Six scores are derived from the Tactual Performance Test which can be used in interpretation. The first score is the total time it takes to finish the three trials. Using a cutoff of 15.7 minutes (942 seconds) is highly effective in discriminating between brain injured and normal patients (Halstead, 1974; Reitan, 1955). Even in the difficult discrimination between acute schizophrenics and brain injured populations, the test is 70 percent effective (Golden, 1977).

The Location Score has also been found to be one of the most sensitive discriminators of brain injured and normal subjects. Wheeler, Burke and Reitan (1963) reported an 85 percent hit rate in a normal population and a 64 percent hit rate in a control population; with psychiatric controls, Golden (1978) reported 77 percent accuracy in the brain injured group and 67 percent accuracy in the controls. As these figures suggest, this score is much less affected by schizophrenia than is the Category Test or Rhythm Test. The Memory score is also highly effective: 74 percent hit rate in normals, 77 percent in brain injured patients, and 80 percent in psychiatric controls. The optimal cutoff point for Memory is between five and six items correct; for Location, it is between four and five correct.

In addition to these scores, the raw scores for the right, left and both hands trials are also useful. A comparison of the right hand and left hand performance is useful in establishing the hemispheric localization of an injury. If the right hand score is 40 percent or more longer than the left hand score, this is suggestive of a left hemisphere injury. If the left hand score is not at least 30 percent better than the right hand score, a right hemisphere injury is suggested. Overall poor performance on all measures is suggestive of a right hemisphere or diffuse injury.

The TPT may also be used to locate an injury in the anterior (front) or posterior (back) areas of the hemisphere. If the Tactual Performance Test on the right hand is performed more poorly than measures of motor skills (Finger Tapping, strength), it suggests posterior injury. If the relationship is reversed, it suggests an anterior injury. Similar conclusions may be reached about the status of the right hemisphere using the left hand performance. Anterior injuries involving the *prefrontal* lobes, however, can often be seen by poor performance on the Tactual Performance Test which are not accompanied by the tactile deficits normally seen in posterior injuries or by motor deficits seen in other frontal injuries.

Trail Making Test

The Trail Making Test, especially part B, is a highly sensitive test of brain dysfunction. Part A requires basic motor and spatial skills from a patient, as well as the ability to count. Part B requires each of the abilities used in part A, as well as the ability to remember and follow a complex plan (alternating numbers and letters) and to be cognitively flexible in executing the plan.

Extensive research has found the Trail Making Test to be very effective in discriminating brain injury and normal controls, with hit rates of about 85 percent. The optimal cutoff point for part A is between 39 and 40 seconds; for part B, between 91 and 92 seconds.

Comparison of the performance on parts A and B yield valuable information. If part A is impaired, but part B performance is better (B is less than twice A), this indicates the problem is basically either spatial (right hemisphere) or due to a dominant hand motor deficit (usually left hemisphere). If part B is impaired compared to the performance on part A (B is greater than three times A), the deficit involves handling verbal material (left hemisphere) or the frontal lobe skills of planning and flexibility. Left frontal disorders may be seen in poor performance on part B and the Category Test without impairment on most other tests. Poor performance on both part A and part B suggests either a diffuse injury or massive involvement of one hemisphere (such as a massive hemorrhage).

A number of studies have questioned the usefulness of the Trail Making Test in psychiatric populations. A good source on the Trail Making Test usually rules out brain damage in a psychiatric population, but a bad score did not necessarily indicate brain damage. Goldstein and Neuringer (1966) emphasized the importance of looking at the qualitative dimensions of performance in psychiatric populations. They found that brain injured patients were less likely to show bizarre behavior when given the test. Schizophrenics were more likely to give up on the test. Organics who failed often had trouble with the alterations required. Using these signs, the authors reported 83 percent in the schizophrenic group and 70 percent accuracy in the brain injured group. Golden (1978), limiting his population to acute schizophrenics and using procedures designed to eliminate problems of motivation and bizarre behavior, found the test had an overall accuracy of 80 percent. In general, then, it appears that subjects who can be motivated to do the test can be discriminated accurately; most of the loss of accuracy comes in the inability to get adequate performance samples from some chronic schizophrenic patients.

Sensory-Perceptual Examination

The presence of lateralized sensory-perceptual dysfunction almost always indicates some kind of damage to the central nervous system. This damage may be in the spinal cord or brain stem instead of the cerebral hemispheres, however, especially in subjects where the only deficits are sensory and motor in nature.

As was observed earlier, suppressions are rare but extremely significant. Golden (1977) found that over 90 percent of the subjects with reliable suppressions were in the brain damaged group, irrespective of the modality in which the suppression occurred. A suppression almost always suggests a destructive lesion in the hemisphere opposite the side of the injury (e.g., right tactile suppression implies a left hemisphere injury). Tactile suppressions imply damage to the opposite parietal lobe; auditory suppressions suggest damage to the opposite temporal lobe; and visual suppressions are related to damage in the opposite occipital lobe. Because of the significance of these signs, it is imperative that the examiner insure that suppressions are reliable and not due to wandering attention on the part of the subject.

Finger Agnosia is most common to injuries of the parietal lobe. The most severe form of finger agnosia problems is seen in left parietal injuries. In the classic form, the subject is unable to perform this task on either hand, showing extremely poor performance (generally at chance levels). In the less severe forms, left parietal injuries may be reflected in a Finger Agnosia deficit on the right hand relative to the left hand. Generally, the errors on the right hand must exceed the errors on the left hand by three or more errors for the results to be reliable. Conversely, three or more errors on the left hand as compared to the right hand implies right parietal involvement.

Fingertip Number Writing can be analyzed in much the same way as Finger Agnosia. Fingertip Number Writing is a more sensitive test than Finger Agnosia, however. Consequently, injuries near the parietal lobe (such as a tumor in the temporal lobe) may affect Fingertip Number Writing more severely than Finger Agnosia. When both are down equally, the injury is likely to be in the parietal lobe itself. Because of the sensitivity of this test, a decline in Tactual Performance Scores without an effect on Fingertip Number Writing is often indicative of a frontal rather than a parietal disorder.

The Coin Recognition Test is difficult to interpret since many clients are unable to recognize coins, even when presented singly. If this is the case, the test cannot be interpreted. If the person can accurately distinguish coins singly but not together, however, this is indicative of an injury to the parietal areas of the hemisphere opposite the side of the errors, especially if other tactile signs are present as well. Impairment on this test alone should be interpreted cautiously.

The Tactile Recognition Test is a more reliable measure of the inability to recognize objects by touch (astereognosis). More errors on one hand than the other strongly indicates brain injury in the opposite parietal lobe. Errors on both hands suggest a diffuse brain injury or an inability to comprehend instructions, as is seen with some injuries to the left hemisphere as well as in severe functional disorders.

Aphasia Exam

Aphasia symptoms are a common result of brain injury. It is especially common to see individuals with cerebrovascular disorders of the left middle cerebral artery with severe aphasic disorders. Consequently, all valid tests of aphasia are generally highly effective in identifying many brain injured patients. Reitan (1959) found that the number of aphasia symptoms were directly related to the likelihood of brain damage. Twenty percent of the patients with no errors had brain damage, while 38 percent of the patients with one error showed brain damage. Eighty-six percent of the patients with two errors had brain injury, while 100 percent of the patients with four or more errors were brain injured. Using the weighted scoring system proposed by Russell, Neuringer and Goldstein (1970), Golden (1978) found that 90 percent of the left brain injured patients had seven or more points, while only 55 percent of the diffuse and 41 percent of the right hemisphere patients showed a total of seven or more points. Only 27 percent of the psychiatric patients showed that many errors.

The Aphasia Test may also be used to localize brain injury. If errors involve the drawing items alone, the injury is likely to be in the right hemisphere. If only verbal items are missed, the injury is probably in the left hemisphere. If both types of items are missed, the injury is likely to be in the left hemisphere or diffuse. Mathematical items may be missed by patients with injuries in either hemisphere.

Finger Tapping Test

Motor functions have long been recognized by clinical neurology as a significant sign of brain dysfunction. This is especially true when one hand performs significantly worse than the other hand. Performance by the dominant hand that is not at least 5 to 10 percent better than the non-dominant hand is generally considered significantly impaired; performance by the nondominant hand which is 20 percent or more below that of the dominant hand is considered poor (Golden, 1978). Lateralization of the injury is to the hemisphere opposite the impaired hand.

Most research on Finger Tapping has looked at the level of performance rather than the comparison of the left and right hands. Wheeler, Burke, and Reitan (1963) found their brain damaged patients showed impairment in level of performance 79 percent of the time, while half the control group also showed impairment. Golden (1977) found similar results for a brain injured group, and somewhat better results for the psychiatric controls (58 percent). In general, the literature suggests that impairment on this motor task is usually seen in brain injured patients, but is also seen frequently in control individuals as well. The test is probably more reliable when the results show a lateralized deficit on one hand compared to the other. The optimal cutoff point for the dominant hand is between 50 and 51 taps; for the nondominant hand, between 45 and 46 taps.

Lateral Dominance

It is usually assumed that the hand a subject writes with is the dominant hand. Most subjects give consistent results: the hand used for writing is used for other tasks as well. Foot dominance is determined by the answers to the two questions involving the football and the bug. Eye dominance is assessed by the ABC Vision Test. Scores of eight or more to either the left or right eye suggest the dominance of that eye; if the scores are seven–three, six–four, or five–five, this suggests that neither eye has clear dominance.

The meaning of mixed dominance, where eye, hand, and foot dominance do not match, is unclear. While it may be associated with brain injury, especially cases of early brain injury, it can also be caused by peripheral factors such as weakness in one eye or arm. It has little meaning by itself consequently; however, if it is combined with other signs suggesting early brain injury (see Chapter 1 on WAIS) then it can be used as an additional piece of confirming data.

If an individual is left handed or mixed dominant, the clinician must evaluate the possibility of verbal functions being located in the right rather than the left hemisphere. In such individuals, many of the score relationships discussed here are reversed, except for those relating to motor and sensory function. In cases where dominance for one side is incomplete, psychological skills such as speech may be represented in both hemispheres. The interpretation is more difficult and more tentative in such individuals.

Strength of grip measures can be interpreted in much the same manner as finger tapping. If the dominant hand is weaker or less than 5 percent better than the nondominant hand, this suggests an injury to the dominant hemisphere. Conversely, if the strength in the nondominant hand is 20 percent or more below the strength of the dominant hand, this may indicate an injury to the nondominant hemisphere. Norms for dynamometers differ with the instrument used.

Impairment Index

The Impairment Index was designed by Halstead (1947) to reflect overall performance on his battery of tests. When Reitan began using the battery clinically, he soon dropped two of Halstead's tests from his battery and from the Impairment Index. The revised Impairment Index included the Rhythm Test, Speech Sounds Perception Test, Finger Tapping, Category Test, Tactual Performance Test, Total Time, Memory and Location. Others have also prepared Impairment Indexes including, along with the Halstead tests, the Trail Making Test, Aphasia Test, the Sensory Exam, and other tests. Each of these Impairment Indexes were calculated in a similar manner. The Index equalled the number of tests in the index which fell beyond a predetermined cutoff point divided by the total number of tests included in the index. For example, Reitan's Index equalled the number of tests impaired divided by seven. Each of these indexes had a minimum score of zero (no impairment) and a maximum score of one (all tests in the brain injured range).

Subsequently, other systems have been suggested. Russell, Neuringer, and Goldstein (1970) rated the performance on each test on a zero (good performance) to five (poor performance) scale. The Impairment Index was then the average of these ratings. Kiernan and Matthews (1976) have suggested converting all scores into T scores and averaging the T scores. The latter has the advantage that T scores can be corrected for age effects, an important factor in several of the tests.

Although this array of different methods for calculating the Impairment Index would appear to make evaluation of it impossible, the results with each index have been remarkably similar. Wheeler, Burke and Reitan (1963) reported that the original Reitan impairment index was 90 percent effective in discriminating brain injured and normal subjects. Similarly, Kiernan and Matthews (1976) reported between 72 and 84 percent accuracy in a more difficult to discriminate population. The results of other studies have been in the same range with most studies reporting discriminations of 80 to 95 percent. The differences between studies have been largely related to the composition of the control and experimental groups.

As might be expected from the discussion of the individual tests, the more schizophrenic the control group the poorer the results that are achieved. With groups of chronic schizophrenics the differentiation between controls and brain injured patients may be minimal. Several studies, however, have identified some of the factors responsible for this, including the lack of motivation, the medication patients are taking, a lack of cooperation, a history of electroconvulsive therapy, and the failure to rule out brain damage as a possible cause in many chronic schizophrenics.

INTERPRETATION OF INDIVIDUAL TESTS

Several major methods of interpretation are employed in examining the effectiveness of the separate tests within the Halstead-Reitan. The first method, the level of performance approach, establishes an optimal cutoff point. Performance worse than the cutoff is classified as brain injured while better performance is classified as normal. The accuracy of these classifications is expressed as the *hit rate*. By chance, the hit rate for a given test is 50 percent. Consequently, hit rates must be significantly above this level for a test to be considered useful.

The second approach is a comparison of performance on one side of the body as compared to the other. This method is generally employed with tests of motor and sensory function. More impairment on one side of the body is taken to indicate brain injury. A similar method compares scores representative of left brain function (verbal skills) to those representative of right hemisphere (nonverbal skills). Significant impairment on one as compared to the other implies brain dysfunction of some kind.

DETERMINING THE PRESENCE OF BRAIN DYSFUNCTION

The presence of brain damage can be inferred in several different ways. The first method involves the Impairment Index. Scores greater than .4 have been found to be highly associated with brain damage. This procedure will miss 10 to 20 percent of the cases with actual brain damage. In general, the cases missed include very mild or fully recovered cases of brain dysfunction, as well as cases of idiopathic epilepsy (cases of epilepsy with no demonstrable etiology). This also includes cases in the areas of the brain which are largely "silent" in the sense that no current test can measure deficits caused by injury in those areas.

In a similar manner, 10 to 30 percent of the cases identified as brain damaged will not be. This can be due to a failure to perform adequate age corrections in older populations. Misidentifications may also occur in psychiatric populations, especially with chronic schizophrenics. This can be minimized by insuring optimal testing conditions: shorter sessions to control for attentional difficulties, discontinuation of medication that interferes with performance on psychological tests, and reinforcements to motivate the client to cooperate. It is also necessary for the clinician to recognize those situations when adequate test data has not been collected and to refuse to reach conclusions based on such data.

Errors may also occur in subjects with low intelligence. Such discrimination is especially difficult since low IQ scores are associated with many forms of brain damage, especially those which occur early in a child's life or result in generalized destruction of the brain. It is important in these cases to be aware of the performance expected of individuals at various IQ levels who are not brain damaged. Those who are brain damaged generally show poorer results, more lateralized motor and sensory deficits, as well as patterns suggestive of a given brain locus or process (see next sections).

IQ can also be used to avoid missing cases of brain injury in high IQ subjects. These subjects may show normal or superior performance after a brain injury and may be missed when examining the level of their performance. Using the IQ, however, can tell the clinician that the "normal" performance is substantially below what would be expected of a given client, a clue which can lead to the correct diagnosis.

In addition to the Impairment Index, performance on other tests may point to brain dysfunction. For example, Reitan (as reported earlier) has found that four or more errors on the Aphasia Test almost always indicates brain damage. Significant lateralized deficits on motor and sensory tests almost always indicates central nervous system dysfunction, except when there are peripheral nerve or muscle disease. The presence of reliable suppressions is almost always related to brain dysfunction, usually of a serious nature.

Conclusions reached by these first two methods should be checked against the last method of inferring brain dysfunction. This method examines the data for patterns of results indicating a particular locus of dysfunction or a specific cause of the dysfunction. This method allows the clinician to recognize brain dysfunction in mild cases, as well as to rule out deficits causes by other problems such as spinal cord damage or schizophrenia.

LATERALIZATION

Lateralization involves the analysis of neuropsychological test results to discover if a brain injury is located in a specific hemisphere. This process requires a knowledge of the effects of brain damage in each hemisphere of the brain and the probable meaning of the performance on any single test or combination of tests within the battery.

Left Hemisphere

The major measures reflecting left hemisphere involvement are verbal tests. Impairment on Speech Sounds, the verbal items on the Aphasia Test, Trail Making Test (part B as compared to part A), and the Verbal tests on the WAIS, and a lower verbal IQ than performance IQ are suggestive of left hemisphere involvement.

Results of any motor or sensory test indicating poor right hand or body performance implies left hemisphere involvement. On finger tapping or grip strength, the right hand should be about 5 to 15 percent faster or stronger than the left hand. Poor right hand performance on the Tactual Performance Test is also indicative of left hemisphere involvement, especially when the left hand performance is 40 percent or more better.

Right Hemisphere

The major measures of right hemisphere involvement are poor ability to draw (especially the Greek cross on the Aphasia Test), poor performance on the WAIS spatial tests (except Digit Symbol), poorer performance on the Rhythm Test as compared to Speech Perception, equal or poorer performance on Trails A as compared to Trails B, and Digit Backwards (with a normal Digits Forward on Digit Span).

Deficits on the left hand or left side of the body on motor or sensory tests indicate right hemisphere dysfunction. If the left hand is nondominant, tapping speed should not be less than 85 percent of the right hand, tapping speed. On the Tactual Performance Test, the left hand speed should be at least 30 percent faster than the right. Overall poor performance on the Tactual Performance Test suggests right hemisphere or diffuse dysfunction, as does poor performance on the Memory scores of the Tactual Performance Test.

Diffuse and General Indications

Several scores are general indicators of brain damage and do not suggest a specific lateralization. The major tests like this are the Category Test and the Total Time and Location scores of the Tactual Performance Test. Digit Symbol is considered a general indicator from the WAIS.

Poor performance on both Trails A and B, on both the right and left hand in a sensory or motor task, low IQ's, and generally poor performance on the WAIS suggests diffuse impairment. Poor overall performance on all tests also indicates a diffuse disorder.

LOCALIZATION

In cases which are found to be lateralized, the injury is often localized within the hemisphere. Localization is the process of determining the locus within the hemisphere. This is done in much the same way as lateralization is determined, matching the test results to general deficits expected from the involvement of each lobe.

The following discussion highlights the major deficits associated with each common locus of injury. It should be recognized that in actual practice the results will vary considerably across individuals. In addition, lesions are not confined to the neat boundaries necessary in describing research results. Finally, the behavioral effects of a lesion are not necessarily restricted to the physical boundaries of a lesion. For example, a tumor may interfere with the function of other areas of the brain by pressure or by disrupting cerebral circulation (Smith, 1975). Any localization, as a consequence, must be considered approximate and a better measure of the behavioral effects of a lesion rather than its physical boundaries.

Frontal Lobes

Many small lesions in some areas of the frontal lobe may show little behavioral deficit, while other lesions may disrupt behavior on a global basis. Bilateral lesions may cause especially marked disintegration of all voluntary behavior. Thus, lesions relatively near each other in these areas may cause markedly dissimilar results.

Lesions of the left prefrontal areas, the most forward parts of the brain, may result in deficits on tests of categorizing and flexibility. Thus, the Category Test and Trail Making Test (part B) may be impaired while other tests on the battery are normal. Such injuries rarely cause deficits on the WAIS or on motor and sensory tests (Smith, 1964, 1966). The right hand on the Tactual Performance will be impaired in a few cases, but no other sensory symptoms will be present.

As the lesion moves back towards the central sulcus the patient is more likely to show severe deficits on Finger Tapping, and in motor speech tasks (speaking, writing). Grip Strength may be affected, as will all tests which have a significant motor component (e.g., Digit Symbol). The Tactual Performance Test, right hand, will be affected but the left hand trial will not be relatively impaired. Speech Sounds and Rhythm will generally be intact.

If the lesion is in the right prefrontal areas, there may be no deficits although Category Test impairment may occur. McFie (1969, 1975) has associated poor performance on Picture Arrangement with right frontal deficits; in other cases Digits Backwards may be affected (Mahan, 1976).

Deficits may sometimes be seen on complex spatial tasks (Block Design, Tactual Performance Test) but not in overall IQ (Benton, 1968; Smith, 1966). As the lesion is moved back, deficits on Finger Tapping (left hand) will be seen. In some cases, there will be deficits on the Rhythm Test.

Temporal Lobes

The temporal lobes are primarily concerned with auditory functions. The presence of auditory suppressions is related to severe injury in the opposite temporal lobe.

The left temporal lobe is responsible for phonemic decoding (Luria, 1966). Low scores will often be seen on Speech Sounds. Rhythm may be impaired, but not as severely as speech sounds. Numerous aphasia symptoms may be seen in speaking, reading, writing, or any task which requires phonemic discrimination. Digit Span will often be impaired, as may Similarities (McFie, 1975).

Lesions to the right temporal will often cause Rhythm deficits, although this is not always the case (Fedio and Mirsky, 1968; Reitan, undated). Deficits may also be seen in Object Assembly, Picture Arrangement, and Digit Symbol (McFie, 1975; Meier and French, 1966).

Visual deficits may occur in deeper lesions since the optic tracts pass through the temporal lobe. If the lesion is in the left temporal, this may cause right upper quadrantanopsia, loss of the upper right visual field. In the right temporal lobe, this may cause left upper quadrantanopsia.

Temporal lobe disorders may also show motor and sensory deficits because of the proximity of the motor and sensory areas of the brain. Generally, these motor deficits are mild; the sensory deficit is seen on the most sensitive tests of sensory function, Fingertip Number Writing, and the Tactual Performance Test. In many cases temporal lobe injuries will look like a cross between a frontal lobe and parietal lobe injury.

Parietal Lobes

The parietal lobes are involved in tactile input and the integration of auditory, visual, and tactile input. Because of the importance of these functions, parietal deficits are generally seen quite clearly on neuropsychological tests.

Deficits in either parietal lobe will generally cause sensory deficits on the opposite side of the body. Depending on the severity and precise location of an injury, there will be deficits on the tests of tactile suppression, the Tactile Form Recognition Test, Finger Agnosia, Fingertip Number Writing, and the Tactual Performance Test. The Tactual Performance Test will be more impaired than the Finger Tapping Test. Fingertapping will be impaired to some degree, as well as other motor tasks since these require Kinesthetic/proprioceptive feedback (motor deficits due to sensory loss is termed ataxia).

Left parietal deficits will result in right sided sensory losses. Deficits will also be seen on the Arithmetic, Digit Span, and Block Design Tests of the WAIS (McFie, 1969) as well as a loss in IQ. Trails B will be poorly performed. Subjects may demonstrate a variety of aphasic symptoms: inability to name objects; dysnomia; reading deficits, dyslexia; writing problems, dysgraphia; and arithmetic problems, dyscalculia. Lesions of the parietal-temporal-occipital junction may cause a complete loss of verbal skills, global aphasia.

Heimburger and his associates (1964) found that the presence of Gerstmann's syndrome was usually associated with left parietal injuries, Gerstmann's syndrome includes finger agnosia, agraphia, acalculia and right-left confusion.

Lesions of the right parietal may result in complete deterioration of performance on the Tactual Performance Test, or a specific loss in the left hand, as well as minor motor deficits. Right parietal lesions also cause deficits in drawing, especially of the Greek cross (construction dyspraxia) (Wheeler and Reitan, 1963; Wheeler, 1963). Deficits are also found on the Trail Making Test (especially part A), Block Design, Picture Arrangement, and arithmetic items that demand "carrying" and spatial orientation (McFie, 1975; Golden, 1977).

A major symptom of right parietal injury, as well as other right hemisphere injuries, is unilateral spatial neglect. In this disorder, patients will ignore the left side of stimulus items. They will draw only the right side of the Greek cross, or read only the right half of a sentence.

Parietal lobe injuries may also cause lower quandrantanopsia, loss of the lower visual field. The loss would be in the left visual field in the right parietal, and the right visual field in the left parietal. In lesions which involve both the parietal and temporal lobe, there may be a complete interruption of the optic tracts. This causes homonymous hemianopsia, a complete loss of the opposite visual field.

Occipital Lobes

Occipital lobe lesions may also cause homonymous hemianopsia, as the occipital lobes are the termination of the optic tracts in each hemisphere. When the deficit is in the right occipital lobe, there is often unilateral spatial neglect as described above. Less extensive deficits in the occipital lobes may cause irregular deficits in the visual field (scotomas).

Occipital deficits may result in visual agnosia, an inability to recognize objects by sight. This will interfere with performance on such tests as

Picture Arrangement, Object Assembly, and Picture Completion. If the deficit is in the left occipital lobe, there may be a loss of the ability to recognize visual verbal stimuli. This can result in an inability to read, dyslexia, or seriously impair reading speed.

Organizing Test Data

With the information outlined above and in Chapter 1, all the poor results on the Test Battery can be classified as indicating left, right, or diffuse brain injury. For example, the normative data presented previously, and in Table 9-1, can be used to classify the data in the sample case presented in Table 9-2.

The Category score in Table 9-2 suggests significant brain dysfunction. The score is placed in a summary column (Table 9-3) labelled "Diffuse/General Impairment." The Speech Sounds score suggests left hemisphere damage and is placed under the left hemisphere column. The Rhythm performance is normal and so is not included in the table. (Some clinicians prefer to include the good tests as well; these can be included by

Table 9-1

Ranges for Brain Injured Performance on the
Halstead-Reitan*

Test	Brain Injured Range
Category Test	>50 errors
Tactual Performance Test—Total Time	>942 seconds
Tactual Performance Test—Memory	<6 correct
Tactual Performance Test—Location	<5 correct
Rhythm Test	>4 errors
Speech Sounds Perception test	>7 errors
Finger Tapping Test (Dominant)	<51 taps
Finger Tapping Test (Nondominant)	<46 taps
Impairment Index	>0.4
Trail Making Test (part A)	>39 seconds
Trail Making Test (part B)	>91 seconds
Suppressions (all modalities)	>0
Finger Agnosia	>2 errors
Fingertip Number Writing	>3 errors
Tactile Form Recognition	>0 errors
Grip Strength (Dominant)	<40 kg.
Grip Strength (Nondominant)	<35 kg.
Aphasia Exam	>6 points or 72 errors

*Norms adopted from Halstead (1947), Reitan (undated), Russell, Neuringer, and Goldstein (1970), Golden (1977), and Golden (1978).

Table 9-2

Sample Case (right-handed, 25 years old, 12th grade education)

Category		Tactile Form Recognition	
78 errors		Right	28 secs/0 errors
		Left	28 secs/0 errors
Speech Sounds		Wechsler Adult Intelligence Scale	
14 errors		Vocabulary	12
Rhythm		Comprehension	10
2 errors		Similarities	10
		Digit Span	7
Tactual Performance Test		Arithmetic	7
Right Hand	600″	Information	11
Left Hand	300″	Digit Symbol	6
Both Hands	240″	Picture Completion	10
Location	3	Block Design	8
Memory	7	Picture Arrangement	8
Total	1140″	Object Assembly	10
Finger Tapping		VIQ	96
Right	48 taps	PIQ	90
Left	48 taps	FSIQ	93
Suppressions		Aphasia	
None		Dyslexia	
Finger Agnosia		Mild Dysarthria	
Right	8 errors	Mild Dysnomia	
Left	3 errors	Trail Making Test	
Fingertip Number Writing		Part A	22 secs
Right	12 errors	Part B	108 secs
Left	5 errors		

putting the name of the test on the form with brackets around the test name.)

The total score on the Tactual Performance Test is placed in the general column. Since the right hand score is 100 percent worse than the left hand score, these scores are placed under the left hemisphere column. The Location score is placed under the general column.

The Finger Tapping Performance of the right hand fails to exceed the left hand score. Consequently, this is placed under the left hemisphere column. Both Finger Agnosia and Fingertip Number Writing show clear right hand deficits and are also listed under the left hemisphere column.

The Wechsler scores show relative deficits on Digit Span and Arithmetic. These are both listed under the left hemisphere column. Of the Performance Tests, Block Design, Picture Arrangement, and Digit Sym-

Table 9-3

Organization of Scores for the Sample Case

Left	Diffuse/General	Right
Speech Sounds (14)	Category (78)	Block Design (8)
TPT (R = 600, L = 300)	TPT Total (1140″)	Picture Arrangement (8)
Finger Tapping (R = L = 48)	Location (3)	
Finger Anosia (R = 8, L = 3)	VIQ = 96, PIQ = 90	
Fingertip Number Writing (RT = 12, L = 5)	Digit Symbol (6)	
Trails B > Trails A (B = 108, A = 22)	<Vocabulary (12)>	
Digit Span (7)	Impairment = .71	
Arithmetic (7)		
Dyslexia		
Dysarthria		
Dysnomia		

bol are relatively impaired. Block Design and Picture Arrangement are listed under the general column. The PIQ and VIQ do not differ sufficiently to suggest lateralization to either hemisphere, nor are they significantly impaired. They are still listed under the general column since they are important for analyzing the overall level of performance, however.

Three verbal aphasic symptoms were found and are listed in the left hemisphere column. On the Trail Making Test, part B, is impaired while part A is normal. Consequently, they are listed under the left hemisphere.

The Impairment Index is calculated last. Of the tests used by Reitan, five are impaired—Category, Speech Sounds, Tactual Performance Test Total, Finger Tapping, and Location. Thus the impairment index is 5/7 or .71. This is listed in the general column.

An examination of the final summary sheet suggests several initial conclusions. First, the Impairment Index and the many poorly performed tests, despite a normal IQ, clearly suggest that this is a case of brain impairment. Second, the overwhelming weight of the data suggests a left hemisphere difficulty.

Once a working hypothesis such as this is formed, the clinician must examine all the results to see if they are consistent with this hypothesis. Examination of the right hemisphere column shows only two tests, Block

Design and Picture Arrangement. Since both of these tests may be affected by left hemisphere damage, these scores are not inconsistent with the hypothesis. The results in the general column are not inconsistent with the hypothesis either, nor are there any tests performed well which should be impaired given such an injury.

In a number of circumstances, however, results might have been found that contradicted the hypothesis. For example, if a left hemisphere injury was hypothesized and the left hand of the Tactual Performance Test was performed much worse than the right, it would be necessary to change the hypothesis.

Overall one of several major hypothesis may be made in a given case:

1. Overall good performance with no significant deficits;
2. Good performance in one hemisphere but significant impairment in the other;
3. Impaired performance in both hemispheres but one considerably worse than the other;
4. Equally impaired performance in both hemispheres;
5. Scattered deficits; both hemispheres have apparent focal deficits;
6. Motor and sensory performance impaired on one or both sides, with cognitive performance intact; and
7. Cognitive performance impaired but motor/sensory abilities intact.

If the final decision involves a significant deficit in one hemisphere, a worse deficit in one hemisphere, or scattered deficits, the data is examined to see if there is a suggestion of localization within the hemispheres.

In the case presented in Table 9-2, there are significant right sensory deficits, impairment on the Tactual Performance Test (right hand), impairment in Block Design, Arithmetic, and Digit Span, and impairment in the Trail Making Test (part B). These deficits closely describe the deficits associated with left parietal disruption. This would be the most likely site for this lesion in this patient. It should be noted that this technique is applicable to any neuropsychological test battery.

PROCESS

Process identification is important in differentiating among neurological conditions as well as between neurological conditions and psychiatric disorders which cause symptoms similar to those of brain dysfunction. Process analysis can also aid the psychologist in recognizing neurological conditions which do not produce strong changes in level of performance but make reliable changes in pattern of performance. These two abilities are highly important in reducing the number of errors made in neuropsychological diagnosis.

The skill of accurately recognizing neurological process is based on familiarity and experience with neuropathological disorders and their neuropsychological correlates. Some of the basic dimensions of those correlates are described below.

Schizophrenia

As has been seen, the discrimination of schizophrenia and brain damage has been a major concern in clinical neuropsychology. The use of a test battery and insuring optimal test conditions reduces some of the problems involved in such a diagnosis. Even under optimal conditions, however, sizable numbers of schizophrenics show a level of performance indicative of brain dysfunction.

Patients with disorders suggesting localized, focal problems can be ruled out as schizophrenia is not likely to produce focal deficits. Patient profiles with scattered motor, sensory, and cognitive disorders, as well as personality test results suggesting psychosis, must be compared to diseases known to produce such patterns (e.g., Parkinson's Disease, Multiple Sclerosis, Multiple Tumors). Multiple sclerosis, for example, may produce motor, sensory and cognitive deficits along with an elevated Sc score on the MMPI. The pattern is predictable, however, and can be separated from other diseases. If a profile cannot be related to any known disorders, schizophrenia becomes likely.

The schizophrenic with diffuse deficits generally shows a pattern different from generalized neurological disorders. Tests measuring higher cognitive skills and attention are severely impaired while basic skills are intact. Some tests which would normally be impaired in a generalized disorder are performed adequately. It is this contradictory pattern and the personality test results that define the schizophrenic pattern.

In cases where a question remains as to diagnosis, retesting within an examination is useful. The results of the psychiatric patient will be inconsistent, while the brain damaged patient will not show sudden regaining of skills over short periods of time.

Several cautions are in order when attempting to make these discriminations in difficult cases. First, it is necessary to always rule out all possible neurological diagnoses. The patient referred for a neuropsychological examination generally presents conflicting features. It is unfair to the patient and referral source to rule out possible alternatives without careful examination.

Second, qualitative dimensions of the patient's behavior must be observed. As Goldstein and Neuringer (1973) have observed, the schizo-phrenic is more likely to be bizarre and unmotivated rather than unable to do a test. Behavior within a test can be revealing. The schizophrenic may be able to perform a problem at one point, for example, but not another.

Third, the effects of drugs and low motivation must be eliminated. If a patient cannot be accurately tested, no valid conclusions can be reached. Many failures reported in the test literature are the result of this significant but often overlooked factor.

Tumors

Tumors occur in a variety of forms, each of which varies in the man-ner it affects neuropsychological test results. There are several common findings, however. All tumors create an area of focal deficit surrounded by an area of more diffuse and less severe deficit. The area of focal deficit varies greatly in severity; the effects may be extremely mild in some tumors, extremely severe in others. In the most severe tumors, brain tis-sue is destroyed and suppressions will be seen if the tumor is in a sensory reception area of the cerebral hemispheres.

The surrounding deficits may also vary in severity. They are nonexis-tent in some tumors, and in others, the entire function of the brain may be disrupted. These secondary effects may be the result of increased pres-sure, edema (swelling of the brain), or disturbances in cerebral circula-tion.

Abscesses, pockets of pus in the brain caused by infection, may re-sult in similar symptoms, as may hematomas, pockets of blood within the brain, and aneurysms, a ballooning of a section of an artery of the brain.

A special type of tumor, metastatic tumors, results from the spread of cancer from other parts of the body to the brain. It is identified because it is usually multiple, causing pockets of focal deficit throughout the brain.

Head Traumas

Head traumas are often characterized by a focal deficit in one hemi-sphere and a somewhat more diffuse and less severe deficit in the opposite hemisphere. The severity of these deficits may vary considerably. In cases in which there is unconsciousness, the severity generally correlates with the length of time it takes a person to awake.

Head trauma may also lead to localized or more severe bleeding in the brain. There are usually more severe and permanent deficits in these injuries; if the bleeding is severe, this may extend the area of injury con-siderably. In some cases, hematomas (pockets of blood) may form, some-times several months after an injury due to slow bleeding in an artery.

Cerebrovascular Disorders

Disruption of the cerebrovascular system is a major cause of brain injury. A common disorder is infarction of an artery, resulting in a lack of oxygen in tissue served by the artery. A common site for infarction is the middle cerebral artery which supplies the motor, temporal, and parietal areas of each hemisphere. These infarctions can result in partial or complete loss of motor and sensory functions on one side of the body. If the left middle cerebral artery is involved, there will also be extensive verbal deficits. If the right middle cerebral artery is involved, there will be severe spatial deficits (e.g., Block Design, drawings) and losses on the Rhythm Test. Similar results, in a more severe form, will be caused by hemorrhage (rupture) of these arteries. In this case, there will also be clear suppressions.

Many cerebrovascular disorders occur after the onset of arteriosclerosis. Since arteriosclerosis causes diffuse brain impairment, patients with cerebrovascular disorders may present a picture of diffuse impairment throughout the brain accompanied by an area of severe focal deficit.

Aneurysms are the result of a ballooning on a part of an artery. Aneurysms will cause mild focal deficits where they are located. Their effects rarely extend beyond this unless they hemorrhage, however. Aneurysms typically have Impairment Indexes of .4 to .6 while infarctions will have indexes of .6 to 1.0, and hemorrhages will result in indexes of .9 to 1.0.

In many cases, cerebrovascular disorders and tumors will produce similar results. For example, a severe tumor near the middle cerebral artery may be difficult to distinguish from an infarction or hemorrhage.

Epilepsy

Epilepsy is generally a secondary result of another neuropathological condition, often caused by the irritation of the brain by a scar, tumor or other space occupying disorder. There is also a large class of epilepsies labelled idiopathic, that is, of unknown origin. A series of articles on epilepsy (Matthews and Klove, 1967; Klove and Matthews, 1966, 1969, 1974) found that epilepsy with known causes showed more severe impairment on the Halstead-Reitan than those labelled idiopathic. At present, however, there is no way to identify the presence of epilepsy by the test battery. Epilepsy is always a possibility, especially in clients with focal lesions.

Alcoholism

Chronic alcoholics have significant deficits on the Halstead-Reitan (Gudeman, Craine, Golden, and McLaughlin, in press). These deficits include tests of frontal lobe activity (Category Test, Trail Making Test, part B), spatial skills (Tactual Performance Test, Rhythm Block Design, Picture Arrangement, Object Assembly), and left sided motor skills (Finger Tapping). The severity of the deficits depend on the chronicity and severity of the alcoholism.

Presenile Dementia

The presenile dementias (Alzheimers and Picks Disease are the major forms) result in generalized deterioration of brain function, including deficits on those tests thought to be resistant to brain damage (e.g., Vocabulary). The Impairment Index in these disorders is usually 1.0.

Parkinson's Disease

Patients with Parkinson's disease show significant impairment on tests of drawing (including a tremor) and on the Category Test, although WAIS scores tend to be normal (Reitan and Boll, 1971). Measures of motor and tactile skills are down, including the Tactual Performance Test and Finger Tapping. These deficits may be bilateral or unilateral. Patients will also have very small writing in an attempt to reduce motor problems. In the later stages of this disorder, there may be generalized impairment across Halstead's basic tests.

Multiple Sclerosis

Multiple Sclerosis (MS) is a degenerative disease of the central nervous system. MS produces sensory and motor symptoms which are often inconsistent, and may show periods of exacerbation and remission. The patients usually show a higher verbal than performance IQ, and show deficits on Finger Tapping, the Tactual Performance Test, and other sensory tests. There may be mild cognitive losses reflected as a borderline score on the Category Test. Auditory problems are rare, but visual deficits may be caused by involvement of the optic nerve (Goldstein and Shelley, 1974; Matthews, et al., 1970; Reitan, et al., 1971; Robbins, 1974). MS patients may also show peaks on the Hypochondriasis and Hysteria scales of the MMPI, a pattern characteristic of conversion hysteria (Cleeland, et al., 1970). Because of the MMPI profile and the inconsistent symptoms, MS is sometimes mistaken for a psychological disorder.

REHABILITATION

Luria (1963) has suggested that when one area of the brain is destroyed, it interrupts the functional systems responsible for behavior. Recovery of any lost abilities depends upon reformulation of the functional systems responsible for those behaviors. The reformulation may take place in one of three ways. First, another area may substitute for the lost area. This is more likely in situations where both hemispheres of the brain are involved in a task. For example, both parietal lobes can be involved in spatial tasks; consequently, loss on one side can be compensated for by increasing the participation of the opposite parietal in the appropriate functional system. One can also involve new areas of the brain by providing an alternate method of doing a task.

The task may be done by involving more basic systems of the brain. For example, the patient may have injury to the motor speech areas and be unable to say the letter "p." Such patients, however, are often able to perform the more basic motion of blowing through pursed lips. Starting at this point, such a response may be shaped into saying "p."

Finally, a functional system may be reformed by including higher centers of the brain. A subject with lesions in the motor area, for example, may be unable to tap his finger on command. If the patient is told to tap out his age, the patient is able to do this since this task involves the higher cortical centers to a greater extent.

The emphasis in each of these situations is that the overt behavior is maintained, although the manner in which the brain executes the behavior has changed. The formation of an effective new functional system depends upon the integrity of the areas which must form the new functional system. Consequently, the neuropsychologist must be interested not only in what deficits are present but what strengths are present as well.

Whichever mechanism may be operating in a given case, it is the job of the rehabilitation neuropsychologist to provide training that enables the brain to efficiently form the most workable alternative functional system. The major technique is to provide a situation in which the brain receives accurate feedback on its performance. This feedback allows the brain to assess the accuracy of its attempts to reformulate the functional system. The tasks must be designed so that the feedback is clear. The lack of clear feedback is one factor limiting the spontaneous improvement that a subject makes without therapy.

PLANNING REHABILITATION PROGRAMS

In order to reach the goals described above, it is necessary to use the neuropsychological examination to fully document the deficits caused by a brain injury. It is important to recognize that all deficits, whether a direct result of a brain injury or of other factors, must be considered if the maximally effective rehabilitation program is to be designed.

The identification process can be done in two ways. First, analysis of neuropsychological test results can reveal underlying deficits. This requires a knowledge of the skills demanded by each test, and a comparison of the patient's performance on tests with overlapping requirements. Second, a knowledge of the locus and cause of a brain injury can be related to experimental information on how the brain works (see Golden, 1978; Luria, 1966, 1973). Combining the information from these two approaches can lead to a detailed analysis of the areas in which a subject is impaired.

In addition to considering the status of the patient's cognitive abilities, it is also necessary to evaluate the patient's emotional status. The client's emotional status can significantly effect the efficiency of rehabilitation programs. In some cases, emotional problems are so severe as to preclude a successful program. In many cases, treatment of the emotional disorder is necessary either as a prelude to treatment or as an integral part of the treatment (see chapters on Personality Assessment).

Several considerations help to set the priorities for rehabilitation. The major goal is the organization of the program so that maximal performance levels may be achieved by the patient with a minimum expenditure of staff and patient effort. Beginning therapy in an area dependent upon skills which have not yet been learned is an inefficient approach, as is putting a patient with low motivation in a program that requires great effort before the motivational problems have been treated.

It is important to determine which deficits, if any, may be due to the emotional disorders patients may be showing. In order to do this, it is necessary for the psychologist to compare the disabilities expected from the client's neurological disorder to those shown. If there are deficits beyond what would be expected, these can be due to the client's emotional status. This is important, since deficits which are due to the patient's emotional reaction may be very resistant to normal rehabilitation treatment.

It is also necessary to assess the importance of the deficits to the patient's life. Some deficits will be more relevant to a patient's occupation, and some more important to them psychologically. For example, the author saw one patient whose motor strength and coordination tested as normal but who felt he was weak. Although he had many more severe problems, it was found that a strength-building program aided considerably in getting the patient's cooperation and making him feel therapy was important.

Finally, the neuropsychologist needs to consider in which areas progress can be made most successfully. Early and obvious success in a rehabilitation program can be a powerful reinforcer to the patient and his family. This is a considerable aid in enlisting the patient's full effort in the rehabilitation program.

ADVANTAGES AND DISADVANTAGES

The primary area in which the Halstead-Reitan has been found to be ineffective is in the chronic schizophrenic population. Numerous testing and interpretation problems exist with this battery as well as other neuropsychological tests in this population. The Halstead-Reitan is an effective tool within acute or milder schizophrenic populations, however.

A second disadvantage to the test battery is the time it takes to administer. In many settings, it is not possible to provide the manpower necessary to administer a test procedure which may take a full working day or more to complete. In other cases, the patient is not capable of such sustained activity (although properly placed rests during the tests will reduce this problem). Many clinicians feel that it is more appropriate to use a shorter, individually chosen test battery (Lezak, 1976; Golden, 1978).

The use of individualized, shorter examinations has its own disadvantages, however. First, it is possible to miss an important deficit if the battery is not selected properly. Since there are no guidelines for such test selection, the accuracy depends on the skills of the individual clinician. Second, this approach does not allow the collection of data on the effectiveness of a test battery, or research on how interrelationships among tests may relate to a given locus or neurological process. Thus, all interpretation must remain largely qualitative and clinical.

Another disadvantage is the dependence of many of the tests in the battery on motor skills. This is especially evident in the spatial tests (e.g., Block Design, Tactual Performance Test, Drawings, Trail Making Test (part A), and Object Assembly). Subjects with severe central or peripheral motor impairment often cannot be tested adequately as a result of this problem. It is necessary in these cases to use alternate tests of these skills which do not demand motor ability, such as Raven's Matrices (see Chapter 4).

Finally, the battery does not cover all possible neuropsychological deficits. Although most of the major deficits required for interpretation are included (as evidenced by the success of the battery), some problems are missed. As a result, many investigators have extended the scope of the battery by adding additional test procedures. The Wisconsin Neuropsychological Laboratory, for example, has developed an additional set of tests aimed primarily at brain stem injuries (Norton and Matthews, 1972). Others have found the Peabody Picture Vocabulary Test useful for patients with expressive speech problems (see Chapter 3). In many cases, specific tests may be added to the battery for individual cases. (See Lezak, 1976, for a review of many available tests in experimental and clinical neuropsychology.)

Adding additional tests has the drawback of again increasing the time of the battery, although it undoubtedly provides a more comprehensive and effective examination. This problem has been partially dealt with by shortening the tests within the Halstead-Reitan in the ways suggested in this chapter, and by developing shorter forms or alternate tests.

The major advantage of the Halstead-Reitan over other neuropsychological batteries and procedures is the extensive validation and experimental work available on the test battery. This allows the clinician to depend on the proven relationships within and between tests to reach conclusions about diagnosis rather than depend on clinical judgment derived from experience and the literature on each individual test. This ability to identify complex test patterns and relationships, such as those identified for alcoholism or multiple sclerosis, greatly increases the value of the test battery. Any standard or individualized test batteries attempting to replace this test would have to develop similar, extensive information.

CASE EXAMPLES

Case 1.   F.R. was a 62-year-old, right-handed male with a ninth-grade education. He was referred for neuropsychological testing because of a gradual loss of sensation in his right side over the preceding three weeks. The neuropsychological examination was part of a more extensive neurological investigation.

Table 9-4 presents the patient's test results. As can be seen from general indicators, the patient's performance was quite impaired. He missed 120 items on the Category Test, was unable to place all ten blocks of the Tactual Performance Test on any of the trials, and failed to remember the location or shape of any of the forms on the Tactual Performance Test. He earned an Impairment Index of 1.0, indicating that all tests on which the index is based were impaired. He also showed severely depressed performance on the Wechsler tests most sensitive to brain damage, the Digit Symbol and Digit Span Tests.

In examining the scores for laterality, several are outstanding. The right-hand tapping was highly impaired compared to the left hand. The right hand was also more impaired on all tests of tactile sensitivity (Finger Agnosia, Fingertip Number Writing, Tactile Form Recognition). The patient was unable to do the Tactual

Table 9-4
Results for Case 1

Wechsler Adult Intelligence Scale		Tactual Performance Test	
Information	7	Left	10:00 (2 blocks in)
Comprehension	7	Left	10:00 (2 blocks)
Arithmetic	6	Left	10:00 (2 blocks)
Similarities	6	Memory	1
Digit Span	2	Location	0
Vocabulary	6	Trail Making Test	
Digit Symbol	3	Part A	84 seconds
Picture Completion	10	Part B	discontinued
Object Assembly	8	Category	
Block Design	8	120 errors	
Picture Arrangement	6	Finger Agnosia	
Verbal IQ	81	Right 9 errors	
Performance IQ	100	Left 0 errors	
Full-scale IQ	79	Fingertip Number Writing	

Peabody Picture Vocabulary		Fingertip Number Writing	
IQ	88	Right 11 errors	
Speech Perception		Left 5 errors	
36 errors		Tactile Form Recognition	
Rhythm		Right 0 errors	
13 errors		Left errors	
Finger Tapping		MMPI	
Right	0	normal	
Left	37	Impairment Index	
		1.0	

Aphasia symptoms: dysnomia, spelling dyspraxia, dysgraphia, dyslexia, dyscalculia, dysarthria.
Dominance:　right hand, right foot, left eye.
Suppressions:　right hand, right ear.

Performance Test with his right hand. He also showed reliable suppressions on the right hand and in the right ear. Trials A was slow, but the patient was unable to finish Trails B. Both the speech perception and rhythm tests were down severely. The patient had numerous signs of aphasia. Performance IQ was significantly greater than Verbal IQ. All of these signs indicate left hemisphere involvement.

It must be recognized that there was a localized lesion in the left hemisphere, probably in the left temporoparietofrontal area. There was not a complete loss of speech skills, however, which suggests that the parietal involvement may be limited.

It is likely, given this evidence, that there has been a serious hemorrhage in the left middle cerebral artery. This is based on the localization of the deficit, the severe effects overall, as well as the suppressions and complete loss of motor movement in the right arm. A secondary possibility would be a tumor. The neurological diagnosis for the patient was hemorrhage of the left middle cerebral artery.

Case 2. Case 2, presented in Table 9-5, was a 26-year-old, right-handed male named M.M. who complained of severe headaches and vomiting. M.M.'s score on the Category Test was normal, although just below the cutoff point. His scores on the Tactual Performance Test, Location, and Trails B were all within the normal range, although there was a minor deficit on the right hand. There was a normal performance on all the tests developed by Halstead. The only deficit on the WAIS was a low score on Digit Span, possibly due to the patient's tendency to be distracted easily. Overall, the performance was good enough to argue against any kind of tumor or space occupying disorder. When neurological tests were completed on this patient, including CAT scan, the final diagnosis was one of schizophrenia with hypochondriacal delusions. The patient was referred for psychiatric treatment.

Table 9-5
Results for Case 2

Wechsler Adult Intelligence Scale		Tactual Performance Test	
Information	9	Right	4 '35"
Comprehension	14	Left	2 '57"
Arithmetic	13	Both	1 '23"
Similarities	9	Memory	7
Digit Span	7	Location	5
Vocabulary	12	Cateogry	
Digit Symbol	14	45 errors	
Picture Completion	10		
Block Design	12	Trail Making Test	
Picture Arrangement	10	Part A	33"
Object Assembly	11	Part B	75"
Verbal IQ	104	Speech Perception	
Performance IQ	114	6 errors	
Full-scale IQ	109	Rhythm	
Impairment Index		3 errors	
0		Tapping Test	
		Right	58
		Left	53
Aphasia symptoms: none.			
Sensory symptoms: none.			

Case 3.   Case 3, P.S. was a 22-year-old, right-handed female with one year of college. The referral was for assessment of residual brain damage after a trauma five months prior to the testing. The results for P.S. are listed in Table 9-6. The overall IQ showed a deficit in intelligence compared to the levels expected of a normal college student. The Category Test score was borderline, but indicative of brain dysfunction. The overall Tactual Performance Test time was well into the brain-injured range, as was the Impairment Index, Location score, and the Trail Making Test (part B). All these indicators suggested that there was moderate brain dysfunction remaining.

A number of signs pointed to a right brain focus. On the WAIS, the performance score was ten IQ points below the verbal score. The patient's lowest scores were on Digit Span (where digits backward was much worse than digits forward), Picture Arrangement, and Block Design. The Rhythm Test was significantly im-

Table 9-6
Results for Case 3

Wechsler Adult Intelligence Scale		Tactual Performance Test	
Information	8	Right	10'10"
Comprehension	7	Left	6'30"
Arithmetic	7	Both	5'00"
Similarities	10	Memory	8
Digit Span	4	Location	17
Vocabulary	7	Category	
Digit Symbol	6	52 errors	
Picture Completion	9		
Block Design	5	Rhythm	
Picture Arrangement	4	10 errors	
Object Assembly	7	Speech Perception	
Verbal IQ	86	4 errors	
Performance IQ	76	Tapping Test	
Full-scale IQ	81	Right	41
Peabody Picture Vocabulary		Left	25
(IQ)	67	Trail Making Test	
Tactile Form Recognition		Part A	36"
Right 1 error		Part B	252"
Left 0 errors		Finger Agnosia	
Grip Strength		Right 4 errors	
Right (kg)	21	Left 3 errors	
Left (kg)	16	Fingertip Number Writing	
Impairment Index		Right 3 errors	
.72		Left 0 errors	

Aphasia symptoms: mild dysnomia, right-left disorientation reversal of key drawings, mild construction dyspraxia.

paired, while the Speech Sounds Perception Test performance was normal. The left hand was considerably reduced (39 percent) in tapping speed compared to the right hand, although both hands were slow. There were signs of left-hand deficits on Fingertip Number Writing, while the right-hand performance remained normal. The left hand was also some 24 percent weaker than the right hand, although both were considerably below the mean for college women on our instrument (45 kg.). P.S. also had mild construction dyspraxia, including a reversal of her key drawing on the aphasia test.

There were a number of good right brain scores as well: The left hand on the Tactual Performance Test performed quite well compared to the right hand: the Trail Making Test (part A) was within normal limits; the memory score of the Tactual Performance Test was quite good; and the left hand on the Tactile Form Recognition (astereognosis) test was normal.

There were also signs of left brain involvement. P.S. showed several aphasia symptoms, although none of them were severe. Her receptive vocabulary, as measured by the Peabody Picture Vocabulary Test, was also down considerably. This suggested a problem in attaching names to pictures. The decrease in the verbal IQ from her expected level was also indicative of left brain involvement. She missed one item on the right hand of the Tactile Form Recognition Test. There was a slight impairment of the right hand on the Tactual Performance Test as compared to the left hand. The Finger Agnosia score suggested somewhat more impairment on the right hand than the left hand, although the difference was not large enough to suggest any localization. Trails B was severely impaired, compared to Trails A, which was normal.

In conclusion, then, the overall pattern of results indicates diffuse brain impairment. There was a more severe focal area in the right frontotemporal area, however. This was seen through the greater impairment in left finger tapping than on the left hand Tactual Performance Test. There were relatively good scores on Object Assembly and the sensory tests. There were also good scores on Trails A and the Memory score of the Tactual Performance Test. There was only mild construction dyspraxia and good learning across trials on the Tactual Performance Test. All of these argue against a primary focus in the parietal area. In addition, the severe impairment of Rhythm and Picture Arrangement (the lowest WAIS score) and Digits backwards argue for an anterior right brain focus.

In the left brain, the deficits were primarily in the parietal area. The right hand of the Tactual Performance was worse than expected when compared to the Finger Tapping Test. There were mild dysphasia symptoms, tactile errors, and both expressive and receptive vocabulary problems. Auditory reception was normal on Speech Sounds Perception. The severe deficits on Trails B suggested a difficulty in handling verbal symbols. The relatively good Category Test argued against a focus in the left frontal lobe. Indeed, the Category Test was normal for a person with an IQ of 81. It was likely that the primary focus of the head injury was either in the right anterior or left posterior areas with the countrecoup effects responsible for the deficits in the opposite hemisphere.

The neurological report noted that P.S. was struck above the right eye during a car accident. She has severe surface lacerations in that area and the right side of her face with no other external evidence of trauma.

10

A Standardized Version of Luria's Neuropsychological Tests

Several alternative approaches exist to the Halstead-Reitan as a comprehensive measure of neuropsychological tests. One alternative is based on the work of the Russian neuropsychologist A. R. Luria. Luria's approach used items selected for their qualitative importance in diagnosing the patient. Rather than using more global measures such as the Bender or the Category test, Luria employs specific measures designed to look at the exact dimensions of the performance of a brain injured patient. Thus, rather than test receptive speech skills with a test like Speech Sounds Perception, Luria gives a series of items dealing with the ability of the patient to understand single letters, groups of letters, words, sentences, sentences with inverted grammatical constructions and sentences with contradictions. By this procedure, Luria is able to identify those specific areas in which a patient is unable to function. Such information can then be used for localizing, identifying, and rehabilitating the neurological patient (as described in the last chapter).

One disadvantage which has interfered with the use of Luria's procedures in the United States has been the lack of standardized procedures and materials for the administration of the test. The latter deficit was corrected by the publication of Luria's Neuropsychological Investigation by Christensen (1975). This publication made standardized material available for Luria's batteries; however, standardized administration or scoring procedures were not provided by Christensen. These were developed in a series of articles by Golden and his associates (Golden, Hammeke, and Purisch, 1978; Hammeke, Golden, and Purisch, 1978; Purisch, Golden, and Hammeke, 1978; Osmon, Golden, Purisch, Hammeke, and Blume,

1978; Lewis, Golden, Osmon, Purisch, and Hammeke, 1979; Marvel, Golden, Hammeke, Osmon, and Purisch, 1979). These studies have largely confirmed the results of Luria's observations using unstandardized procedures, and suggest that these procedures can be highly effective in identifying and localizing brain dysfunction.

ADMINISTRATION AND SCORING

The Standardized version of Luria's Neuropsychological Investigation contains 269 items. Each item is administered separately and represents a specific aspect of function. Each item, except for a few exceptions, differs in some aspect from all other items on the test. The items vary along such dimensions as complexity, degree of difficulty, mode of stimulus input (auditory, verbal, tactile), mode of answering (open ended, motor, speech, multiple choice), speeded or nonspeeded, and amount of information available. In this way ten major areas of neuropsychological performance are explored: motor skills, rhythmic and pitch abilities, tactile abilities, expressive speech skills, receptive speech abilities, reading, writing and arithmetic skills, memory skills, visual-spatial skills, and intellectual ability. An example of a page of items from the protocol can be seen in Figure 1 of the manual.

Each item is scored in one of a number of ways depending on the item content. The scoring techniques include accuracy, speed, quality of response, time to make a response, trials to a criterion level, and number of responses. After a raw score is determined for each item, it is translated into a scaled score of zero, one, or two. A scale score of zero is indicative of a response seen in normals. A score of one suggests a response intermediate to that of the typical normal and typical brain injured patient. A score of two is indicative of a response similar to that of the typical brain injured patient on the item. The administration protocol of the test contains the normative data necessary to determine the scale score for any given raw score on each item.

After the scores for each item are determined, the 11 primary summary scales are scored. These summary scale scores are the sum of the individual scaled scores on each item within a given area. The following summary scores are employed:

Motor Functions

This scale includes both simple and complex motor skills. The items on the scale involve simple timed motor tasks, simple motor tasks without visual feedback, simple motor tasks which are produced by imitation, simple and complex motor movements directed by verbal commands, and bilateral motor coordination. In addition, the scale evaluates mouth and tongue movements including simple movements and series of movements, and the ability of the subject to spontaneously draw and copy simple geometric shapes.

Rhythmic and Pitch Skills

The first half of this section evaluates pitch skills: the ability to determine whether two tones have the same pitch, to determine which of two tones is higher, and to reproduce increasingly complex tonal sequences. The second half of the section evaluates rhythmic skills: identifying the number of tones in a sequence, identifying whether rhythmic patterns are the same, and producing rhythmic patterns on verbal command.

Tactile Functions

This section evaluates simple and complex tactile and kinesthetic functions. All items in this section are given to the subject while he or she is blindfolded. The subject must identify where he or she is touched, whether a touch is sharp or blunt, discriminate between a hard and soft touch, identify numbers and letters written on the hands, reproduce a movement of one arm which is flexed by the examiner and identify common objects by touch alone.

Visual (Spatial) Functions

This section evaluates basic visual and spatial functions, except for construction skills which are evaluated in the motor section. The items require subjects to recognize simple objects presented to them, to identify photographs and line drawings, to identify objects presented in a mixed-up jumble, to discern pictures where only part of the gestalt is visible, to solve problems similar to those found in Raven's Matrices (Chapter 2), and to work with three-dimensional piles of blocks and two-dimensional rotations.

Receptive Speech

This section evaluates the subject's ability to correctly understand a wide variety of material presented auditorially. The initial section evaluates the subjects skills in understanding simple phonemes, phonemic combinations, series of phonemes, and phonemes presented in different pitches. The second part of the section evaluates simple word comprehension, comprehension of simple sentences, and comprehension of sentences involving contradictions, prepositions, possessive constructions, spatial relationships, logical relationships, inverted grammatical structures, and complex or compound constructions.

Expressive Speech

This section evaluates an individual's skill to express material orally. This includes the repetition of phonemes, and the repetition of successively more difficult words. The section also evaluates the ability to repeat increasingly complex sentences, as well as repeating automatic and simple sequences (such as the days of the week). The section also measures a subject's ability to spontaneously discuss a topic in response to pictures, a story, and a theme. Finally, the subject must organize words into intelligible statements.

Writing

This section evaluates basic writing skills, including simple spelling, the ability to copy letters and words from cards, from memory, and from dictation. Spontaneous writing skills are also evaluated.

Reading

The Reading section parallels the writing section. The subject must reproduce sounds from letters, name individual letters and their sounds, read syllables, words of varying complexity, sentences, and short stories.

Arithmetic

This section covers a wide range of skills related to mathematical abilities. These skills include number recognition (both Arabic and Roman Numerals), the comparison of numbers, simple arithmetic skills (addition, subtraction, multiplication, and division), and simple algebraic problems. Two items cover the ability to subtract 7 and 13 from 100 continuously, similar to the tasks seen on most mental status exams.

Memory

This section evaluates a wide range of mnestic processes. Subjects are reexamined on their ability to memorize a list of items over several trials, to memorize pictures and other nonverbal stimuli, to memorize short verbal lists with and without interference, to memorize a story, and to associate verbal labels with pictures.

Intellectual Processes

This section covers a wide range of intellectual processes. This includes a number of items similar to those on the WAIS Comprehension, Picture Arrangement, Arithmetic, Similarities, and Vocabulary subtests. In addition, subjects must explain the theme of a picture, what is funny about a picture, and to make logical comparisons.

In addition to these basic 11 sections, three additional summary scores are calculated. The Left Hemisphere score consists of all items in the motor and tactile sections which require the use of the right hand alone. The Right Hemisphere score consists of all items in the Motor and Tactile sections which require the use of the left hand alone. The final scale, Pathognomonic, consists of 31 items which are especially sensitive to brain damage. These items, rarely missed by non-brain injured patients, are missed by brain injured patients much more frequently than other groups of patients.

After raw scores are determined for each summary index, they are plotted on the profile sheet (see example in case presentations at end of this chapter). From the left hand column of the profile sheet, T scores (with a mean of 50 and a standard deviation of ten) can be read for each score. These T scores can be averaged across all 14 indices to yield a Total score which can act as a quick summary of the individual's level of performance.

CLINICAL INTERPRETATION

Individual Scales

Of the 269 items on the 14 scales, 252 were found to be significantly discriminate between brain injured and normal patients at the .05 level, while the remaining 17 items were significant at the .20 level (Golden, Hammeke, and Purisch, 1978). A follow-up study found the individual scales able to discriminate between brain injured and normal patients between 74 and 96 percent of the time, while the scales were able to discriminate between brain injured and schizophrenic patients between 58 and 78 percent of the time. Overall, the test was able to discriminate 93 percent of the time when normal controls are used and 88 percent of the time when schizophrenic controls are employed.

Several rules appear to maximize the discrimination between brain injured and non-brain injured patients. In general, a T score above 60 in an otherwise normal person or a T score greater than 70 in a patient with a psychiatric history is indicative of brain damage. If three or more scales are above these cutoff points, the patient has a 90 percent chance of being brain damaged, while two scales above the cut-off strongly suggests the possibility of brain damage. Of all the scales, the Pathognomonic scale is the most reliable indicator of brain damage. When this scale is significantly above the cutoff points or is the high point for the entire profile, the chances of brain damage are quite high. In some mild or largely recovered cases, a high Pathognomonic score may be the only prominent indicator of residual brain dysfunction.

Other signs may also indicate brain damage. An overall Total score which is ten or more T score points higher than the T score for Intelligence may be suggestive of significant brain dysfunction. A memory score which is elevated above the cutoff and ten or more points higher than all other scales (except Intelligence) may indicate the presence of noncortical brain damage and may suggest atrophy of the brain.

Qualitative signs of brain damage may also be elicited on the test as it is given. Observation of significant problems in visual-constructive tasks may suggest brain injury, as are significant signs of perseveration (repetition) in drawing or expressive speech items. Reading only the right half of the line and other related symptoms may indicate unilateral spatial neglect (discussed in the chapter on the Benton). Lateralized motor or tactile performance, when there is no peripheral injury to an arm, is also highly suggestive of brain damage. This is indicated by a score on the Left or Right Hemisphere index which is ten or more points greater than the score on the opposite index.

Localizing Brain Damage

Several important rules are useful for localizing brain damage with the Luria battery. First, a comparison of the Left Hemisphere and Right Hemisphere scores is able to lateralize a brain disorder about 80 percent of the time. This works maximally well with lesions involving the major motor and tactile areas of the brain.

Injuries in the frontal areas of the two hemispheres are characterized by deficits in evaluation, planning, and motor functions. In general, this causes a greater deficit on the Motor scale as compared to the Tactile scale. Left frontal patients score very high on Pathognomonic (averaging above 80). Left frontal injuries also show significant deficits on the Expressive scale as compared to the Receptive scale. In addition, motor impairment will usually be bilateral, with both the Left and Right scales raised above normal levels.

Right frontal injuries do not show strong expressive language deficits. Rather, the Receptive score is usually more impaired than the Expressive score. An examination of the individual test items indicate that items involving spatial relationships, logical analysis, inverted sentence structure and the like show more impairment than deficits in more basic word understanding seen in left temporal injuries. Memory and Intelligence scores will generally be the best in right frontal injuries.

Impairment to the sensorimotor areas of the brain—the precentral and postcentral gyri which control motor output and tactile input—show unique deficits. In general, the Left or Right Hemisphere score will be elevated as much as 20 points or more over the opposite scale. Thus, if the injury occurs in the left hemisphere the Left score will be significantly higher while right hemisphere injuries will produce the opposite result. In general, large Left-Right differences exceeding 20 points almost always imply the involvement of the sensorimotor areas.

If the injury occurs in the left sensorimotor areas, both the Left and Right scales will be elevated above 60 although the Left scale will be considerably higher. The Motor scale will generally exceed the Tactile scale as well, due to the disruption of the complex motor items on the Motor scale. These deficits will be accompanied by both Expressive and Receptive deficits in addition. If the injury occurs in the right hemisphere, the Motor and Tactile scores will tend to be equal. High Pathognomonic scores are characteristic of injuries in either hemisphere.

Injuries to the temporal lobe affect verbal and nonverbal auditory stimuli. If the injury is to the right hemisphere, Motor scores tend to be higher than Tactile scores, usually because of the items on the Motor scale dealing with construction abilities. There will often be significant deficits on Intelligence and impairment of the nonverbal items on the Memory scale. The rise on Memory is generally much higher than seen in other right hemisphere injuries, but less than that associated with left hemisphere injuries of similar severity.

If the injury occurs to the left temporal lobe, there will be significant impairment in the Receptive, Rhythm, Memory, Reading, Writing, and Arithmetic scores. The Expressive score may be impaired, but is generally ten or more T score points below the Receptive score. Motor and Tactile scores are generally equal, and less severe than in Frontal or Parietal injuries.

Injuries to the parietal-occipital areas generally produce poor Tactile as compared to Motor scores, although injuries in the more posterior parts of the hemisphere may cause equal impairment in these scales. If the injury occurs on the right hemisphere, there will be extensive impairment in drawing tasks on the Motor scale, usually consisting of spatial rather than perseverative problems. In right parietal injuries, the worst scores will typically be on Tactile, Arithmetic, and Pathognomonic. In the left hemisphere, the parietal injury produces impaired scores on Arithmetic, Reading, Writing, and Intelligence. Motor and Tactile scores will be equal in more posterior injuries, while Tactile scores are worse if the lesion involves the post central gyrus. Receptive Language may be impaired, primarily in items involving more complex word and sentence discrimination, except for those lesions which closely involve the temporal lobe as well. In the latter case of parietal-temporal injuries, nearly all items on the Receptive scale can be missed.

Although extensive localization can be made with the quantitative scores alone, it is important for the user to use the more qualitative results offered by the test. Specifically, an analysis of the items within and across the Luria scales allows for a qualitative understanding of the patient's basic deficits. This information, in turn, can be used to localize and identify brain disorders when used with a comprehensive theory of brain function (e.g., see Golden, 1978; Luria, 1973). Even without such a theoretical background, the user is usually able to delineate the specific areas of deficits a patient possesses. This is useful for vocational and rehabilitative planning, as discussed in the last chapter.

ADVANTAGES AND DISADVANTAGES

The Luria test offers some major advantages as a neuropsychological test battery. First, the test takes two-and-one-half hours to administer as opposed to test batteries like the Halstead-Reitan which takes six or more hours to administer. The test allows the user to break general functions (like Receptive Speech) into specific skills and deficits. This is of use in both detailing a patient's deficits and in diagnosing a patient's disorder. The qualitative nature of the items allows for the understanding of the patient on a more clinical level, while the quantitative indices allow for the use of research and the insights available from a quantitative approach (as discussed in the last chapter).

The Luria has several disadvantages as well. First, the test does not have the extensive background or use represented by the Halstead-Reitan tests and other test batteries. Secondly, although the test offers potentially more information, the most valuable information requires that the user be aware of the theoretical system on which the test is based. This, indeed, is a drawback of almost all tests offering qualitative observations.

The best initial readings on Luria's tests and theories can be found in Luria (1973). (Readers without any background in this area may first wish to read Golden (1978). A second, but more advanced test, can be found in Luria (1966). For qualitative information on the specific test items contained in the standardized battery, the best source is Christensen (1975), whose manual details both Luria's theories and the intended role of each item. With this background, the reader should have sufficient theoretical information to appreciate the integrated standardized-qualitative approach used in the interpretation of the Luria battery.

There is a strong relationship between the advantages and disadvantages of the Luria techniques. The test's comprehensiveness, ease of use, accuracy, and administration time are based upon the combined standardized and qualitative interpretive system. Use of the test without considering both aspects of the interpretation results in a significant loss of information which interferes considerably with the clinical efficacy of the battery.

CLINICAL EXAMPLES

Because of the length of a Luria protocol, it is not possible to reproduce an entire test record in order to give the reader a full feeling for the potential of the test as well as the problems in dealing with a large set of items. Consequently, the case examples included here will only examine the conclusions which can be reached from the more formal quantitative aspects of the test. The reader should remember, however, that in actual clinical practice such an evaluation would consist of a qualitative evaluation as well. In addition, the final report would integrate the results from the two methods in order to fully describe the patient's problems.

Case 1. As can be seen in Figure 10-1 the Right Hemisphere score is significantly elevated over the Left Hemisphere score, suggesting lateralization to the right hemisphere, although both hemispheres appeared impaired. The Tactile score is significantly higher than the Motor score, suggesting a parietal rather than a frontal focus. Receptive Language is greater than Expressive Language, as is usually seen in right hemisphere injuries, while Rhythm, Reading, Writing, and Memory are the best scores in the profile. Overall, this is highly suggestive of a clear focus in the right parietal area including the sensory strip in the post central gyrus. This was subsequently confirmed by CAT scan.

Case 2. This second case (Figure 10-2) presents a clear lateralization to the right hemisphere. In addition, Motor scores are significantly higher than the Tactile score and Expressive Language is elevated above Receptive Language (somewhat rare in right hemisphere injuries). There is an elevation in Arithmetic as well. Overall, this points to a clear serious involvement of the right frontal area, with possibly a great deal of injury to motor speech structures either in the left hemisphere or in the lower brain areas. (The case was a 14-year-old with a serious gunshot wound involving the right frontal lobe and some lower cortical structures, the latter injury causing a partial paralysis of the speech musculature).

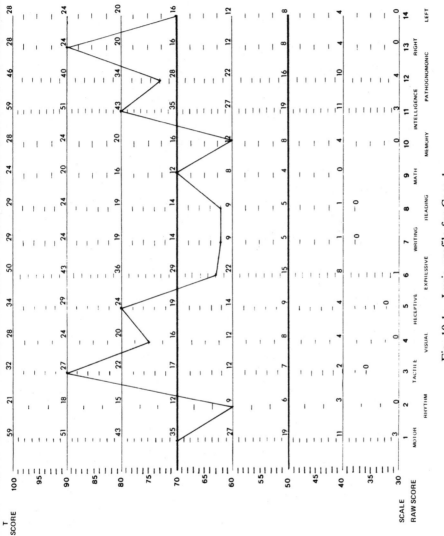

Fig. 10-1. Luria profile for Case 1.

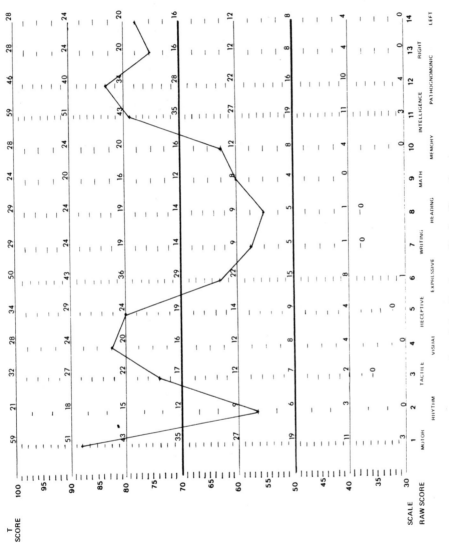

Fig. 10-3. Luria profile for Case 3.

Case 3.   The third case (Figure 10-3) does not show a clear lateralization as the Left and Right Hemisphere scores are quite close (one raw score point). Motor functions are more impaired than tactile functions, suggesting some frontal localization. Since the pattern does not suggest direct sensor-motor involvement, this would have to be in the prefrontal areas. There is significant visual impairment, suggesting a right hemisphere focus, as well as considerable loss on Receptive as opposed to Expressive Language, consistent with a right hemisphere focus. Relatively good scores on Reading, Writing, Math, and Memory are also consistent with this diagnosis. The Pathognomonic score is somewhat elevated for a lesion limited to the right frontal/temporal area, however, suggesting either a fast growing tumor or some bilateral involvement. The lack difference between the Right and Left Hemisphere scores, however, argue against an acute, lateralized disorder as generally one side of the body will be significantly more impaired. As a result, the pattern suggests a bilateral injury but with the worst effects and primary focus in the right hemisphere. (The patient had a right frontal, slow growing tumor which was extended into the left hemisphere as well.)

References

Aita, J. A., Armitage, S. C., Reitan, R. M., and Rabinowitz, A. The use of certain psychological tests in the evaluation of brain injury. *Journal of General Psychology,* 1947, *37:*25.

Bachrach, H., and Mintz, J. The Wechsler Memory Scale as a tool for the detection of mild cerebral dysfunction. *Journal of Clinical Psychology,* 1974, *30:*58.

Balthazar, E. E. Cerebral unilateralization in chronic epileptic cases: The Wechsler Object Assembly Subtest. *Journal of Clinical Psychology,* 1963, *19:*169.

Balthazar, E. E., and Morrison, D. H. The use of Wechsler Intelligence Scales as diagnostic indicators of predominant left, right, and indeterminate unilateral brain damage. *Journal of Clinical Psychology,* 1961, *17:*161.

Barron, F. An ego strength scale which predicts response to psychotherapy. *Journal of Consulting Psychology,* 1953, *17:*327.

Bartz, W. R. Relationship between Wechsler, Beta, and Shipley-Hartford scores. *Psychological Reports,* 1968, *22:*676.

Bender, L. A. *Visual Motor Gestalt Test and Its Clinical Use.* American Orthopsychiatric Association Research Monograph, No. 3, New York: American Orthopsychiatric Association, 1938.

Benton, A. L. A visual retention test for clinical use. *Archives of Neurology and Psychiatry,* 1945, *54:*212.

Benton, A. L. Differential behavioral effects in frontal lobe disease. *Neuropsychologia,* 1968, *6:*53.

Benton, A. L. *The Revised Visual Retention Test* (4th ed.). New York: Psychological Corporation, 1974.

Benton, A. L., and Spreen, O. Visual Memory Test: The simulation of mental incompetence. *Archives of General Psychiatry,* 1961a, *4:*79.

Benton, A. L., and Spreen, O. Zur Simulation intellektueller Leistungsdefekte im Benton-Test. *Psychologische Beitraege,* 1961b, *7:*147.

Black, F. W. The utility of the Shipley-Hartford as a predictor of WAIS Full Scale IQ for patients with traumatic head injuries. *Journal of Clinical Psychology,* 1974, *30:*168.

Boerger, A. R., Graham, J. R., and Lily, R. S. Behavioral correlates of single-scale MMPI code types. *Journal of Consulting and Clinical Psychology,* 1974, *42:*398.

Boller, F. Latent aphasia: Right and left "nonaphasic" brain damaged patients compared. *Cortex,* 1968, *4:*245.

Boller, F., and Vignolo, L. A. A latent sensory aphasia in hemisphere-damaged patients: An experimental study with the Token Test. *Brain,* 1966, *89:*815.

Bonner, L. W. Comparative study of the performance of Negro seniors of Oklahoma City High Schools on the WAIS and the PPVT. *Dissertation Abstracts,* 1969, *30:*921A.

Borgatta, E. F., and Corsini, R. T. The Quick Word Test and the WAIS. *Psychological Reports,* 1960, *6:*201.

Brilliant, P. J., and Gynther, M. D. Relationships between performance on three tests for organicity and selected patient variables. *Journal of Consulting Psychology,* 1963, *27:*474.

Bruhn, A. R., and Reid, M. R. Simulation of brain damage on the Bender-Gestalt Test by college students. *Journal of Personality Assessment,* 1975, *39:*244.

Canter, A. H. *The Canter Background Interference Procedure for the Bender-Gestalt Test.* Nashville: Counselor Recordings, 1976.

Carson, R. C. Interpretative manual to the MMPI. In J. N. Butcher (Ed.), *MMPI Research Developments and Clinical Applications.* New York: McGraw-Hill, 1969.

Cattell, R. B. *Personality and Motivation Structure and Measurement.* Yonkers-on-Hudson, New York: World Book Company, 1957.

Cattell, R. B. *Personality and Mood by Questionnaire.* San Francisco: Josey-Bass, 1973.

Cattell, R. B., Eber, H. W., and Tatsuoka, M. M. *Handbook for the Sixteen Personality Factor Questionnaire (16PF).* Champaign, Illinois: Institute for Personality and Ability Testing, 1970.

Cattell, R. B., and Warburton, F. W. *Objective Personality and Motivation Tests.* Champaign, Illinois: University of Illinois Press, 1967.

Christensen, A. L. *Luria's Neuropsychological Investigation.* New York: Spectrum, 1975.

Cleeland, C. S., Matthews, C. G., and Hopper, C. L. MMPI profiles in exacerbation and remission of Multiple Sclerosis. *Psychological Reports,* 1970, *27:*373.

Cohen, J. Wechsler Memory Scale performance of psychoneurotic, organic, and schizophre ic groups. *Journal of Consulting Psychology,* 1950, *14:*371.

Colonna, A., and Faglioni, P. The performance of hemisphere-damaged patients on spatial intelligence tests. *Cortex,* 1966, *2:*293.

Costa, L. D., and Vaughan, H. G., Jr. Performance of patients with lateralized cerebral lesions. I. Verbal and perceptual tests. *Journal of Nervous and Mental Disease,* 1962, *134:*162.

Costa, L. D., Vaughan, H. G., Jr., Levita, E., and Farber, N. Purdue Pegboard as a predictor of the presence and laterality of cerebral lesions. *Journal of Consulting Psychology*, 1963, *27*:133.

Crochelet, Y. Considérations sur L'apport de L'exarien médicopsychologique dans l'expertise du syndrome postcommotionnel subtectif des traumatisés craniens. *Acta Psychiatrique Belgian*, 1970, *70*:233.

Cronholm, B., and Schalling, D. Intellectual deterioration after focal brain injury. *Archives of Surgery*, 1963, *86*:670.

Dahlstrom, W. G. Prediction of adjustment after neurosurgery. *American Psychologist*, 1954, *9*:353.

Dahlstrom, W. G., Welsh, G. S., and Dahlstrom, L. E. *An MMPI Handbook: Volume I. Clinical Interpretation*. Minneapolis: University of Minnesota Press, 1972.

Dahlstrom, W. G., Welsh, G. S., and Dahlstrom, L. E. *An MMPI Handbook: Volume II. Research Applications*. Minneapolis: University of Minnesota Press, 1975.

Davis, W. E., and Dizonne, M. F. Relationships between the Quick Test and the WAIS. *Psychological Reports*, 1970, *26*:457.

Delprato, D. J., and Jackson, D. E. The effects of seating arrangement upon WAIS Digit Span and Digit Symbol performance. *Journal of Clinical Psychology*, 1975, *31*:88.

Dennerll, P. D. Prediction of unilateral brain dysfunction using Wechsler Test scores. *Journal of Consulting Psychology*, 1964, *28*:278.

Dothring, D. G., Reitan, R. M., and Klove, H. Changes in patterns of intelligence test performance associated with homonymous visual field defects. *Journal of Nervous and Mental Disease*, 1961, *132*:227.

Donahue, D., and Sattler, J. M. Personality variables affecting WAIS scores. *Journal of Consulting and Clinical Psychology*, 1971, *36*:441.

Drake, L. E., and Oetting, E. R. *An MMPI Codebook for Counselors*. Minneapolis: University of Minnesota Press, 1959.

Dunn, L. M., and Markwardt, F. C. *Peabody Individual Achievement Test*, Circle Pines, Minnesota: American Guidance Service, 1970.

Edinger, J. D. WAIS Picture Arrangement and premorbid social competence among process schizophrenics. *Journal of Personality Assessment*, 1976, *40*:52.

Fedio, P., and Mirsky, A. F. Selective intellectual deficits in children with temporal lobe or centrencephalic epilepsy. *Neuropsychologia*, 1969, *7*:287.

Fernald, L. D., Fernald, P. S., and Rines, W. B. Purdue Pegboard and differential diagnosis. *Journal of Consulting Psychology*, 1966, *30*:279.

Fields, F. R. J., and Whitmyre, J. W. Verbal and performance relationships with respect to laterality of cerebral involvement. *Diseases of the Nervous System*, 1969, *30*:177.

Finlayson, M. A. J., Johnson, K. A., and Reitan, R. M. Relationship of level of education to neuropsychological measures in brain-damaged and non-brain-damaged adults. *Journal of Consulting and Clinical Psychology*, 1977, *45*:536.

Firetto, A. C., and Davey, H. Subjectively reported anxiety as a discriminator of digit span performance. *Psychological Reports*, 1971, *28*:98.

Fisher, M. Left hemiplegia and motor impersistence. *Journal of Nervous and Mental Disease,* 1956, *123:*201.

Gilberstadt, H., and Duker, J. A. *A Handbook for Clinical and Acturial MMPI Interpretation.* Philadelphia: Saunders, 1965.

Goldberg, L. R. Diagnosticians vs. diagnostic signs: The diagnosis of psychosis vs. neurosis from the MMPI. *Psychological Monographs,* 1965, *9:*79.

Goldberg, L. R. Objective diagnostic tests and measures. *Annual Review of Psychology,* 1974, *25:*343.

Golden, C. J. The identification of brain damage by an abbreviated form of the Halstead-Reitan Neuropsychological Battery. *Journal of Clinical Psychology,* 1976, *32:*821.

Golden, C. J. Validity of the Halstead-Reitan Neuropsychological Battery in a mixed psychiatric and brain-injured population. *Journal of Consulting and Clinical Psychology,* 1977, *45:*1043.

Golden, C. J. *Diagnosis and Rehabilitation in Clinical Neuropsychology.* Springfield, Illinois: Charles C Thomas, 1978.

Golden, C. J. *Learning Disabilities and Brain Dysfunction.* Springfield, Illinois: Charles C Thomas, 1978.

Golden, C. J. and Anderson, S. M. Short form of the Speech-Sounds Perception test. *Perceptual and Motor Skills,* 1977, *45:*485.

Golden, C. J., Hammeke, T., and Purisch, A. Diagnostic validity of a standardized version of Luria's neuropsychological investigation. *Journal of Consulting and Clinical Psychology,* 1978, in press.

Golden, C. J., Sweet, J. J., and Osmon, D. C. The MMPI in the diagnosis of brain damage: A comprehensive evaluation. *Journal of Personality Assessment,* 1979, in press.

Goldstein, G. The use of clinical neuropsychological methods in the lateralization of brain lesions. In J. Dimond, and J. G. Beaumont (Eds.), *Hemisphere Function in the Brain.* New York: Wiley, 1974.

Goldstein, G., and Neuringer, C. Schizophrenic and organic signs on the Trail Making Test. *Perceptual and Motor Skills,* 1966, *22:*347.

Goldstein, G., and Shelley, C. H. Univariate vs. multivariate analysis in neuropsychological test assessment of lateralized brain damage. *Cortex,* 1973, *9:*204.

Goldstein, G., and Shelley, C. H. Neurodiagnosis of Multiple Sclerosis in a neuropsychiatric setting. *Journal of Nervous and Mental Disease,* 1974, *158:*280.

Good, P. K. E., and Brantner, J. B. *The Physician's Guide to the MMPI.* Minneapolis: University of Minnesota Press, 1961.

Gough, H. G. The F minus K dissimulation index for the MMPI. *Journal of Consulting Psychology,* 1950, *14:*408.

Graham, F. K., and Kendall, B. S. Memory-for-Designs Test: Revised general manual. *Perceptual and Motor Skills, Monograph Supplement,* No. 2–VIII, 1960, *11:*147.

Graham, J. R. *The MMPI: A Practical Guide.* New York: Oxford, 1977.

Granick, S. Brief tests and their interrelationships as intellectual measures of aged subjects. American Psychological Association, *Proceedings,* 1971, *7;*599.

Grossman, H. J. *Manual on Terminology and Classification in Mental Retardation* (Rev. ed. 1973). Baltimore: American Association on Mental Deficiency, Garamond/Pridemark Press, 1973.

Grundvig, J. L., Ajax, A. E., and Needham, W. E. Screening organic brain impairment with the Memory-for-Designs Test. Validation of comparison of different scoring systems and exposure times. *Journal of Clinical Psychology,* 1973, *29:*350.

Grundvig, J. L., Needham, W. E., and Ajax, A. E. Comparison of different scoring and administration procedures for the Memory-for-Designs Test. *Journal of Clinical Psychology,* 1970, *26:*353.

Gudeman, H. E., Craine, J. F., Golden, C. J., and McLaughlin, D. Higher cortical dysfunction associated with long-term alcoholism. *International Journal of Neuroscience,* 1977, *8:*33.

Gudeman, H. E., Golden, C. J., and Craine, J. F. The role of neuropsychological evaluation in the rehabilitation of the brain-injured patient. A program in neurotraining. *JSAS Catalogue of Selected Documents in Psychology,* 1978, *8:*30. (Ms. No. 1693)

Hain, J. D. The Bender-Gestalt Test: A scoring method for identifying brain damage. *Journal of Consulting Psychology,* 1964, *28:*34.

Halstead, W. C. *Brain and Intelligence.* Chicago: University of Chicago Press, 1947.

Hammeke, T., Golden, C. J., and Purisch, A. A standardized, short, and comprehensive neuropsychological test based on the Luria Neuropsychological Evaluation. *International Journal of Neuroscience,* 1978, in press.

Hammer, E. F. An experimental study of symbolism on the Bender-Gestalt. *Journal of Projective Techniques,* 1955, *18:*335.

Hanvik, L. J. Some psychological dimensions of low back pain. (Doctoral dissertation, University of Minnesota, 1949)

Hanvik, L. J. MMPI profiles in patients with low back pain. *Journal of Consulting Psychology,* 1951, *15:*350.

Hartje, W., Kerstechensteiner, M., Poeck, K., and Orgass, B. A cross validation study on the Token Test. *Neuropsychologia,* 1973, *11:*119.

Hathaway, S. R., and Meehl, P. E. *An Atlas for the Clinical Use of the MMPI.* Minneapolis: University of Minnesota, 1951.

Hedlund, J. L. MMPI clinical scale correlates. *Journal of Consulting and Clinical Psychology,* 1977, *45:*739.

Heilbrun, A. B. Lateralization of cerebral lesion and performance on spatial-temporal tasks. *Archives of Neurology,* 1959, *1:*282.

Heimburger, R. F., Demyer, W., and Reitan, R. M. Implications of Gerstmann's Syndrome. *Journal of Neurology, Neurosurgery, and Psychiatry,* 1964, *27:*52.

Holland, T. R. Wechsler Memory Scale paired associate learning in discrimination of brain-damaged and non-brain-damaged psychiatric patients. *Perceptual and Motor Skills,* 1974, *39:*227.

Hovey, H. B. Brain lesions and five MMPI items. *Journal of Consulting Psychology,* 1964, *28:*78.

Howard, A. R. Diagnostic value of the Wechsler Memory Scale with selected groups of brain-damaged patients. *Journal of Consulting Psychology*, 1950, *14:*395.

Hulicka, I. M. Age differences in Wechsler Memory Scale scores. *Journal of Genetic Psychology*, 1966, *109:*135.

Hunt, W., Quay, H., and Walker, R. E. Validity of diagnostic judgment as a function of amount of test information. *Journal of Clinical Psychology*, 1966, *22:*154.

Hutt, M. L. *The Hutt Adaptation of the Bender-Gestalt Test* (2nd ed.). New York: Grune & Stratton, 1969.

Hutt, M. L. The projective use of the Bender-Gestalt Test. In A. I. Rabin (Ed.), *Projective Techniques in Personality Assessment*. New York: Springer, 1968.

Isenberg, S. J., and Bass, B. A. Effects of verbal and nonverbal reinforcement on the WAIS performance of normal adults. *Journal of Consulting and Clinical Psychology*, 1974, *42:*467.

Jastak, J. F., and Jastak, S. R. *The Wide Range Achievement Test. Manual of Instructions*. Wilmington, Delaware: Guidance Associates, 1965.

Karson, S. Second-order personality factors and the MMPI. *Journal of Clinical Psychology*, 1958, *14:*313.

Karson, S. The Sixteen Personality Factor Test in clinical practice. *Journal of Clinical Psychology*, 1959, *15:*174.

Karson, S. Validating clinical judgments with the 16 PF test. *Journal of Clinical Psychology*, 1960, *16:*394.

Karson, S. Second-order personality factors in positive mental health. *Journal of Clinical Psychology*, 1961, *17:*14.

Karson, S., and O'Dell, J. W. *A Guide to the Clinical Use of the 16 PF.* Champaign, Illinois: Institute for Personality and Ability Testing, 1976.

Karson, S., and Pool, K. B. The construct validity of the Sixteen Personality Factors Test. *Journal of Clinical Psychology*, 1957, *13:*245.

Keiffer, D. M., and Golden, C. J. The Peabody Individual Achievement Test with normal and special school populations. *Psychological Reports*, 1978, *42:*395.

Keiser, T. W. Schizotype and the Wechsler Digit Span Test. *Journal of Clinical Psychology*, 1975, *31:*303.

Kiernan, R. J., and Matthews, C. G. Impairment index versus T score averaging in neuropsychological assessment. *Journal of Consulting and Clinical Psychology*, 1976, *44:*951.

Kljajic, I. Wechsler Memory Scale indices of brain pathology. *Journal of Clinical Psychology*, 1975, *31:*698.

Klove, H., and Matthews, C. G. Psychometric and adaptive abilities in epilepsy. *Epilepsia*, 1966, *7:*330.

Klove, H., and Matthews, C. G. Neuropsychological evaluation of the epileptic patient. *Wisconsin Medical Journal*, 1969, *68:*296.

Klove, H., and Matthews, C. G. Neuropsychological studies of patients with epilepsy. In R. M. Reitan, and L. S. Davison (Eds.), *Clinical Neuropsychology: Current Status and Applications*. Washington: Winston, 1974.

Knox, W. J., Grippaldi, R. High levels of state or trait anxiety and performance on selected verbal WAIS subtests. *Psychological Reports*, 1970, *27:*375.

Koppitz, E. M. *The Bender-Gestalt Test for young children*. New York: Grune & Stratton, 1963.

Koppitz, E. M. The Bender-Gestalt Test and Visual Aural Digit Span Test and reading achievement. *Journal of Learning Disabilities,* 1975, *8:*154.

Kratochwill, T. R., and Brody, G. H. Effects of verbal and self-monitoring feedback on Wechsler Adult Intelligence Scale performance in normal adults. *Journal of Consulting and Clinical Psychology,* 1976, *44:*879.

Krug, S. E. *Psychological Assessment in Medicine.* Champaign, Illinois: Institute for Personality and Ability Testing, 1977.

L'Abate, L., Vogler, R. E., Friedman, W. H., and Chusid, T. M. The diagnostic usefulness of two tests of brain damage. *Journal of Clinical Psychology,* 1972, *39:*508.

Ladd, C. E. WAIS performances of brain damaged and neurotic patients. *Journal of Clinical Psychology,* 1964, *20:*114.

Levine, J., and Ferstein, A. Differences in test performance between brain damaged, schizophrenic, and medical patients. *Journal of Consulting and Clinical Psychology,* 1972, *39:*508.

Lewinsohn, P. M. Dimensions of MMPI change. *Journal of Clinical Psychology,* 1965, *21:*37.

Lewis, G., Golden, C. J., Osmon, D. C., Purisch, A., and Hammeke, T. Localization of brain dysfunction by a standardized version of Luria's neuropsychological investigation. Manuscript submitted for publication, 1979.

Lezak, M. D. *Neuropsychological Assessment.* New York: Oxford University Press, 1976.

Logue, P. E., and Allen, K. WAIS predicted Category Test score with the Halstead Neuropsychological Battery. *Perceptual and Motor Skills, 33:*1095, 1971.

Luria, A. R. *Restoration of Function after Brain Injury.* New York: MacMillan, 1963.

Luria, A. R. *Higher Cortical Functions in Man.* New York: Basic, 1966.

Luria, A. R. *The Working Brain.* New York: Basic, 1973.

McAndrews, C. The differentiation of male alcoholic outpatients from nonalcoholic psychiatric patients by means of the MMPI. *Quarterly Journal of Studies on Alcohol, 26:*238, 1965.

McFie, J. The diagnostic significance of disorders of higher nervous activity. In P. J. Vinken, and G. W. Bruyn (Eds.), *Handbook of Clinical Neurology* (Vol. III). New York: Wiley, 1969.

McFie, J. *Assessment of Organic Intellectual Impairment.* New York: Academic Press, 1975.

McGuire, F. L. A comparison of the Bender-Gestalt and Flicker Fusion as indicators of CNS involvement. *Journal of Clinical Psychology,* 1960, *16:*276.

McIver, D., McLaren, S. A., and Phillip, A. E. Inter-rater agreement on Memory-for-Designs Test. *British Journal of Social and Clinical Psychology,* 1973, *12:*194.

McManis, D. M. Memory-for-Designs performance of brain damaged and non-brain damaged psychiatric patients. *Perceptual and Motor Skills,* 1974, *38:*47.

McKeever, W. F., May, P. R. A., and Tuma, A. H. Prognosis in Schizophrenia: Prediction of length of hospitalization from psychological test variables. *Journal of Clinical Psychology,* 1965, *21:*214.

Mack, J. L. A. A comparative study of group test estimates of WAIS verbal, performance and full scale IQs. *Journal of Clinical Psychology,* 1970, *26:*177.

Mahan, H. Sensitivity of WAIS tests to focal lobe damage. Privately Mimeographed, 1976.

Maloney, M. P., and Ward, M. P. *Psychological Assessment: A Conceptual Approach.* New York: Oxford University Press, 1976.

Marks, P. A., and Seeman, W. *Acturial Description of Abnormal Personality.* Los Angeles: Western Psychological Services, 1963.

Marvel, G., Golden, C. J., Hammeke, T., Osmon, D. C., and Purisch, A. The effects of age and education on a standardized version of Luria's neuropsychological tests. Manuscript submitted for publication, 1979.

Matthews, C. G., Cleeland, C. S., and Hopper. C. L. Neuropsychological patterns in Multiple Sclerosis. *Diseases of the Nervous System,* 1970, *31:*161.

Matthews, C. G., and Klove, H. Differential psychological performance in major motor, psychomotor and mixed classifications of known and unknown etiology. *Epilepsia,* 1967, *8:*117.

Maxwell, E. Validities of abbreviated WAIS scales. *Journal of Consulting Psychology,* 1957, *21:*121.

Meier, M. J. Neuropsychological predictors of motor recovery after cerebral infarction. Paper read atthe 82nd Annual Convention of the American Psychological Association, New Orleans, September, 1974.

Meier, M. J., and French, L. A. Longitudinal assessment of intellectual function following unilateral temporal lobectomy. *Journal of Clinical Psychology,* 1966, *22:*22.

Meyer, V., and Jones, H. G. Patterns of cognitive test performance as functions of the lateral localization of cerebral abnormalities in the temporal lobe. *Journal of Mental Science,* 1957, *103:*758.

Monroe, K. L. Note on the estimate of the WAIS full-scale IQ. *Journal of Clinical Psychology,* 1966, *22:*79.

Nikols, J. Mental deficit, schizophrenia and the Benton Test. *Journal of Nervous and Mental Disease,* 1963, *136:*279.

Norman, R. P., and Wilensky, H. Item difficulty of the WAIS Information subtest for a chronic schizophrenic sample. *Journal of Clinical Psychology,* 1961, *17:*56.

Norton, J. C., and Matthews, C. G. Psychological test performance in patients with subtentorial versus supratentorial CNS disease. *Diseases of the Nervous System,* 1972, *33:*312.

O'Dell, J. W. Method for detecting random answers on personality questionnaires. *Journal of Applied Psychology,* 1971, *55:*380.

Ogilvie, R. D. Correlation between the Quick Test and the WAIS as used in a clinical setting. *Psychological Reports,* 1965, *16:*497.

Orgass, B., and Poeck, K. Clinical validation of a new test for aphasia: An experimental study on the Token Test. *Cortex,* 1966, *2:*222.

Orme, J. E. Bender design recall and brain damage. *Diseases of the Nervous System,* 1962, *23:*329.

Osmon, D. C., and Golden, C. J. Minnesota Multiphasic Personality Inventory correlates of neuropsychological deficits. *International Journal of Neuroscience,* 1978, in press.

Osmon, D. C., Golden, C. J., Purisch, A., Hammeke, T., and Blume, H. The use of a standardized battery of Luria's tests in the diagnosis of lateralized cerebral dysfunction. *International Journal of Neuroscience,* 1978, in press.

Parker, J. W. The validity of some current tests for organicity. *Journal of Consulting Psychology,* 1975, *21:*425.

Pascal, G. R., and Suttell, B. J. *The Bender-Gestalt Test: Its quantification and validity for adults.* New York: Grune & Stratton, 1951.

Paulson, M. J., and Lin, T. Predicting WAIS IQ from Shipley-Hartford scores. *Journal of Clinical Psychology,* 1970, *26:*453.

Peck, D. F. The conversion of Progressive Mayrices and Mill Hill Vocabulary raw scores into deviation IQs. *Journal of Clinical Psychology,* 1970, *26:*67.

Pedrini, D. T., and Pedrini, L. N. *The Pedrini Supplementary Aid to the Administration of the Stanford-Binet Intelligence Scale (Form L–M): A Handbook.* Los Angeles: Western Psychological Services, 1970.

Pennington, H., Galliani, C. A., and Voegelle, G. E. Unilateral electroencephalographic dysrhythmia and children's intelligence. *Child Development,* 1965, *36:*539.

Perret, E. The left frontal lobe of man and the suppression of habitual responses in verbal categorical behavior. *Neuropsychologia,* 1974, *12:*323.

Pool, D. A., and Brown, R. The PPVT as a measure of general adult intelligence. *Journal of Consulting and Clinical Psychology,* 1970, *34:*8.

Pringle, R. K., and Haanstad, M. Estimating WAIS IQs from Progressive Matrices scores. *Journal of Clinical Psychology,* 1971, *27:*479.

Purisch, A., Golden, C. J., and Hammeke, T. The discrimination of schizophrenic and brain injured patients by a standardized version of Luria's neuropsychological tests. *Journal of Consulting and Clinical Psychology,* 1978, in press.

Quattlebaum, L. F., and White, W. F. Relationships between two quick screening measures of intelligence for neuropsychiatric patients. *Psychological Reports,* 1969, *24:*691.

Rapaport, D., Gill, M. M., and Schafer, R. *Diagnostic Psychological Testing,* New York: International Universities Press, 1970.

Reed, H. B., Reitan, R. M., and Klove, H. Influence of cerebral lesions on psychological test performance of older children. *Journal of Consulting Psychology,* 1965, *29:*247.

Reitan, R. M. *Neuropsychological Methods of Inferring Brain Damage in Adults and Children.* unpublished manuscript, undated.

Reitan, R. M. Investigation of the validity of Halstead's measures of biological intelligence. *A.M.A. Archives of Neurology and Psychiatry,* 1955, *73:*28.

Reitan, R. M. Affective disturbances of brain damaged patients. *Archives of Neurology and Psychiatry,* 1955, *73:*530.

Reitan, R. M. The effect of brain lesions on adaptive abilities in human beings. 1959, unpublished manuscript.

Reitan, R. M., and Boll, T. J. Intellectual and cognitive functions in Parkinson's disease. *Journal of Consulting and Clinical Psychology,* 1971, *37:*364.

Reitan, R. M., Reed, J. C., and Dyken, M. L. Cognitive, psychomotor and motor correlates of Multiple Sclerosis. *Journal of Nervous and Mental Disease,* 1971, *153:*218.

Robbins, S. L. *Pathologic Basis of Disease.* Philadelphia: Saunders, 1974.

Russell, E. W. Validation of a brain damage versus schizphrenia MMPI key. *Journal of Clinical Psychology,* 1975, *31:*659.

Russell, E. W. WAIS factor analysis with brain damaged subjects using criterion measures. *Journal of Consulting and Clinical Psychology,* 1972, *39:*133.

Russell, E. W., Neuringer, C., and Goldstein, G. *Assessment of brain damage. A neuropsychological key approach.* New York: Wiley-Interscience, 1970.

Sattler, J. M. Effects of cues and examiner influence on two Wechsler subtests. *Journal of Consulting and Clinical Psychology,* 1969, *33:*716.

Sattler, J. M. *Assessment of Children's Intelligence.* Philadelphia: Saunders, 1974.

Savage, R. D. Intellectual assessment. In P. Mittler (Ed.), *The Psychological Assessment of Mental and Physical Handicaps.* London: Methuen, 1970.

Shaw, D. J., and Matthews, C. G. Differential MMPI performance of brain damaged versus pseudoneurologic group. *Journal of Clinical Psychology,* 1965, *21:*405.

Shaw, J. H. Comparability of PPVT and WAIS scores with schizophrenics without brain damage. Unpublished study, Nampa State School, Nampa, Iowa, 1961, quoted in C. B. Ernhart, The correlation of PPVT and WAIS scores for adult psychiatric patients. *Journal of Clinical Psychology,* 1970, *26:*470.

Shearn, C. R., Berry, D. F., and Fitzgibbons, B. Usefulness of the Memory-for-Designs Test in assessing mild organic complications in psychiatric patients. *Perceptual and Motor Skills,* 1974, *38:*1099.

Silverstein, A. B. Reappraisal of the validity of a short form of Wechsler's scales. *Psychological Reports,* 1970, *26:*559.

Smith, A. Changing effects of frontal lesions. *Journal of Neurology, Neurosurgery, and Psychiatry,* 1964, *27:*511.

Shith, A. Intellectual functions in patients with lateralized frontal tumors. *Journal of Neurology, Neurosurgery, and Psychiatry,* 1966, *29:*52.

Smith A., Verbal and nonverbal test performances of patients with "acute" lateralized brain lesions (tumors). *Journal of Nervous Mental Deficiency,* 1966, *70:*595.

Smith, A. Neuropsychological testing in neurological disorders. In W. J. Friedlander (Ed.), *Advances in Neurology* (Vol. 7). New York: Raven Press, 1975.

Spreen, O., and Benton, A. L. Neurosensory Center Comprehensive Examination for Aphasia. Victoria, B.C.: Neuropsychology Laboratory, Department of Psychology, University of Victoria, 1969.

Sterne, D. M. The Benton, Porteus, and WAIS Digit Span Tests with normal and brain-injured subjects. *Journal of Clinical Psychology,* 1969, *25:*173.

Sterne, D. M. The Hooper Visual Organization Test and the Trail Making Test as discriminants of brain damage. *Journal of Clinical* 1973, *29:*212.

Sydiaha, D. Prediction of WAIS IQ for psychiatric patients using the Ammons Full Range Picture Vocabulary and Raven Progressive Matrices. *Psychological Reports,* 1967, *20:*823.

Todd, J., Coolidge, F., and Satz, P. The Wechsler Adult Intelligence Scale discrepancy index: A neuropsychological evaluation. *Journal of Consulting and Clinical Psychology,* 1977, *45:*450.

Tymchuk, A. J. Comparison of the Bender error and time scores from groups of epileptic, retarded, and behavior problem children. *Perceptual and Motor Skills*, 1974, *39:*71.

Von Kerekjarto, M. Wahrnehmungstests zur Diagnose und Differentialdiagnose der Multiplen Sklerose, Eine Untersuchung mit dem Benton Visuellen Merkfaehigkeitstest, dem Goldstein-Scheerer Mosaiktest und dem Halstead Taktilen Leistungstest. *Zeitung Experimentalen und Angelwalten Psychologie*, 1961, *8:*369.

Walker, M. Perceptual coding, visuo-motor and spatial difficulties and their neurological correlates. *Developmental Medicine and Child Neurology*, 1965, *7:*543.

Walker, R. E., Sannito, T. C., and Firetto, A. C. The effect of subjectively reported anxiety on intelligence test performance. *Psychology in the Schools*, 1970, *7:*241.

Walker, R. E., and Spence, J. T. Relationship between digit span and anxiety. *Journal of Consulting Psychology*, 1964, *28:*220.

Watson, C. G. An MMPI scale to separate brain damaged from schizophrenic men. *Journal of Consulting and Clinical Psychology*, 1971, *36:*121.

Watson, C. G. The separation of NP hospital organics from schizophrenics with three visual motor screening tests. *Journal of Clinical Psychology*, 1968, *24:*412.

Watson, C. G., and Klett, W. G. Prediction of WAIS IQs from the SH, AGCT, and Revised Beta Examination. *Journal of Clinical Psychology*, 1968, *24:*338.

Watson, C. G., and Thomas, R. W. MMPI profiles of brain damaged and schizophrenic patients. *Perceptual and Motor Skills*, 1968, *27:*567.

Wechsler, D. *The Measurement and Appraisal of Adult Intelligence*. Baltimore: Williams & Wilkins, 1958.

Wechsler, D. *Wechsler Adult Intelligence Scale. Manual*. New York: Psychological Corporation, 1955.

Wechsler, D. A. A standardized memory scale for clinical use. *Journal of Psychology*, 1945, *19:*87.

Weiner, I. B. *Psychodiagnosis in Schizophrenia*. New York: Wiley, 1966.

Welsh, G. S. An extension of Hathaway's MMPI profile coding system. *Journal of Consulting Psychology*, 1948, *12:*343.

Welsh, G. S., and Dahlstrom, W. G. (Eds.), *Basic Readings on the MMPI in Psychology and Medicine*. Minneapolis: University of Minnesota Press, 1956.

Wheeler, L., Burke, C. H., and Reitan, R. M. An application of discriminant functions tt the problems of predicting brain damage using behavioral variables. *Perceptual and Motor Skills*, 1963, *16:*417. (Monograph Supplement)

Wheeler, L., and Reitan, R. M. Predictions of brain damage from an aphasia screening test, an application of discriminant functions and a comparison of a non linear method of analysis. *Perceptual and Motor Skills*, 1963, *17:*63.

Williams, R. L. The BITCH-100: A culture specific test. *Journal of Afro-American Issues*, 1975, *3:*103.

Willis, J., and Ehrlick, S. Tangible reinforcement and feedback effects on the IQ scores of college students. *Journal of Clinical Psychology*, 1975, *31:*463.

Winder, P., O'Dell, J. W., and Karson, S. New motivational distortion scales for the 16-PF. *Journal of Personality Assessment,* 1975, *39:*532.

Yates, A. J. The validity of some psychological tests of brain damage. *Psychological Bulletin,* 1954, *51:*359.

Zimmerman, I. L., and Woo-Sam, J. M. *Clinical Interpretation of the Wechsler Adult Intelligence Scale.* New York: Grune & Stratton, 1973.

Zwann, E. J., DeVries, E., and Van Dijk-Bleker, H. De Benton Test: Aspecten bedoeld en onbedoeld. *Nederl. Tijdschr. Psychol. Grens.,* 1967, *22:*427.

Author Index

Aita, J., 40
Ajax, A., 147
Allen, K., 173
Anderson, S., 173
Arber, N., 145

Bachrach, H., 149
Bartz, W., 40
Bass, B., 2
Bender, L., 129, 130, 132
Benton, A., 127, 184
Berry, D., 147
Blume, H., 202
Boerger, A., 75
Boll, T., 193
Boller, F., 144
Bonner, L., 43
Borgatta, E., 39
Brantner, J., 75
Brilliant, P., 126, 135, 147
Brody, G., 2
Brown, R., 43
Bruhn, A., 135
Burke, C., 174, 178, 185

Canter, A., 132, 136
Carson, R., 69
Cattell, R., 110, 113, 114

Christensen, A., 202
Chusid, T., 126
Cleeland, C., 194
Choen, J., 149
Colonna, A., 41
Corsini, R., 39
Costa, L., 145
Craine, J., 2, 193
Crochelet, Y., 126
Cronholm, B., 126

Dahlstrom, L., 75
Dahlstrom, W., 75
Davey, H., 16, 18
Davis, W., 39
Delprato, D., 2
DeVries, E., 126
Dizonne, M., 39
Donahue, D., 4
Drake, L., 75
Duker, J., 75
Dunn, L., 51

Eber, H., 110
Edinger, J., 21
Ehrlick, S., 2

Fernald, L., 145
Fernald, P., 145
Ferstein, A., 135
Finlayson, M., 15
Firetto, A., 16, 18

Fischer, M., 167
Fitzgibbons, B., 147
French, L., 31, 184
Friedman, W., 126

Gilberstadt, H., 75
Gill, M., 2, 15, 17, 18, 20, 22
Goldberg, L., 135
Golden, C., 2, 18, 19, 21, 30, 31, 40, 51, 54, 75, 136, 146, 152, 153, 173, 174, 176, 177, 178, 185, 193, 195, 196, 202, 203, 206, 209
Goldstein, G., 166, 170, 176, 177, 191, 194
Good, P., 75
Gough, H., 69
Graham, F., 146
Graham, J., 75
Granick, S., 39
Grippaldi, R., 16
Grundvig, J., 147
Gudeman, H., 2, 193
Gynther, M., 126, 135, 147

Haanstad, M., 40
Hain, J., 132, 135
Halstead, W., 159, 173

Hammeke, T., 202, 203, 206
Hartje, W., 144
Hathaway, S., 75
Hedlund, J., 75
Heinburg, R., 185
Holland, T., 149
Howard, A., 149
Hulicka, I., 148
Hunt, W., 15
Hutt, M., 130, 131, 132, 133, 136, 142

Isenberg, S., 2

Jackson, D., 2
Jastak, J., 46, 48
Jastak, S., 46, 48
Johnson, K., 15

Karson, S., 110, 113, 114
Keiser, T., 16, 18
Kerstechensteiner, M., 144
Kieffer, D., 54
Klett, W., 40
Knox, W., 16
Koppitz, E., 135
Kratochwill, T., 2
Krug, S., 110, 119

Ladd, C., 22
Levine, J., 135
Levita, E., 145
Lewis, G., 203
Lezak, N., 143, 151, 196
Lily, R., 75
Lin, T., 40
L'Ivate, L., 126
Logue, P., 173

Luria, A., 51, 184, 194, 195, 203, 209, 214

McFie, J., 2, 18, 31, 183, 184, 185
McGuire, F., 135
McIver, D., 147
McKeever, W., 18
McLaren, S., 147
McLaughlin, D., 2, 193
McManis, D., 147
Mack, J., 40
Mahan, H., 31
Marks, P., 75
Marvel, G., 203
Markwardt, F., 51
Matthews, C., 193
Maxwell, E., 13
May, P., 18
Meehl, P., 75
Meier, M., 31, 184
Mintz, J., 149
Monroe, K., 40

Needham, 147
Neuringer, C., 162, 170, 176, 177, 191
Nikols, J., 126
Norman, R., 15

O'Dell, J., 110
O'Dell, K., 114
Oetting, E., 75
Ogilvie, R., 39
Orgass, B., 144
Orme, J., 135
Osmon, D., 75, 202, 203

Parker, J., 40, 149
Pascal, G., 132
Paulson, M., 40

Pedrini, D., 37
Pedrini, L., 37
Peck, D., 42
Perret, E., 146
Phillip, A., 147
Poeck, K., 144
Pool, D., 43
Pringle, R., 40
Purisch, A., 202, 203, 206

Quattlebaum, L., 39
Quay, H., 15

Rapaport, D., 2, 15, 17, 18, 20, 22
Reid, M., 135
Reitan, R., 15, 159, 174, 177, 178, 193
Rines, W., 145
Robbins, S., 193
Rocker, M., 15
Russell, E., 166, 170, 177

Sannito, T., 18
Sattler, J., 2, 4, 38
Savage, R., 40
Schafer, R., 2, 15, 17, 18, 20, 22
Schalling, D., 126
Seeman, W., 75
Shaw, J., 43
Shearn, C., 147
Shelley, C., 193
Smith, A., 183, 184
Spence, J., 18
Spreen, O., 127
Sterne, D., 126
Suttell, B., 132
Sweet, J., 75
Sydiaha, D., 39

Tatsuoke, M., 110
Tuma, A., 18
Tymchuk, A., 135

Van Digk-Bleker, H., 126
Vaughan, H., 145
Vogler, R., 126
Von Kerekjarto, M., 126

Walker, R., 15, 18
Warburton, F., 110
Watson, C., 40, 147
Wechsler, D., 4, 5, 7, 8, 15, 18, 21, 22, 147, 148
Weiner, I., 20
Welsh, G., 62, 75
Wheeler, L., 174, 178, 185
White, W., 39

Wilensky, H., 15
Williams, R., 33
Willis, J., 2
Woo-Sam, J., 9, 17, 18

Yates, A., 40

Zimmerman, I., 9, 17, 18
Zwann, E., 126

Subject Index

ABC Test of Occular Dominance, 171
Acting out behavior, 101
Alcohol addiction, 102
Alcoholism, 191
Alzheimer's disease, 19
Ammons Full Range Picture Vocabulary Test, 38–39
Anxiety, 16, 18, 19, 115–116, 117, see MMPI and Sixteen PF
Asphasia Screening Test, 170
Arithmetic, 31, 205
  administration, 5
  interpretation, 16–17
Auditory memory, 18

Bender-Gestalt, 143, 147
  administration, 130–132
  advantages, 142
  background interference procedures example, 156
  clinical interpretation, 135–141
  disadvantages, 142
  history, 129
  interpretative strategies, 141

item examples, 131
item interpretation, 139–141
patient example, 155
purpose, 130
scoring, 132–135
Benton Visual Retention Test, 143, 147
  administration, 121–123
  advantages, 128
  disadvantages, 128
  discriminative validity, 126–127
  item example, 122
  normative data, 125–126
  qualitative evaluation, 127–128
  scoring systems, 123–125
Block Design, 20, 31
  administration, 8–9
  scoring, 11–12
Boldness, 112–113
Brain damage, 18, 20, 21, 22, 28–30, 40, 50–51, 126–127, 130, 136, 143–214
  diagnosis, 180–181
  diagnosis by WAIS, 30–32
  early, 31

Brain damage *(continued)*
   lateralization, 181–182, 207
   localization, 183–186, 207–209
   MMPI, 98–100
   test case examples, 153–158

Category Test, 161–163, 172–173
Cerebral vascular disorders, 191,
   192
Coin recognition, 169
Comprehension, 6, 31
   interpretation, 15–16
   scoring, 11
Comprehension Subtest, 5
   administration, 4–5
Computer interpretation, 64–65
Conformity, 112

Depression, 19, 20, 127, *see also*
   MMPI
Difference between two subtests,
   23
Diffuse brain injury, 31
Diffuse lesions, 126
Digits Backwards, 6, 18, 31
Digits Forward, 6
Digit Span, 30, 31
   administration, 6
   interpretation, 18–19
   scoring, 11
Digit Symbol, 30
   administration, 7–8
   illustration, 7
   interpretation, 19–20
   scoring, 11
Dominance, 111
Dynamometer, 171

Egostrength, 111
Emotional sensitivity, 113
Environment, 24
Epilepsy, 191, 192
Expressive speech, 205

Extroversion, 116–117, *see also*
   MMPI *and* Sixteen PF

Finger Agnosia, 169
Finger Tapping Test, 170–172,
   178
Fingertip Number Writing, 169
Formation, 31
Frontal lobe, 183–184, 207–208

Grip Strength, 171
Guilt, 114–115

Halstead-Reitan
      Neuropsychological
      Battery, 129, 159–201, *see
      also listings for individual
      tests in the Battery*
   advantages, 196, 197
   case examples, 197–201
   disadvantages, 196–197
   illustration, 161–179
   organizing test results,
      186–189
   purpose, 160–161
Head trauma, 191
Hooper Visual Organization Test,
   150–151
Hypochondriasis, *see* MMPI
Hypomania, *see* MMPI
Hysteria, *see* MMPI

Imagination, 114
Impulsivity, 112
Independence, 118
Information, scoring, 11
Information Subtest,
      administration, 3–4
   interpretation, 14–15
Intellectual processes, 205, 206
Intelligence, 110–111
Introversion, 116–117, *see also*
   MMPI *and* Sixteen PF

I.Q., 19–36
    difference scores, 28–30
    interpretation, 23–28
    interpretation of low scores,
        26–28

Lateral Dominance Examination,
        170–171, 178–179
Lateralization, 181–182, 207
Learning disabilities, 50–51
Left frontal lesions, 31
Left handedness, 7
Left hemisphere, 143, 182
Left parietal lesions, 31
Left temporal lesions, 31
Localization, 183–186, 207–209
Luria Neuropsychological
        Battery, 149, 202–214
    advantages, 209
    case examples, 210–214
    disadvantages, 209
    theory, 209–210

Memory, 205
Memory for Designs, 126, 146–147
    illustration, 157
Minnesota Multiphasic
        Personality Inventory,
        57–106, see also MMPI,
        purpose, 58
MMPI, 129
    accuity, 96–97
    acting out behavior, 101
    administration, 58–61
    advantages, 102
    alcohol addiction, 102
    cannot say scale, 65
    case examples, 103
    chronicity, 96–97
    clinical interpretation, 63–106
    clinical scales, 75–84
    depression, 76–77
    disadvantages, 102–103

faking bad profile, 73
faking good profile, 73
F-scale, 66–68
functional disorder, 98–100
hypochondralisis, 76
hypomania, 83
hysteria, 77–78
K-scale, 68–69
lie scale, 65
malingering profile, 74
masculinity-femininity, 79–80
masculinity-femininity scale,
        113
organic disorder, 98–100
paranoia, 80–81
profile coding, 62–63
profile invalidity, 69–75
profile invalidity, illustrations,
        70–74
prognosis, 100–101
psychasthenia, 81–82
psychopathic deviate, 78–79
psychosis, 97–98
random profiles, 70–72
scales, 61
schizophrenia, 82
scoring, 61–62
social introversion, 84
suicide, 100–101
two point codes, 84–96
        12/21, 85–86
        13/31, 86–87
        14/41, 87
        18/81, 87–88
        19/91, 88
        23/32, 88
        24/42, 88–89
        26/62, 89–90
        27/72, 90
        28/82, 90
        29/92, 90–91
        34/43, 91
        36/63, 91

MMPI *(continued)*
  two point codes: 38/83, 91–92
    39/93, 92
    45/54, 92
    46/64, 92–93
    47/74, 93
    48/84, 93
    49/94, 93–94
    68/86, 94
    69/96, 94–95
    78/87, 95
    89/98, 95–96
  validity scale, 65–75
Motivation, 24
Motor Skills, 19
Multiple Sclerosis, 193–194

Neurosis, 27
Neurotics, 22

Object Assembly, 31
  administration, 10–11
  interpretation, 22
  scoring, 11–12
Occipital lobe, 185–186, 208–209

Paranoia, *see* MMPI
Parietal lobe, 184–185, 208–209
Parkinson's Disease, 192
Pattern Analysis, 22–23
Pattern Analysis, Stanford-Binet,
    38
Peabody Individual Achievement
    Test, 51–55
  administration, 52, 53
  advantages and disadvantages,
    55
  and Wide Range Achievement
    Test, 54
  example, 56
  interpretation, 53–54, *see*
    educational interpretation
    under the Wide Range
    Achievement Test

  scoring, 53
Peabody Picture Vocabulary Test,
    42–43
Picture Arrangement, 31
  interpretation, 21–22
  scoring, 11–12
Picture Completion
  administration, 8
  interpretation, 20
  scoring, 11
Premorbid intelligence, 19, 20
Presenile dementia, 193
Process, 189–194
Psychiatric disorders, diagnosis
    by WAIS, 32
Psychopathic deviate *see*
    MMPI
Psychotherapy, prognosis,
    100–101
Purdue Pegboard, 144–145

Quick Test, 39–43

Reading, 205
Rebelliousness, 115
Reben's Progressive Matrices,
    40–42
  illustration, 41
Receptive speech, 204–205
Rehabilitation, 194–196
  planning, 195–196
Reitan Indiana Aphasia
    Examination, 177–178
Reitan-Klove Sensory Perceptual
    Exam, 167–170
Retardation, 26–28
Rhythm, 204
Rhythm Test, 163–164
Right frontal lesions, 31
Right hemisphere, 182
Right hemisphere lesions, 126
Right parietal lesions, 31
Right temporal lesions, 31

Schizophrenia, 19, 21, 22, 27, 114, 127, 136, 190–191, *see also* MMPI
Schizophrenics, 14, 15, 16, 17, 18, 20
Screening batteries, 152
Seashore Rhythm Test, 163–164
Self sufficiency, 115
Sensory Motor Areas, 208
Sensory Perceptual Examination, 176–177
Shipley-Hartford, 39–40, 43
Shrewdness, 114
Similarities, 6, 31
  interpretation, 17–18
  scoring, 11
Similarities Subtest, 4
  administration, 5–6
Sixteen PF
  administration, 108–109
  advantages and disadvantages, 118–119
  case examples, 119–120
  factor 1, 116–117
  factor 2, 117
  factor 3, 118
  factor 4, 118
  factor 5, 118
  faking bad scale, 109
  intepretation, 110–119
  interpretative strategy, 118–119
  motivational distortion scale, 109
  purpose, 107–108
  scale A, 110
  scale B, 11
  scale C, 111
  scale E, 111
  scale F, 112
  scale G, 112
  scale H, 112–113
  scale I, 113
  scale L, 113–114
  scale N, 114

  scale O, 114–115
  scale Q1, 115
  scale Q2, 115
  scale Q3, 115–116
  scale Q4, 116
  second order factors, 116–119
  validity scales, 109
Sociopathy, 118
Spatial reasoning, 21
Speech Sounds Perception Test, 163, 173
Stanford-Binet, 36–39
Stroop Color and Word Test, 145–146
Suicide, 100
Suppression, 167–169
Suspiciousness, 114

Tactile Form Recognition Test, 169–170
Tactile Functions, 204
Tactual Performance Test, 164–166, 174–175
Temporal lobe, 184, 208
Test batteries, 151–153
Testing the limits, 4–5, 6, 7, 8, 9, 10, 11
Token Test, 143–144
Tough poise, 118
Trail Making Test, 166–167, 175–176
Tumors, 191

Validity scales, 64, 65–75
Visual Memory, 19
Visual Skills, 22
Visual-spatial functions, 204
Vocabulary, 31
  interpretation, 19
  scoring, 11
Vocabulary Subtest, 4
  administration, 6–7

WAIS, 36, 37, 38, 39, 40, 43, 47,
    48, 130, 148, 178, 205
  administration and scoring,
    3–13
  advantages, 33
  brief forms, 13
  case examples, 34–35
  disadvantages, 33–34
  history, 1
  interpretation, 13–32
  I.Q., 12–13
  purpose, 1–2
Warmth, 110
Wechsler Adult Intelligence Scale,
    see Chapter 1 and also,
    WAIS *and individual*
    subtest listings

Wechsler-Bellevue, 1
Wechsler Memory Test, 147–149
Wide Range Achievement Test,
    17, 45–51, 52
  administration, 46–47
  advantages, 51
  brain damage, 50–51
  disadvantages, 51
  educational interpretations,
    48–49
  example, 55, 56
  learning disabilities, 49–50
  scoring, 47
  scoring issues, 47–48
Writing, 205

a
b
c
d
e
f
9 g
0 h
1 i
8 2 j